FORTRESS HALIFAX

PORTRAIT OF A GARRISON TOWN

To Uncle Reg
Happy Birthday
Love Andrew & Alexia

Fortress Halifax

Portrait of a Garrison Town

— Mike Parker —

NIMBUS
PUBLISHING LTD

Nimbus Publishing Limited
PO Box 9166
Halifax, NS B3K 5M8
(902) 455-4286

Printed and bound in Canada

Design: Arthur Carter, Paragon Design Group

Library and Archives Canada Cataloguing in Publication

    Parker, Mike, 1952-
    Fortress Halifax : portrait of a garrison town / Mike Parker.
    Includes bibliographical references.
    ISBN 1-55109-494-0

1. Halifax (N.S.)—History, Military. 2. Halifax (N.S.)—History.
3. Halifax (N.S.)—History, Military—Pictorial works. 4. Halifax
(N.S.)—History—Pictorial works. I. Title.

FC2346.4.P37 2004   971.6'22   C2004-905135-0

We acknowledge the financial support of the Government of Canada
through the Book Publishing Industry Development Program
(BPIDP) and the Canada Council for our publishing activities.

ACKNOWLEDGEMENTS

My thanks to Nimbus Publishing; Clare Goulet; Gary Castle; Arthur Carter; Ray Beck; Garry Shutlak and all the staff at Nova Scotia Archives and Records Management, especially Gail Judge, who toiled tirelessly in search of elusive images; Miriam Walls and Parks Canada for permission to access images and archival material; Helen, Emily, and Matt for their patience and support.

Table of Contents

New Brunswick

Cape Breton Island

Prince Edward Island

Fredericton

Sydney

Louisbourg

Fort Beauséjour

Fort Lawrence

Camp Debert

Saint John

Nova Scotia

Canso

Minas Basin

Stanley

Aldershot

Greenwood

Fort Edward

Bay of Fundy

Halifax

Fort Sackville

Dartmouth

Fort Anne

Cornwallis

Atlantic Ocean

Lunenburg

Yarmouth

.... denotes Prince Edward's Military Telegraph, 1790s

Introduction

"Halifax was a fortress, nothing more, and the civilians were interlopers. Nevertheless the civilians slowly multiplied in the shadow of the forts, grumbling at military occupation and rule but somehow proud of it, taking visitors to see the forts and barracks, flocking to every garrison sham fight and parade, and eagerly boarding the ships of the fleet on visiting days. The sound of the drum, the twitter of naval pipes, have been magic music to Haligonians all down through the years."
—Thomas Raddall, *Halifax: Warden of the North*

In their seemingly endless struggle for domination of the New World colonies, Britain and France waged four North American wars. Each one of these—from King William's War (1689–97) to the French and Indian War (1754–63)—was part of a larger European campaign, and, on every occasion, Nova Scotia proved a major battleground.

France laid claim to Acadie—the Maritime Provinces and part of Quebec's Gaspé Peninsula—in 1603, building a habitation two years later at Port Royal along the Annapolis River in western Nova Scotia. The fur trade monopoly was dealt a severe blow in 1613 when Samuel Argall, an English privateer from Virginia, burned the French settlement to the ground. Despite this and other early setbacks, French-Acadian roots took hold over the next century, during which time the two warring nations handed ownership of Acadie back and forth.

Scots were the first to fortify Nova Scotia: Sir William Alexander the Younger, by authority of the Charter of New Scotland granted to his father in 1621 by King James I of England, built a fort in 1629 at the confluence of the Annapolis and Allain's Rivers. Charles Fort, named for then King Charles I, remained only three years under Scottish control before Acadie reverted back to France in 1632, with the Treaty of Saint-Germain-en-Laye. Renamed Port Royal, the fort fell to the English in 1654, was returned to France by treaty in 1667, and was captured again in 1690 by colonial militia from Boston. They left immediately, however, allowing the French to rebuild. Following two failed sieges by New Englanders in 1707, a third attempt in 1710 was bolstered by British regulars and succeeded. The name was changed again, this time to Fort Anne, and the town around it to Annapolis Royal, in honour of Queen Anne of England. Another fifty years of intermittent fighting would ensue, but this was effectively the beginning of the end for French aspirations in Acadie.

The 1713 Treaty of Utrecht concluded Queen Anne's War, the second North American war (1702-13), and ceded what turned out to be permanent possession of Nova Scotia and Newfoundland to Britain. France retained Isle Royale (Cape Breton), retreating there to construct a new fortress, Louisbourg. The British set up colonial government at Fort Anne, then forgot about it. On paper, they owned Nova Scotia. In reality, the French and their Indian allies held control. Governor Phillips wrote in 1720, "This has been hitherto no more than a mock government, its authority never yet having been extended beyond cannon-shot of the fort." Only Annapolis Royal and the centuries-old seasonal fishing village of Canso three hundred miles away flew the Union Jack, where "any English speaking person who ventured out of the narrow limits of the settlements carried his life in his hands." Canso was insignificant and could be taken at will. Fort Anne, on the other hand, despite its dilapidated ramparts, would survive nearly forty years of intermittent attacks from French and Indian raiding parties, the tiny garrison of only three hundred men, led by the stalwart Major-General Paul Mascarene and provisioned by New England allies, standing firm.

Open conflict erupted in 1744 with King George's War, third of the North American wars (1744-48). Canso was attacked and burned the first year. A motley force of New England militia then surprised the world in 1745 by capturing Louisbourg. Euphoria soon dissipated when this "Dunkirk of the West" was returned to France in 1748 by the Treaty of Aix-la-Chapelle. Such a mockery was made of the London government, and the Bostonians who backed the expedition with their money and blood were so outraged, that British authorities were coerced into taking definitive action. Another three years of entreaty from Governor Shirley of Massachusetts were needed, however, to put the wheels in motion for building a secure naval base to counter Louisbourg and for settling Nova Scotia with subjects loyal to the crown.

The site chosen for Halifax in 1749 was an area known as Chebucto (from Mi'kmaq *Che-book-took* meaning "at the biggest harbour") on Nova Scotia's south coast, a narrow isthmus "not more than a mile and a half in width, [which] offers very great facilities for a defensive position and is well calculated to arrest an Enemy's further progress." The harbour, the second largest natural harbour in the world after Sydney, Australia, is formed in part by an expansive basin twenty-two miles in circumference, with water depths reaching two hundred and fifty feet. Long a summer encampment for native Mi'kmaq, French fishermen used Chebucto as early as 1698, and in 1711 France sent engineer Pierre-Paul Delabat to conduct a survey and to map defensive positions for possible settlement. The Treaty of Utrecht quashed those plans, forcing the French to build on Isle Royale. In 1746, a French fleet of more than seventy warships and transports commanded by Duc d'Anville sailed from Brest bound for Chebucto. There it was to rendezvous with French forces from the West Indies before launching attacks bent upon retaking Louisbourg, capturing Fort Anne and wrecking havoc upon the New England colonies. However, d'Anville ill-fated expedition fell victim to storms, shipwreck, scurvy, and typhus long before reaching the Nova Scotia coast, leaving more than 2,400 dead and hopes of victory dashed. France's loss was Britain's gain: Her Royal Engineers built batteries in later years on the exact sites identified in Delabat's plans.

Halifax was named in honour of George Montague, Earl of Halifax and head of the Lords of Trade and Plantations, who were in charge of financing the venture. Commanding the expedition was thirty-six-year-old Colonel Edward Cornwallis, described by Thomas Raddall as "incorruptible, a very rare quality in colonial governors of his time." The Cornwallis legacy, however, has been somewhat tarnished in recent years (one example being the decision to place a bounty on Mi'kmaw scalps, including women and children). The decisions Cornwallis made two and a half centuries ago on conducting warfare in a hostile environment continue to evoke controversy among modern-day sensibilities,

with some critics condemning him as one of the most vilified personages in history.

The British established several outposts within the first year of founding Halifax. Blockhouses were built at Sackville, Windsor, and Chignecto, the latter being Fort Lawrence, erected on the isthmus separating Nova Scotia from present-day New Brunswick. The French also built a fort at Chignecto in 1750-51 (Fort Beauséjour) with hopes of containing British forces inside Nova Scotia. A stalemate ensued for the next few years with the English "all but prisoners in their own forts." Halifax, while never directly attacked by the French or Indians, did lose a number of settlers to raiding parties. "Many stragglers were cut off during the first years of the settlement," writes Thomas Akins, "particularly along the western side of the Basin, where the best firewood was to be obtained. It was at length found necessary to send out an armed body when fuel or lumber was required. The enemy usually retired before a regular, organized force."

An attempt was made to expand English rule in Nova Scotia with the establishment of Dartmouth in 1750 across the harbour from Halifax. A more ambitious undertaking three years later involved predominately German and Swiss immigrants, or "Foreign Protestants," who were ferried sixty miles down the coast to where the fortified town of Lunenburg was laid out on an easily defended peninsula. In 1754, a third settlement was built at Lawrencetown, ten miles east of Dartmouth; unlike Dartmouth and Lunenburg, however, this venture was abandoned in 1757 "owing to its exposed situation and distance from Halifax."

The French and Indian War, the fourth and last of the North American wars, erupted throughout the colonies in 1754; two years later it spread to Europe as the Seven Years' War. Some military minds in England at the time had yet to grasp the geography of their colonial holdings. The Duke of Newcastle, for example, is claimed to have asked for suggestions as to how best Nova Scotia could be defended against French attack. When advised to reinforce Annapolis Royal, his reply was, "Annapolis? Annapolis? Where is Annapolis?" A map was subsequently produced to orientate his lordship. Ignorance aside, Britain applied the coup de grâce to colonial French holdings at Louisbourg,

Quebec, and Montreal several years before the 1763 Treaty of Paris ended the Seven Years' War and returned stability to Nova Scotia for the first time in more than a century. Nothing was left to chance a second time. Louisbourg was blown up and torn down, with some of its French building stone brought to Halifax and used in shaping this English fortress town.

War and rumours of war would keep Imperial forces in Halifax until the early 1900s. Such was not the case for the rest of Canada. Running an empire and maintaining foreign policy was not only expensive but it drained manpower resources. During the Crimean War in the mid-1850s, the Canadas (Ontario and Quebec) were faced with mass withdrawal of British troops to fight the Russians in a campaign so disastrous for Britain that it would lead to a complete restructuring of the army command. A Canadian Militia Act of 1855 authorized the raising of a paid five thousand-man force to fill the void in the upper provinces. Another round of downsizing followed Canadian Confederation in 1867 as self-governing dominions of the empire were expected to shoulder responsibility for their own defence. On October 4, 1870, headquarters for command of British North America moved from the Canadas to Halifax. A year later, all remaining Imperial forces were withdrawn from the country with the exception of garrisons at Halifax and Esquimalt that were retained for protecting the Royal Navy yards. A handful of British officers were assigned to various artillery schools for the purpose of instructing militia.

It should be emphasized that, historically, the strategic importance of Halifax far outweighed that of the west coast. Tension between the United States and Britain in the 1840s over trading rights in the Pacific Northwest gave rise to a military presence at Esquimalt. In 1848, the first Royal Navy warship visited the harbour and in 1855, three hospitals were built in anticipation of being needed for returning wounded from the Crimea. In 1856, a Naval Depot for the Pacific Squadron was opened. The Admiralty later authorized "a small establishment for the custody, etc. of stores and provisions for HM ships in the north Pacific" when Esquimalt replaced Valparaiso, Chile, in 1865 as headquarters of the Royal Navy's Pacific Squadron. Not until 1887, however, was a naval dockyard completed, one hundred and twenty-eight years after the King's Yard was established at Chebucto and only eighteen years prior to Britain completing its pull-out from Canada.

Halifax is steeped in military history. Its harbour floor is strewn with the hulks and refuse of seven colonial era wars and two world wars; its now silent ramparts once stood guard over every regiment in the British army. More than two hundred and fifty years ago, the first Imperial forces landed at Chebucto; one hundred years have elapsed since the last were called home. Only photographs, nameless images for the most part, remain as testament to their presence and passing. Much of the structural legacy left behind has long since disappeared, swept away by time and the changes it has brought. People today, oblivious to the past, walk over and drive through spaces at one time reserved as "Property of Imperial Government." Scores of books and academic treatises cover much of this history in minute detail; while these are invaluable for heritage conservation and for research purposes, they can prove tedious for the armchair historian looking for an informative yet entertaining read. A few works of "popular history" have been produced, the most noteworthy by master storyteller Thomas Raddall, whose 1948 classic *Halifax: Warden of the North* won a Governor-General's Award for creative non-fiction.

Fortress Halifax was conceived with the amateur history enthusiast in mind, but hopefully scholars will glean something of value in it as well. The sheer number and diversity of events and the volume of documentation are beyond the scope of a single book. Choices regarding subject matter are meant to be representative, not comprehensive. Drawing upon images from circa 1856 to 1945, the intent is to provide a portrait, or more accurately a photo-essay, that puts a face to the past, taking the reader back to the Halifax immortalized by Rudyard Kipling in *The Song of the Cities*:

"Into the mist my guardian prows put forth,
Behind the mist my virgin ramparts lie,
The Warden of the Honour of the North,
Sleepless and veiled am I!"

1. GATE AND DRAWBRIDGE, FORT GEORGE, CITADEL HILL, 1926

CHAPTER I

SENTINELS OF THE PAST

Parks Canada historians have categorized the development of Fortress Halifax in two "distinct phases." For the first sixty or so years of its existence, the town was "a standby military and naval outpost of empire to be held in readiness for war but as cheaply as possible." From 1749 to 1815, defensive works were bolstered only during times of crisis, such as the Seven Years' War (1756-63), American Revolutionary War (1775-83), Napoleonic Wars (1796-1815), and War of 1812 (1812-15). In each case, new batteries were erected and existing ones were restored to some semblance of battle readiness. Stop-gap measures at best, these defences invariably were allowed to languish into a state of decay following the cessation of hostilities. With Nelson's victory at Trafalgar in 1805, any realistic threat of French attack upon Halifax dissipated. The Americans, however, were looked upon with increasing trepidation. "For almost a century after the American Revolution," writes historian Roger Sarty, "the protection of British North America against the United States posed one of the two most difficult defence problems for the British Empire; the other was India's frontier with Afghanistan." Realizing at long last the need for a permanent fortress to defend Britain's only North Atlantic base of operations for the Royal Navy, bureaucrats loosened purse strings in the early 1820s and began an expensive second phase of re-tooling Halifax defences that would last nearly eighty years.

The first order of business for Edward Cornwallis in 1749 was to construct landward defensive works to protect his fledgling enterprise from marauding Indians. Five small stockaded forts connected by a palisade (see map, page 5) were completed within the first year, enclosing the town perimeter to the water's edge. By the early 1750s, three peninsular blockhouses—North, Middle and South—had been erected to seal off the narrow isthmus and to provide protection for soldiers patrolling a military road that ran from present-day Fairview on the Bedford Basin to the Northwest Arm. Royal Engineers then turned their attention to the town's undefended waterfront. Three shore batteries mounting forty-four guns (North, Middle, and South) were built in 1755, using more than nine thousand logs and squared timbers, which were banked with sods and earth. While these defensive measures effectively encapsulated early Halifax, they were by no means the only works then in progress. A blockhouse was built across the harbour in 1750 to provide limited security against Indian incursions upon the recently settled and isolated hamlet of Dartmouth. Three additional forts—George's Island (1750), Eastern Battery (1754), and Grand Battery (1761)—formed the main seaward defence line for the first hundred years until they were replaced by heavier armed batteries at Point Pleasant and the harbour approaches.

The fall of Louisbourg in 1758 negated any further threat of Indian attack upon Halifax, resulting in the removal of the town palisade and rapid deterioration of most earthen batteries and blockhouses. The American Revolutionary War and perceived threat of overland attack (there was then no navy to contend with) led to the building of several new fortifications concentrated primarily around the naval dockyard. Halifax proved to be of more than passing interest to George Washington who, at the behest of the French, sent a spy—"upon whose firmness and fidelity we may safely rely"—to infiltrate the town and report back on the state of defences. James Bowdoin, a draftsman who would later become the first president of the American Academy of Arts and Science, was chosen for the assignment. In a letter to Bowdoin dated May 15, 1780, General Washington stressed that "it may be of infinite importance to obtain the information required, and I should hope it may be done. Our very good Friends and Allies have it much at heart, and view the reduction [capture] of Halifax as a matter of great consequence, as being the Arsenal of support to the Enemy's fleet in these seas and in the West Indies…." On May 31, 1780, Bowdoin submitted his report, including detailed sketches of the harbour defences, and even water depths. Washington's reply of June 14, 1780 may explain in part why neither the Americans nor French took a crack at Halifax. "The plan and table of reference are very intelligible and satisfactory, and convey a clear idea of many points, about which I was uninformed before…. The place appears to be very strong and to have had much attention paid to its security latterly…."

Halifax was built on the steep eastern slope of a drumlin or "glacial rubbish heap" which factored significantly in military planning for decades and caused more than one Royal Engineer to throw up his hands in frustration. "I am aware that any work placed on it must be defective," wrote Colonel James Arnold in 1824. "Every Officer who has been here seems almost to have given the case up in despair." Arnold was referring to the deceptive first impression that the hill gave from the harbour side. Rising to a height of 255 feet, the hill looked like an engineer's dream, instead of the nightmare it came to be. Parks Canada historian J. J. Greenough explains the defects in his book *The Halifax Citadel 1825-60: A Narrative & Structural History*: "Contrary to popular belief, the element absent in the composition of its summit is solid bedrock. It is an inconvenient place to build anything…. As the land was cleared around the new town-site, the truth became apparent. From the harbour the hill was indeed imposing; from the landward side, it was less so. Viewed from the swamp behind it, it was only an egg-shaped hillock, rising sixty or seventy feet from the bottom of the swamp, with a crest just big enough for a small redoubt [a field work entirely closed on all sides, usually of a square or polygonal shape]. Less than seven hundred yards away to the southwest was a second hill, more substantial but lower. From a military point of view, the second hill (Camp Hill) and the swamp (now the central common) proved to be more important than Citadel Hill's imposing view of the harbour, for their very existence severely limited any possible alterations to the chosen site. While the soil of the drumlin permitted it to be hacked down to a more convenient

shape, this could only be done to a limited extent. Only massive cutting could alter the fundamental shape of the crest, which was inconveniently narrow for regular fortifications and this was inadvisable: any great reduction in the overall height would make it impossible for the hill to dominate the swamp, let alone Camp Hill."

The military would jealously maintain its grip on much of the common land well into the 1800s, which caused more than its share of confrontations with residents and civic authorities faced with urban expansion. In 1749, however, and for many years after, it was the one direction from which a land-based assault upon Halifax could be realistically launched and must therefore be defended.

Despite the hill's shortcomings, it remained central to strategic planning and was therefore the focus of British engineers, who built a citadel near the summit. A citadel, according to the Funk and Wagnalls Dictionary, is "a fortress commanding a city." Four were constructed in Halifax between 1749 and 1856, the last, since restored, is Canada's most visited national historic site. The first three, erected in 1749, 1761, and 1794 "were poor things at best." Built predominately of logs and sods, they were hastily thrown together and deteriorated rapidly in the variable Maritime weather. "The first, a simple log fort designed solely to keep out Indians, had lasted less than a decade," writes Greenough. "The second was an octagonal blockhouse surrounded by field fortifications which wound over the crest and down the slopes in all directions and had an equally brief and undistinguished career…. [The] third citadel, an enormous improvement on its predecessors, suffered from the same impermanence."

The 1794 arrival in Halifax of Prince Edward, commander-in-chief of military forces in Nova Scotia, signaled the most ambitious refurbishing of defences undertaken during this first phase. Being the fourth son of King George III, Edward had more than a little pull when it came to accessing the oft-times stingy royal treasury, and it was during his tenure that the third citadel was built—"four regular bastions connected by curtains [walls] which enclosed a log and earth cavalier which served as a gun platform and barracks." The design suffered too much from the lack of space atop the hill to be of practical use, and when altered to fit, the final product looked "ludicrous." Edward also had several older batteries demolished and newer ones built. While most lasted only a short time, the Prince of Wales Tower at Point Pleasant remains to this day; this massive, round stone fort is often referred to as a "Martello Tower," named for a stone keep on Cape Mortella in Corsica. So impressed were the British by its ability to withstand a naval bombardment in 1793-94 that two hundred similar towers were built throughout the British Isles, Cape Colony (South Africa), and British North America between 1796 and 1850. Five of the sixteen Martello towers erected in Canada were in Halifax. The first three were closer in design to the original medieval-type Martello Tower than those built in the British Isles eight years after work had commenced on Edward's towers. None of the Canadian towers, of which eleven remain, were ever attacked. With Edward's departure in 1800, a prolonged period of stagnation set in until the War of 1812, which prompted yet another round of building, including the last two stone towers.

With growing distrust of the Americans (resulting from two wars within thirty years) and fearing an attack without formal declaration of war (despite the Rush–Bagot Agreement of 1817, which demilitarized the Great Lakes), Britain entered the second building phase of Fortress Halifax in 1825 by sending a commission of Royal Engineer officers, headed by James Carmichael Smyth, to examine British North American defences. Prioritization led to the decision that Halifax was "the principle [sic] point to defend" while Upper and Lower Canada "could only hope at best to act upon the defensive." Smyth's recommendations led to the building of the fourth citadel, a star-shaped ironstone and granite fort. Problems immediately arose. The hill had first to be cut down twenty feet and levelled to accommodate the design, which resulted in delays as the ruins of three earlier citadels were cleared. Thanks to penny-pinching politicians, faulty architectural plans, shoddy workmanship, and a failure to account for the harsh climate, the stone and masonry walls buckled and crumbled. When work commenced in 1828, engineers estimated that the fort would take six years to complete at a cost of £116,000; the final tally twenty-eight years later was £242,122.

So much effort and money were expended on the citadel that other defences circa 1830–50 were left to fall apart. Things changed in the 1860s with advances in weaponry. The introduction of heavy rifled ordnance led to increased spending to revamp batteries (circa 1862–72) in order to accommodate the new guns as well as to withstand their attack. The American Civil War (1861–65) produced a victorious Northern Union Army of massive size and unknown intentions. Cross-border raids into Canada (1866–70) by the Irish–American Fenian Brotherhood—bent upon driving the British out of Ireland by instigating an American–Anglo war in North America—also kept Britain vigilant. (The Fenians were, in reality, a minor irritation that more than anything helped Canadians decide favourably upon Confederation in 1867.) The American threat to the British largely disappeared on May 8, 1871, with the signing of the Treaty of Washington "between Her Majesty and the United States of America for the Amicable Settlement of all Causes of Difference Between the Two Countries." There was a brief war scare between December 1895 and January 1896 over the Venezuelan boundary dispute, but this was "the last occasion of apprehended hostility between the two nations."

Chapter One, "Sentinels of the Past," focuses upon the key outposts and the principal Halifax fortifications that earned the garrison town the nickname "Gibraltar of British North America" in the late 1800s. Please note: the Halifax Citadel—the name by which today's fifty-acre national historic site is commonly known—will be referred to throughout the accompanying text and chapters as "Fort George," in keeping with its traditional name of two hundred years.

1. York Redoubt, showing Battery No. 2 armed with 10-inch rifled muzzle loader, 1873. In distance is McNab's Island with Sherbrooke Tower to right.

2. Line drawing of principal forts, blockhouses, and batteries that comprised the early Halifax defence system. This map appeared in Harry Piers' classic reference book *The Evolution Of The Halifax Fortress 1749-1928*. Piers (1870-1940) was the long-time curator of the Provincial Museum and librarian of the Provincial Science Library.

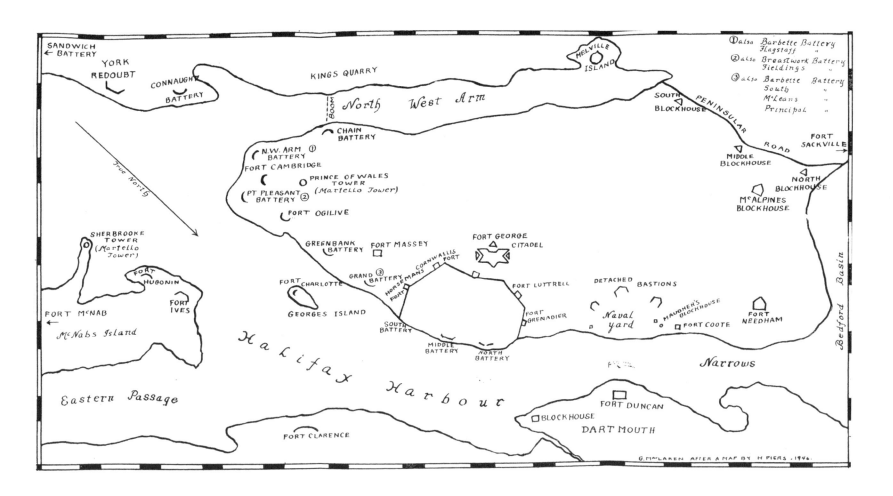

The British built a small blockhouse at Piziquid (Windsor) in 1750, on a hill overlooking the confluence of the Avon and St. Croix Rivers, near the Minas Basin. Its strategic purpose was to guard against attack by Acadians and Indians on Halifax, to interrupt trade with the French fortress of Louisbourg, and to maintain lines of communication and travel with the Bay of Fundy. Fort Edward is significant in that it is the oldest surviving blockhouse of two hundred built in Canada. Based upon a standard military design, Fort Edward is representative of the fourteen blockhouses erected at Halifax between 1750 and 1808. "Blockhouse" is derived from the German *blochaus*, meaning "a house which blocks a pass"; these sturdy forts were cheap and quick to construct from materials at hand and were impervious to muskets and arrows. The fire-power of those at Halifax were bolstered with forty small swivel cannons. Interestingly, all blockhouses built by the British during their conquest of Acadie were prefabricated at Halifax by French workers, then transported, by troops, in pieces to the field and assembled on site.

4. FORT SACKVILLE BARRACKS C.1878.

In September 1749, three months after landing at Chebucto, Governor Cornwallis ordered Gorham's Rangers to proceed to Bedford Basin and establish an outpost fort near the mouth of the Sackville River. Their mission was to protect the vulnerable British flank from surprise attack and to provide support for the troops at Minas and Annapolis. By December, a road eighteen feet wide had been hacked thirty miles through the trackless forest to Minas, only a day's march from Halifax should reinforcements be needed. Exactly what the original fort at Sackville entailed is unclear; circa 1755, it was described as occupying one acre of land, a hundred feet above low water, upon which a picket stockade enclosed a blockhouse and barracks garrisoned by fifty men armed with muskets, swivel guns, and one cannon. After the British and Mi'kmaq signed a Treaty of Peace & Friendship in 1760, Fort Sackville's strategic value diminished considerably. Its primary purpose during much of the nineteenth century was to be a look-out post for deserters from Halifax. Remnants of the fort remained until the early 1900s.

5. PRINCE EDWARD ORDERED THESE FIELD OFFICERS' QUARTERS BUILT IN 1797 AT FORT ANNE, ANNAPOLIS ROYAL. IN 1917, FORT ANNE WAS DESIGNATED CANADA'S FIRST NATIONAL HISTORIC SITE.

After the founding of Halifax, the British retained a small garrison at Fort Anne for another century. The following order was issued on January 15, 1803: "A detachment consisting of two subalterns, two sergeants, three corporals, two drummers, one bugler, and seventy-eight privates of the 29th Regiment to march to Annapolis [135 miles] on Monday morning next, at second gunfire, agreeably to a route with which the commanding officer will be furnished by the Deputy Quartermaster General, who will provide extra coats and blankets as may be necessary for the detachment." The interior of Nova Scotia remained a wilderness for many years, the only means of reaching Annapolis overland being an Acadian footpath that connected with the military road cut in 1749 to Minas. A Halifax-to-Windsor stage coach didn't operate until 1815, and it was 1856 before the province's first railway connected the towns, two years after British troops had been withdrawn from the Annapolis and Windsor outposts. Halifax detachments bound for garrisons at Saint John and Fredericton, New Brunswick, would often travel to Windsor, then board vessels to cross the Bay of Fundy.

6. FORT GEORGE, CITADEL HILL, 1923. THE TWO PROMINENT
BUILDINGS WERE BARRACKS. TO THE RIGHT IS THE "CAVALIER,"
WHICH REMAINS TODAY. THE OTHER IS THE "BRICK BLOCK," A
THREE-STOREY BARRACKS BUILT C.1900 AND DEMOLISHED IN
1953. THE SMALL STRUCTURES AT OPPOSITE CORNERS WERE
MAGAZINES.

Pictured here is the fourth and last citadel to anchor Fortress Halifax. The fort's design—adapted to fit within the parameters imposed by the constricted, narrow hilltop—was based upon the Vauban principles in which all British Royal Engineers were schooled. Sebastien Vauban (1633-1707) was a French military engineer during the reign of Louis XIV, and his genius in conducting siege warfare was "legendary." From directing more than fifty assaults against fortified towns, Vauban mastered the art of not only breaking down defences but also building them to withstand attack. One source credits him with erecting or strengthening one hundred and sixty fortresses. His star-shaped design, as illustrated here, provided for clear lines of cannon and musket fire to all points outside the walls, leaving no place for an enemy to hide. Vauban's creativity carried over to other areas: he is credited with introducing the socket bayonet as well as ricochet gunfire, whereby a cannon ball was fired to bounce across the ground, taking out several targets in its path.

7. THE "DITCH OF DEATH," FORT GEORGE c.1879.

A Royal Engineer holds a ten-foot survey stick at the base of Fort George's ironstone "escarp of flank," or inner wall. To breach the citadel defences, an invading force would have faced the daunting task of crossing this "Ditch of Death," a dry moat encircling the fort's stone and earthen ramparts. A withering fusillade of cross-fire could be brought to bear on the ditch. Protected within the "escarp of flank," defenders were able to fire small-arms through loop holes, or short-barreled cannons filled with grape and canister shot from twenty strategically placed gun ports. Complementing the "escarp of flank" was the "counterscarp," an outer wall of the ditch facing the fort (left in photo), which had a musket gallery for snipers built throughout the perimeter, a gallery consisting of corridors and chambers cut with loop holes. To add to an attacker's woes, engineers constructed countermines beneath the expansive slopes, or glacis, leading to Fort George. These underground chambers (connected to the fort by passageways) contained explosive charges that could be detonated in the event of siege. By the late 1800s, with any threat of attack more imagined than real, the "Ditch of Death" was commonly used for picnics, vegetable gardens, and a shooting range—as evidenced by the improvised target.

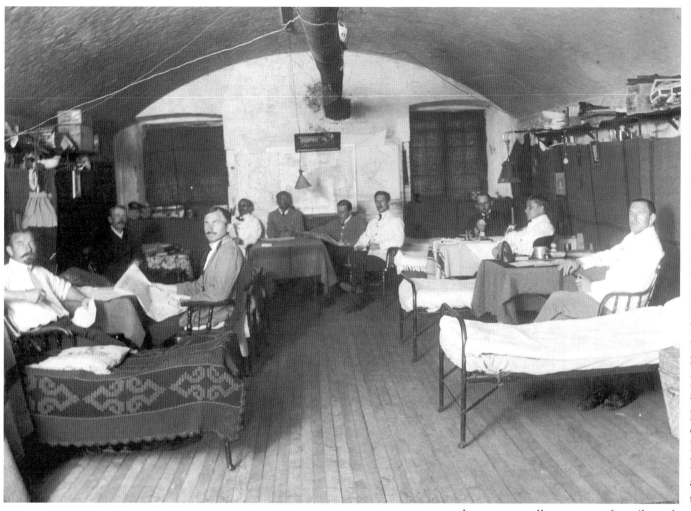

"Casemates" were reinforced, bomb-proof, vaulted rooms built within the thick ramparts of a fort. Within the walls of Fort George were sixty brick and masonry casemates (each of one or two storeys) buried beneath ten to twenty-five feet of earth. When completed in 1848, all these casements were damp and most leaked, which caused a ten-year headache for engineers until the issue was partially corrected with "Claridge's Patent Seyssel Asphalt" waterproofing. Casemates served a variety of purposes—barrack and office space, cook house, mess, canteen, library, school, recreational room, jail, ablution room, latrine, and general store; as well as storage for oil, coal, wood, ammunition, and fire-fighting apparatus; and trade shops for tailors, shoemakers, carpenters, blacksmiths, plumbers, and barbers. Some casemates were defensive in nature, designed with loop holes and embrasures for muskets and cannons. Seven arched rooms in the cavalier building were technically classified as casemates as well; one of their later uses, as featured here, was to house German POWs during World War One.

8. INTERIOR OF CAVALIER CASEMATE AT FORT GEORGE c.1915.

9. CAVALIER, FORT GEORGE 1877.

Plans of the fourth citadel called for three sturdily built, flat-roofed cavaliers to serve as barracks and gun platforms. The ironstone cavalier featured here, the largest and only one actually constructed, housed 322 men. (Barrack casemates under the ramparts replaced the other two proposed cavaliers.) Armed with seven 32-pound rooftop cannons facing west—the direction from which a land attack would be launched—the two-storey cavalier was higher than the ramparts and thus theoretically provided a clear field of fire. However, chimneys blocked gunners' viewplanes, building walls could not sustain thunderous cannon reverberations, and the flat-timbered roof, covered with earth and stone, leaked—all of which made it impractical for a gun platform. Strangely, the only access from ground level to upper storeys was by way of exterior staircases in the wooden verandahs that were intended to be removed during a siege to prevent catching fire. Modifications circa 1875 raised the top of the cavalier and converted it to barracks with a peaked roof. A fire in 1889 destroyed the roof and upper level, but these were soon repaired.

During the fourth citadel phase, two identical granite magazines, with a combined capacity of 3920 barrels of gunpowder, were built to replace a stone, bomb-proof magazine from the War of 1812. For safety, magazines were constructed to specific design plans as closely as the on-site cramped conditions permitted. The Fort George magazines were placed at opposite ends of the parade ground and enclosed behind blast walls ten feet high and three feet thick.

Despite strict regulations for the storage and handling of gunpowder, the occasional accident happened, sometimes with fatal results. On Dominion Day 1868, two artillerymen were mortally wounded while firing a salute to celebrate Canada's first anniversary of nationhood. An inquest held at the Military Hospital determined "that the deceased, Robert Bennett and James McHugh, came to their death accidentally by the premature explosion of a cartridge which they were in the act of ramming into a gun on the Citadel Hill on Wednesday, July 1st 1868. The jury are of the opinion that no blame is to be attached to any person, every proper precaution having been taken against accidents."

During the 1890s, the north magazine was converted to a canteen; in 1901-02, a brick building was erected in its place, which for many years served as a canteen, recreational room, and mess. The south magazine, which remains today, saw service during World War Two, first as a wet canteen, then as the operations room for anti-aircraft defences.

11. FORT GEORGE SIGNAL MASTS, LATE 1800s.

An effective means of communication was essential to link Fort George with surrounding fortifications. Outposts at the harbour approaches—Sambro Island lighthouse, Camperdown, and York Redoubt—were the first line of defence to relay early warning in the event of a seaborne attack. Two signaling masts had been erected at Fort George by the late 1700s, although there is evidence to suggest a rudimentary system was put in place at the time of Halifax's founding. A commercial mast, the taller at 117 feet above the ramparts, flew a series of pennants, discs, and flags to announce the arrival and departure of marine traffic. Identification charts were widely circulated to familiarize the general public with their meanings. The military signal mast measured seventy-eight feet in height and also used a series of flags and balls (substituted with lanterns at night) strung on yard-arms to send communiqués from Fort George throughout the town defences. When Prince Edward assumed command of military forces at Halifax in 1794, a more complicated, secretive coded telegraph system was introduced, a system it is believed he had become familiar with in Europe. With French privateers threatening British North America in 1797, Edward looked to expand his telegraph to outposts in Nova Scotia and New Brunswick and by 1798, a direct link had reached the garrison at Annapolis via Windsor. From Annapolis, a message was relayed by boat to Saint John, New Brunswick, then sent again by visual telegraph to the garrison at Fredericton. The system "worked admirably" with communication times in ideal weather conditions cut from three or four weeks to a mere forty-eight hours. On one occasion, Edward issued an order by telegraph to flog a Halifax soldier while he was in Annapolis Royal inspecting Fort Anne. A system of relay stations built on high ground, seven to eight miles apart, stretched from Halifax to Fredericton. Some stations were separated by fifteen miles of water, but signals atop a flagstaff could still be discerned at that distance with a telescope. Six soldiers manned each post, which consisted of a wooden building with an observatory on the roof. Proposed plans called for expansion of the telegraph into Quebec.

Norman Studio
9605

12. SAMBRO ISLAND, SHOWING FOGHORN STATION, LIGHTHOUSE KEEPER'S RESIDENCE, AND FLAGSTAFF, 1877. BUILT IN 1758, SAMBRO ISLAND LIGHTHOUSE IS THE OLDEST OPERATIONAL LIGHTHOUSE IN NORTH AMERICA. LOCATED TWO NAUTICAL MILES BEYOND THE HARBOUR ENTRANCE, IT WAS THE FIRST LINE OF DEFENCE IN ALERTING HALIFAX TO POSSIBLE ATTACK.

Edward's dream of a telegraph to Quebec died on the outskirts of Fredericton because it was too expensive to build and maintain. Large numbers of troops were needed to operate it, viewplanes had to be continually cut out, and bad weather obscured visibility. Had it not been for the fact that Britain and France were at war when plans were initially conceived, the telegraph might never have been built. As it was, when Edward left in 1800 and peace was signed two years later, the telegraph fell into disrepair—though it was still maintained at Halifax for many years, the greatest distance between points being Fort George to Sambro (eleven miles), with York Redoubt and Camperdown as relay stations. The arrival of the electric telegraph to Halifax in 1869 signaled a new era in military communications. As a footnote, there was a third telegraph in the early days, with the Admiralty operating a separate set of naval signals. Neither army or navy shared code books, apparently an accepted operational procedure at colonial outposts.

13. GATE AND DRAW-BRIDGE TO FORT CHARLOTTE, GEORGE'S ISLAND, HALIFAX HARBOUR c.1876.

While the main purpose of Fort George was to protect against an overland attack, George's Island was the first defensive position to be fortified to guard against a seaborne assault. Governor Edward Cornwallis describes this in a July 23, 1749 letter to the Duke of Bedford, Secretary of State: "George's Island lies very convenient for a battery to defend both the harbor and the town. It contains about ten or twelve acres.... I have now a guard there and stores, and propose to build a magazine upon it for powder." Clearing of land began in July 1750, and by November, seven heavy cannons and a field-work of sods were in place. George's Island filled many roles over the years. In 1751, Halifax's first jail—His Majesty's Gaol—was erected there; four years later it served as a detention area for Acadians awaiting deportation, and for French prisoners of war from 1755 to 1763. George's Island also contained a naval and quarantine hospital and was frequently used for Admiralty hangings.

14. FORT CHARLOTTE UPPER SOUTH BATTERY, GEORGE'S ISLAND C.1879.

By the 1830s, George's Island was the most heavily armed fortress in Halifax. The evolution of ordnance from smooth-bore cannons to rifled guns in the 1860s led to a complete rebuilding of defences between 1864 and 1870. Masonry and stone replaced the sod-and-timber ramparts of earlier days, as featured here and on the facing page. Two powerful batteries—consisting of huge, rifled muzzle loading cannons—were erected on a tier system facing seaward, the lower battery buried underground. In fact, much of the new Fort Charlotte was a subterranean labyrinth within in the bowels of George's Island: storehouses, powder magazines, and barracks connected by rail tracks, tunnels, and corridors. Rapid developments in military technology in the late 1800s (including the introduction of breech-loading guns, submarine mines, and torpedoes) lessened Fort Charlotte's importance as key harbour defences were moved far-

ther seaward to intercept increasingly heavier armed, ironclad warships, and speedy torpedo boats. When electricity was installed at Halifax forts in 1886, Fort Charlotte assumed an important role in the science of mine-laying warfare in its use as an assembly and storage site for submarine harbour mines.

15. FORT CLARENCE, SHOWING OUTER PARAPET AND DRAW-BRIDGE ENTRANCE OVER NORTH DITCH C.1880.

A "strong battery" was erected in 1754 on the Dartmouth shore opposite George's Island, where the Woodside Imperial Oil Refinery is located today. Originally named the Eastern Battery but changed in 1798 to Fort Clarence, the battery's primary purpose was to work in conjunction with Fort Charlotte to guard the eastern harbour channel from naval attack. There were two distinctive parts to the early Fort Clarence: a shoreline battery, mounting 12- and 24-pound smooth-bore cannons, and an earthen fort set back on higher ground. In 1863, Fort Clarence was completely rebuilt of concrete, ironstone, granite, and brick during the military construction frenzy that enveloped Halifax over the paranoia of possible attack from the United States. When completed circa 1874, the fort mounted eleven 9-inch, twelve-ton rifled muzzle loaders protected within underground bomb-proof "gun rooms" or casemates. The only accessible entry point to the fort was through this imposing gateway, behind which was a dry ditch, twenty-eight feet deep and thirty feet wide, the ditch spanned by a hand-cranked drawbridge on rails that could be withdrawn into the main defensive works.

15. FORT CLARENCE, SHOWING OUTER PARAPET AND DRAWBRIDGE ENTRANCE OVER NORTH DITCH C.1880.

16. NORTHWEST ARM BATTERY, POINT PLEASANT 1870.

In July 1762, during the Seven Years' War, Halifax received news that the French had captured St. John's, Newfoundland, and there was a flurry of activity to bolster sagging defences. One of several measures taken was the hasty erection of two batteries along the shore at Point Pleasant, marking the most seaward position yet fortified. Point Pleasant Battery, mounting eight 24-pound smooth-bore cannons, faced the main channel leading into the harbour. Northwest Arm Battery was erected four hun-dred yards to the west, its ten 9-pound guns trained on the entrance to the Northwest Arm to prevent an enemy from landing forces. To solid-ify the battery's defensive position, a timber-and-chain boom 720 feet long was stretched across the inlet waters, its anchor point at the Northwest Arm Battery still referred to as Chain Rock. Threat of attack dissipated within the month, peace was restored in 1763, and both bat-teries were allowed to fall into disrepair until the next crisis; in 1775, with the outbreak of the American Revolution, they were rebuilt again.

17. FORT OGILVIE, POINT PLEASANT, C.1880. THE ARTILLERY-MAN AND LITTLE GIRL INDICATE THAT ROYAL ARTILLERY FAMILIES WERE STAYING AT THE FORT, POSSIBLY IN BUILDING TO LEFT.

In 1793, at the beginning of the Napoleonic Wars, the British built Fort Ogilvie on a hill above Point Pleasant Battery "to augment cross-channel fire." Originally an earthen fort armed with six 24-pound cannons, it was completely rebuilt and enlarged in 1862 during the American Civil War and equipped with ten of the newly introduced rifled muzzle loaders. Further improvements made in 1888 included concrete gun emplacements mounted with breech-loading cannons.

Fortifications were commonly named for army and naval officers or for royalty. Fort Ogilvie, for example, honoured Brigadier General James Ogilvie, commander-in-chief at Halifax from 1789 to 1794, while Dartmouth's Fort Duncan was named for Henry Duncan, Royal Navy Commander and Commissioner of HM Dockyard. Prince Edward left several royal tributes: in 1798, he ordered the citadel to be thereafter known as Fort George for his father the King, and Fort Charlotte on George's Island for the Queen Mother. Five other forts and towers he named for three brothers—George, Prince of Wales; Frederick, Duke of York; and William, Duke of Clarence (later King William IV).

18. CAMBRIDGE BATTERY, BUILT 1862-68 AT POINT PLEASANT, WAS NAMED FOR THE DUKE OF CAMBRIDGE, A COUSIN OF QUEEN VICTORIA AND COMMANDER-IN-CHIEF OF THE BRITISH ARMY FOR MORE THAN FORTY YEARS. THE PICKET FENCE INDICATES LITTLE CONCERN, AT THAT TIME, FOR A REAR ATTACK.

York Redoubt in 1869. It would be ten years, however, before telegraphic communication between Fort George and the outlying Halifax forts was completed. By then, Alexander Graham Bell's invention had already changed the future course of communication, and in the early 1890s, the telephone rendered the electric telegraph obsolete, much as the latter had done to Edward's manual signal masts.

With its elevated position and powerful arsenal of 18-ton rifled muzzle loading cannons, Cambridge Battery provided "greater command" of McNab's Island, Northwest Arm, and the seaward approaches than either Point Pleasant or Northwest Arm Batteries. An interesting feature of this photo is the telegraph pole in the foreground. Communication was of increasing strategic importance by the mid 1800s, with the ever-expanding British Empire then covering twenty percent of the earth's surface. As such, Britain was a leader in the development and spread of the electric telegraph. In the 1850s an electric telegraph system already connected Nova Scotia with parts of eastern Canada and the United States, and a trans-Atlantic cable was completed in 1866. The Fenian scare of 1866 led to the establishment of the electric military telegraph at Halifax with the first equipment and operators in place at Fort George, Cambridge Battery, and

An "advanced post on the commanding summit of a rugged granite cliff" was erected four miles from Halifax along the west shore of the harbour, circa 1793-95. In the words of Prince Edward, it was meant "to annoy enemy shipping on their first entrance into the harbour." The battery of 32-pound smooth-bore cannons required no seaward protection due to their height above water and to the inability of war ships to elevate ordnance. Named for the Duke of York, the crude battery was entirely rebuilt and enlarged into a powerful fortress in 1863-77 and again in 1888-93, making it "the keystone in the Halifax defence system."

The first, self-propelled torpedo was developed in 1866 by Englishman Robert Whitehead; in 1877, the Royal Navy introduced the torpedo boat—a fast, small surface vessel designed in part to attack harbours. Torpedo boats were soon adopted by the world's major navies, which necessitated measures to counter this deadly menace. At Halifax in the late 1800s, York Redoubt became the control centre for electrically detonated mine-fields supported by searchlights and quick-firing batteries.

20. VIEW OF SOUTH GUN POSITIONS AT YORK REDOUBT, c.1880. THE FORT THEN MEASURED 1,760 FEET LONG BY 660 FEET WIDE, WITH A HEIGHT ABOVE SEA LEVEL VARYING FROM 150 TO 234 FEET.

Two types of mines were developed during the nineteenth century. Contact mines, being "blind and unintelligent," destroyed both friendly and hostile vessels. Controlled mines, on the other hand, were more practical as they could be manually released and detonated individually or in clusters from shore using underwater electronic cables. The latter formed the basis of Halifax's submarine mining defence. Initial plans for submarine mining were undertaken in 1880, with storage and test facilities erected circa 1885 at York Redoubt and Fort Charlotte. 1889 saw the construction, at York Redoubt, of a forward command observation post equipped with depression range finder, firing mechanisms, and maps of the harbour minefield. Powerful searchlights along the cliffs and at Point Pleasant Battery illuminated the harbour at night. York Redoubt remained operational until the mid 1950s, serving as barracks for troops awaiting shipment overseas during World War One, then as the Fire Command Post for harbour defences in World War Two.

A unique component of early defences were the five stone and masonry towers erected between 1796 and 1814. The Prince of Wales Tower, built in 1796-98 on the highest elevation at Point Pleasant (125 feet above sea level), gave it "command" of Fort Ogilvie as well as the Northwest Arm and Point Pleasant Batteries four hundred yards distant. Because the Prince of Wales Tower was strategically positioned to protect the lower fortifications against a land attack from the rear, and to guard the Northwest Arm from enemy vessels, all trees south of the tower were cleared away to provide an open field of fire to the harbour. The massive, two-storey structure was twenty-six feet high and seventy-two feet in diameter, with walls eight feet thick, and floors planked with thirty-six-inch-thick timbers. The multi-purpose tower was designed to be a gun platform, "self-defensible battery keep," barracks for two hundred men, powder magazine, and arms store. Two fireplaces vented through the wall provided heat, but the interior remained cold and damp, making it generally unsuitable for barracks or powder storage in the early years. Forty-three loopholes for muskets and four gun-ports for cannons were cut into the walls; the parapet supported twelve heavy guns. Until the War of 1812, munition stores included one hundred rounds for each cannon, seventy-two muskets, twelve pistols, ten thousand ball cartridges, and thirty boarding pikes. A vertical cylindrical hollow shaft, thirteen feet in diameter, ran through the tower's centre and hoisted ammunition to the roof. Leakage was a constant problem, and the conical roof featured here was added in 1825; it was adapted for cannons to fire through or could be removed altogether in the event of a prolonged attack. In the early 1860s, the tower was completely renovated into a self-defensible magazine for powder and shells; introduction of rifled artillery in the 1870s rendered its defensive capability obsolete, but it remained a magazine for Point Pleasant batteries until 1881.

cled by a ditch seven feet wide and eight feet deep, with entry by an exterior staircase to the roof; this staircase was replaced in 1812 with a lower level door and drawbridge. With smaller dimensions than the Prince of Wales Tower, this tower's base measured fifty feet in diameter, tapering to thirty-five feet at the parapet with six foot thick walls cut throughout for musket loopholes and cannon gun-ports. Because sandstone could not endure the ravages of maritime weather, nor withstand the punishment inflicted by rifled muzzle loaders, ten feet of the upper storey was removed in 1863 and the remaining tower converted to a small barracks and reinforced magazine. In 1889, another level was demolished, leaving the basement as a magazine; the accumulated rubble was used to build a wharf at Ives Point on McNab's Island, but within a year this, too, had deteriorated so badly that it had to be rebuilt in ironstone. "From this time on," writes Harry Piers, "as new forts were constructed farther out the harbour, the value of Fort Clarence decreased." In 1900, two 4.7-inch quick-fire guns were mounted on top of what remained of the old tower to ward off torpedo boat attacks. Between 1906 and 1913, the fort was completely stripped of its armament, then sold in 1927 as part of a thirty-four-acre land deal to the Imperial Oil Company, which had built a refinery in 1916 adjacent to the military site. The last vestiges of Fort Clarence were demolished during World War Two.

22. THE LOWER STOREY OF DUKE OF CLARENCE TOWER WAS ALL THAT REMAINED AT THE TIME OF THIS C.1878 PHOTO.

Duke of Clarence Tower was unique among the five stone towers in that it stood three storeys high and was constructed of sandstone, the others being ironstone and granite. Built circa 1798 at Fort Clarence to replace an earlier barracks, the tower could accommodate 164 men. It was encir-

23. DUKE OF YORK TOWER, YORK REDOUBT.

Perched atop a cliff 230 feet high, the medieval-looking Duke of York Tower, incorporated into York Redoubt defences in 1798, would have been an imposing sentinel to vessels entering Halifax harbour. In addition to a gun-platform and barracks, the thirty-foot-high tower formed part of Edward's visual telegraph system from 1797 to 1879, relaying messages between Fort George and Camperdown at Portuguese Cove inside Chebucto Head. The Duke of York Tower was extensively damaged by fire circa 1896, after which the upper storey was removed, leaving the remaining structure for coal storage. Remains of the tower, along with old gun emplacements, stone buildings, and large segments of the outer masonry walls are preserved today as a National Historic Site.

24. SHERBROOKE TOWER WAS BUILT AT MAUGERS BEACH ON McNAB'S ISLAND, DIRECTLY ACROSS THE CHANNEL FROM YORK REDOUBT. IT WAS THIS LIGHT WHERE ABRAHAM GESNER, IN 1851, FIRST TESTED HIS NEW INVENTION, KEROSENE, AS A REPLACEMENT FOR WHALE OIL.

The last two stone towers were built during the War of 1812. Fort Charlotte Tower on George's Island lasted from 1812 to 1877. Construction of Sherbrooke Tower started in 1814 but, due to expense overruns, was suspended before completion of the second storey; work resumed in 1826 and was finished within two years. During that time, a lighthouse was recommended for McNab's Island, and the provincial legislature allotted funds for its construction. However, a decision was made instead to incorporate the light atop Sherbrooke Tower, "thereby permitting a commanding site for the light and a free sweep for the tower's guns over the whole of the channel." The province was permitted to roof in the tower on condition it not hinder firing the guns, the military would accrue no expense, and, should the need arise, the roof and light "must be subject to removal." Of the five towers, Sherbrooke Tower was the only one originally designed to be bombproof, having been built of squared granite facing outside of brick. The tower's base formed the foundation of a replacement lighthouse erected during World War Two.

25. IVES POINT BATTERY, MCNAB'S ISLAND, LOOKING WEST TOWARD HALIFAX WITH GEORGE'S ISLAND VISIBLE, c.1876. THE FORT WAS NAMED FOR CAPTAIN BENJAMIN IVES, AN ORIGINAL HALIFAX SETTLER WHO SERVED WITH PEPPERELL AT LOUISBOURG. MCNAB'S—AT THREE MILES LONG AND ONE MILE WIDE—IS THE LARGEST ISLAND IN HALIFAX HARBOUR.

Steps to fortify McNab's Island were initially taken in 1762 during the Seven Years' War. Plans called for the building of a ten-gun battery on the northwest point of the island, which could support the fire-power of newly completed Point Pleasant and Northwest Arm Batteries. Work ceased after only one month, however, due to lack of manpower and was cancelled in 1763 with the declaration of peace. Not until a century later, in 1865, did construction resume with growing fears of an attack from the south during the American Civil War. Completed in 1870, Ives Point was ideally situated, being equidistant (2200 yards) from Fort Ogilvie to the west and Fort Clarence to the east. A two-year project to strengthen the parapets and magazines using concrete began in 1888. When completed, Fort Ives boasted a new quick-fire battery comprised of six 6-inch guns having a maximum range of ten thousand yards, with the capability to penetrate 11.5 inches of wrought iron at one thousand yards. The fort was activated in World War One as part of the harbour defences but was abandoned for World War Two.

26. FORT McNAB, SHOWING 10-INCH BREECH-LOADING GUN, c.1895. THIS WAS REPORTEDLY THE ONLY 10-INCH BREECH LOADER EVER MOUNTED IN HALIFAX AND, AT THIRTY-TWO TONS, WAS TWICE THE WEIGHT OF EARLIER 10-INCH RIFLED MUZZLE LOADERS WHICH WERE MOUNTED IN FORTS DURING THE 1870S AND 1880S.

McNab's Island was originally known as Cornwallis Island as Governor Edward Cornwallis, in 1749, deeded much of the land to his nephews. In 1782, Peter McNab purchased the island, which stayed in the McNab family for 150 years. In the 1860s, the British Admiralty acquired large portions of the island to build additional harbour defences. Work began on Fort McNab in 1889; when completed five years later, it was the farthest seaward battery, being nearly four-and-a-half miles from the centre of Halifax. Fort McNab was intended to guard the harbour entrance from Chebucto Head and Sambro Ledges to Lawrencetown and Cole Harbour. An interesting feature of the fort was the private McNab cemetery within its walls, where family members continued to be interred until the early 1900s. During World War Two, the fort served as a plotting room and radar post.

27. FORT HUGONIN, McNAB'S ISLAND, c.1899. NOTE GUN SHIELDS, WHICH AFFORDED BETTER PROTECTION FOR ARTILLERYMEN.

Fort Hugonin was constructed in 1899 on a slight elevation along the west shore between Ives Point and McNab's Cove. Named for Peter McNab's son-in-law, Captain Roderick Hugonin, the fort was armed with the latest 4.7-inch quick-fire guns and served as an observation station for the harbour mine field. Fort Hugonin, in conjunction with Fort McNab, could direct a withering fusillade onto the unprotected far shore below York Redoubt or onto torpedo boats running up the harbour. The fort was turned over to the navy in 1942 and used as an instrument centre for degaussing ships to neutralize magnetic mines.

28. UNLOADING RIFLED MUZZLE LOADING GUNS, HALIFAX
c.1873.

Land and sea battles were fought for three hundred years using smooth-bore cannons made of iron, brass, or bronze. It has been said that a gunner from the days of the Spanish Armada in 1588 would have had little difficulty operating the ordnance mounted at Halifax in the 1850s. This changed dramatically in the 1860s with the advent of rifled muzzle loaders. By the late nineteenth century, new-age weaponry weighed eight times that of the old smooth-bores and could fire heavier, more explosive projectiles ten times farther and with greater accuracy. The rifled muzzle loaders (RMLs) being unloaded in this picture weighed twelve tons, which necessitated the installment of a fifteen-ton crane to replace an older model used to hoist five-ton smooth-bores. The 1870s and 1880s saw seventy-seven RMLs of varying sizes mounted in eight forts. Although capable of reaching targets at six thousand yards, RMLs were most effective at two thousand yards, making them ideal for defending Halifax Harbour, as key entry points were within the two-thousand-yard range and several forts overlapped fields of fire to provide a deadly defensive blanket.

29. 59TH COMPANY ROYAL ARTILLERY PRACTICE ON 6-INCH BREECH LOADING GUN AT FORT OGILVIE C.1904.

Despite their killing power, rifled muzzle loaders were ponderous to handle and had a slow rate of operation. In the smooth-bore era, a gun crew could fire one round per minute. A well-trained, eleven-man RML crew took two-and-a-half minutes to load, sight, and fire a 10-inch gun. Speed in late-nineteenth-century warfare was essential for Halifax gunners trying to hit heavily armoured, fast-moving warships or elusive tor-pedo boats. In the late 1870s, improved breech-loading guns were intro-duced, some later models weighing 27 tons with the capability to fire 380-pound shells up to 34,000 yards. The Royal Navy began mounting breech loading guns in 1884 on its warships. Breech loaders were first recommended for Halifax in 1886 and while more expensive than RMLs, fewer were needed to do the job. Quick-fire guns—small light breech loaders capable of six shots per minute—were added to some for-tifications in 1900-01 to guard against torpedo boat attacks.

30. Fort George southwest ramparts, with 64-pound RML c.1880.

Due to myopic political foresight, Fort George was a money pit from day one, eating up some £300,000 prior to 1825 to restore and revamp temporary works in times of war and crisis. Nearly that much again was spent until the fourth citadel was completed in 1856. By then, rifled ordnance had rendered it obsolete and, although adapted for the new guns, time had run out. Originally designed to protect Halifax from a land-based attack, Fort George did serve for a short time in the late 1800s as a sea battery of minor importance, covering the inner harbour north of George's Island to the Dartmouth shore. The emphasis then, however, was on keeping warships as far to seaward as possible, and by the 1890s the key installations were Fort McNab, Fort Ives, and York Redoubt, with support from Forts Hugonin, Cambridge, Ogilvie, Clarence, Charlotte, and Point Pleasant. In the late 1800s, more than £200,000 were spent to transform these works into bastions capable of withstanding modern weaponry. By 1900, Fort George's "defensive usefulness had ended once and for all," its military role reduced to that of a barracks and administrative centre. The last fort built during the British period was Sandwich Battery, about half a mile south of York Redoubt at Ferguson's Cove. Completed just before the remaining troops left in 1906, it mounted four breech-loading guns and, with Fort McNab, could engage enemy vessels up to six miles out to sea. In less than three decades, several of these relics would be dusted off for duty during two world wars.

CHAPTER 2

THE KING'S YARD

For all the importance attributed to the establishment of Halifax as a naval and military base in 1749, only three sloops of war were initially assigned for its protection. As surprising as this may seem, "It can be stated quite bluntly," writes W. A. B. Douglas, "that the Lords of the Admiralty had no intention of maintaining a strong naval force in the new colony. The opposite was true—they would bend over backwards to avoid a direct naval confrontation with France in Nova Scotia. Financial retrenchment may have influenced them to some degree, but diplomatic considerations were the prime factor prompting such an attitude." However, this attitude would change.

With Halifax proving itself an immediate irritant to the French, an unofficial colonial war soon broke out in Nova Scotia. Britain was well aware that French naval vessels out of Louisbourg maintained lucrative trade and often illicit smuggling contacts with Mi'kmaq and Acadians as well as with enterprising New Englanders. From 1750-55, the onus for patrolling and providing a semblance of naval presence in coastal waters fell to the provincial marine or sea militia. Under directives from the governor, a flotilla of eleven vessels—owned and crewed predominately by American colonials who had years of experience in such matters—maintained Halifax's "lifeline" with Boston and with outposts at Annapolis, Minas, Canso, Chignecto, and Lunenburg.

A change in Imperial policy came in 1755, when Admiral Edward Boscawen sailed into Halifax Harbour with a fleet of nineteen warships and eight thousand men, bent upon a campaign to sever French supply lines and to settle matters once and for all. Fort Beauséjour was captured in short order and renamed Fort Cumberland. The next step was the detention and expulsion of Acadians, an agonizing and controversial ordeal that lasted eight years.

Halifax was ideally suited for a dockyard, its spacious, deep-water harbour capable of holding the entire Royal Navy, its virgin forests overflowing with timber and resin for vessel repair and construction. Boscawen immediately made arrangements for the procurement of a careening wharf where ship bottoms could be scraped of barnacles, which impaired speed and manoeuverability. He then ordered part of his fleet to winter at Halifax (to be ready for a spring blockade of the St. Lawrence River) and withdrew the rest to warmer West Indian climes.

The outbreak of the Seven Years' War thrust Halifax into a strategic naval position that it would maintain intermittently for nearly two centuries. Things moved slowly at the outset. The first Naval Storekeeper was assigned in 1756, and naval supplies valued at £16,000 were shipped out from England; by 1758, expenditures would more than double. In February 1759, the King's Yard was officially established at Halifax on nine acres of land to the south of today's MacDonald Bridge. Successful campaigns were launched against Louisbourg (1758), Quebec (1759), and Montreal (1760), which secured British dominance in North America. During the invasion scare of 1762—triggered by French forces capturing St. John's Newfoundland—the Royal Navy shored up Halifax defences. Admiral Lord Colville moved his flagship *Northumberland* mid channel, between Point Pleasant and McNab's Island, to serve as a floating battery. An armed sloop was placed in the southeast passage near the Dartmouth shore and another moored inside the chain boom, closing off the Northwest Arm. These moves were significant in that they demonstrated the added fire-power an attacker would have faced from naval warships, had the static harbour defences been breached.

The King's Yard retained its importance for a short time following the Seven Years' War. It served as an advance base for ships of the North America and West Indies Squadron assigned to enforce the navigation laws as ruled upon by the Vice-Admiralty Court at Halifax, which maintained jurisdiction on "any and all causes of a maritime origin." During the years of peace in the late 1760s, the Yard's role was scaled back considerably to pre-1755 status. But with the American Revolution and Napoleonic Wars, the Yard again reverberated with the sounds of hammer and adze, and a three-hundred-man Naval Yard Volunteer Force was raised to defend the King's Yard in the event of an American attack. The War of 1812 saw the dockyard at its peak of operation, with 1,600 men employed. British warships came and went regularly between assignments that involved blockading the American coast, chasing down privateers, and escorting invasion forces against targets such as Castine and Washington.

The Napoleonic Wars and War of 1812 have been romanticized as a time when "the town and port were bright with the pomp and circumstance of glorious war." A prominent Haligonian of the period, however, remembered it differently.

"What times these are indeed. This latest war inflates Halifax's general economy as well as its incidence of public disturbance. The town is a virtual quay and cockpit at Shrovetide. Ruffians rule the streets, and vagrants the alleys. There is no place for an honest man out-of-doors at night, and for honest women…one doubts seeing them on the streets even at mid-day. Black eyes and a cracked-skull have now become the marks of a night on the town…. The lower courts are crowded with cases of riot and assault, and mine own docket a full catalogue of manslaughter and murder."

Press gangs and privateers are two elements, from that period, to which Halifax has become inextricably linked. The Royal Navy was an equal opportunity employer. Only half its seamen were English, the remainder being a melting pot of Irish, Scots, Blacks from the West Indies and Americas, Africans, Scandinavians, Italians, French, even Americans. Many volunteered, others were "pressed." In times of peace, Britain did not maintain a large navy, which meant that when war came—as it did so often in the late eighteenth and early nineteenth centuries—the search for crews was on. In 1800, the Royal Navy required

130,000 men for its ships. Thomas Raddall writes in *Hangman's Beach*,

"The English were futile on land [but] the sea was another matter. [The] French built better ships, and manned them with capable seamen, but…[could not]…produce sea-fighters as the English did. For all their talk of freedom, as if they had invented it, the English notoriously made slaves of their poor to man their warships. They snatched up *canaille* from their streets and jails and forced them into their ships…keeping them aboard for years without a foot to shore, flogging them savagely for any slackness, hanging any man who uttered a word against his fate. Men kept at sea in such a manner had only one outlet in their hard and cruel lives, the chance of battle, in which they fought like wolves."

The Impress Service was the Royal Navy's "recruiting" tool, with roots dating back to the eleventh century. Press gangs of eight to twelve men, accompanied by an officer, were set loose upon the streets to "convince" males between the ages of eighteen and fifty-five, preferably with sea experience, to accept the King's Shilling (see Chapter 6) and sign on willingly; those who declined were taken by force. Thomas Akins describes this in his *History of Halifax City*:

"On the 6th January an armed party of sailors and marines assisted by soldiers and commanded by naval officers, seized in the streets of the town some of the inhabitants and several coasters belonging to Lunenburg, who had come up in their vessels to sell their produce; they bound their hands behind their backs, carried them through the streets and lodged them in the guardhouses, from which they were conveyed on board the ships of war in the harbour."

Armed guards posted about a ship were under orders to shoot any man who made an attempt to run or swim to freedom. In many cases, press gangs roamed at will, but in Halifax permission was often needed before filling their quota. "Two press warrants were issued this year [1797] by the council—one on 31st January to Admiral Murray for twenty-four hours in the town, and another in October to Admiral Vandeput for two months through the province." Sailors from merchant ships were highly prized, with one merchant seaman considered the equal of any three others brought in by the press gangs. Merchant seamen earned four times the wage paid in the Royal Navy, where an ordinary seaman earned nineteen shillings ($2.28) monthly, with an able seaman earning, twenty-four shillings ($2.88). The only limit imposed as to how many could be taken from a merchant crew (officers and apprentices were exempted) was that sufficient men must remain to sail the vessel. Some merchant seamen carried "tickets" which supposedly protected them from the press, but this was not always the case. A naval captain could and often did exchange his worst sailors for a merchant ship's best, a completely legal circumvention of the law. Six thousand seamen suspected of being British subjects were forcibly removed from American vessels between April 1809 and September 1810 and "pressed" into service aboard His Majesty's warships. And impressment was the first reason cited by President James Madison in his War Message of June 1812. Not until the 1850s and the Crimean War did impressment disappear. On April 1, 1853, Queen Victoria introduced an initial ten-year naval engagement period for those eighteen years of age and older; a pension was payable after twenty years service.

Marine historian Dan Conlin describes privateers as "privately owned warships, licensed and regulated by the state to attack enemy shipping and keep a share of what they captured." He credits privateers for presenting "a strong case to be considered as sea-going militia." Seventeen privateers were licensed out of Halifax in the Seven Years' War, a number that grew to seventy-seven during the American Revolution.

"Privateering had evolved by 1793 an elaborate system to regulate its activities and distribute its proceeds. A group of interested merchants posted a bond of £1500, pledging themselves worth the amount should there be any violation of the King's instructions and regulations for private ships of war. That bond obtained a commission from the Governor to operate a private warship along with a warrant from the Court of Vice-Admiralty to issue a Letter of Marque and Reprisal. The Letter of Marque authorized the privateer to bring captured vessels, called prizes, to Vice-Admiralty's Prize Court for adjudication. The Vice-Admiralty Judge would rule whether the capture was legal. This decision was based on affidavits of the privateer crew, captured documents and interrogation of captured mariners, who answered a long detailed list of questions about their vessel and cargo called 'the standing interrogatories.' If the capture was judged legal, the vessel and its cargo were 'condemned,' that

is ordered to be auctioned. Once the court and administrative fees were deducted, the privateer owners, officers and crew were free to divide the remainder according to their own agreement. Royal Navy crews were also entitled to a share in their captures and used the same court system. The capture, judgement, sale, resale and distribution of captured ships by both privateers and the navy created a sort of industry, sometimes called 'prize making' that involved many players in Nova Scotia society" (Conlin).

While privateers sailing the Caribbean were often "pressed" for men, it appears that those operating out of Halifax had an amiable working relationship with the Royal Navy on station as well as with certain captains in the West Indies. Privateers often served as the eyes and ears for the navy, providing valuable information and intelligence on enemy movement. The importance of privateers to Imperial interests in Halifax is illustrated by the fact that their cannons and shot were often supplied from government stores. A case in point was the town of Liverpool on Nova Scotia's south shore, which operated nearly half the privateers sailing out of Nova Scotia. Captains there were loaned twenty-seven cannons and sixteen hundred pounds of shot from stores at the King's Yard. The Napoleonic Wars were, according to Dan Conlin, the "last hurrah" for privateering, and "the practice was generally outlawed by the Declaration of Paris in 1856."

Drastic changes were in store for Halifax with the cessation of hostilities in 1815. There had always been a scaling back of dockyard activity in peacetime. But on this occasion, the royal coffers were drained after nineteen years of nearly continuous war with France and after the immense expense incurred fighting two combatants simultaneously in the War of 1812. Following the American Revolution, Britain had become concerned about future attacks upon Halifax and began looking for a more secure base of operations. She found it eight hundred miles away: in 1795, work began on a dockyard and resupply depot at Bermuda for ships travelling between Halifax and the West Indies. A formidable fortress was built on the island between 1814 and 1863, using a labour force of ten thousand convicts. In 1819, Halifax was downgraded to a depot and the dockyard moved to Bermuda. There is debate as to what effect this had upon the garrison town, considering the fleet still summered in Halifax. Some claim it was a terrible economic blow, while others say the damage was minimal. The February 16, 1918 *Acadian Recorder* gives this retrospective analysis:

"The reduction of the Dockyard establishment in 1819 was a great loss to the town. A large force of workmen were thrown out of employment without any provision from the government. This change was viewed by the inhabitants as an extremely injudicious one. It was the current opinion, at that time, that it was brought about by one of the admirals on the station, who taking offence at some occurrences in the town, took this means of showing his revenge. It was pointed out when the change was being made that Bermuda had none of the advantages that Halifax possessed for an effective Dockyard. It was by no means suited for a receptacle of those articles which, continuously assailed by the climate and insects peculiar to the place, soon decay. Moreover, Bermuda was still less calculated for the hospital, to the success of which the dampness of the atmosphere and the scarcity and high price of provisions, seemed to impose insurmountable impediments.

"Independently of these objections, it was the opinion of experienced persons that the work could not be completed in the manner designed, from obstacles of a broad nature, which could never be overcome or removed. The Dockyard at Halifax, on the contrary, was situated on a fine commodious harbour in a healthy climate, and in a country abounding with provisions of all kinds. It was not long after the project for the removal of the Dockyard was carried out when it was found, in many respects, not to have realized the advantages contemplated by the change.

"A few years after the removal, the shears, a gigantic apparatus at the Yard, used for throwing down vessels was demolished. The shears was a very conspicuous object, and stood so high that it could be seen from most parts of the town. The Royal Standard floated from the staff which surmounted the shears on the King's and Queen's birthdays, and other public holidays."

There is still uncertainty and debate over what precipitated the move to Bermuda. Perhaps it was strategic thinking. Then again, the weather might have been a factor. The British first garrisoned the West Indies in 1678, and by 1742 the Royal Navy was wintering there.

According to historian Peter Landry, "Up to 1740 there was not much thought given by the Royal Navy to have any kind of a systematic patrol of the North Atlantic coast. Indeed, it was in March of 1742, that [Admiral Peter] Warren was to make *Proposals for the Better Employing His Majesty's Ships Stationed on the Coast of North America*: 'The severity of the winter from the middle of November to the latter end of March is sufficient protection to the colonies to the northward of Virginia. I propose that the ships stationed at New York and New England and one of those at Virginia should, about the middle of November, proceed to Barbados or Antigua…. They should continue on the station till 20 Mar., and would probably intercept the Spanish privateers who fit out at Havana about that time in order to cruise on our trade to the northward.'

"The Admiralty put Warren's suggestions into effect and made him in charge of the squadron. Thereafter, the West Indies had a presence (certainly in the winter) and a seasonal presence along the eastern coast of North America." With the disease-infested West Indies a killing ground for Imperial forces, perhaps a move to Bermuda was thought more healthy, although medical history shows this to have not been the case.

Still another reason for moving the dockyard from Halifax might have been economics. The Royal Navy is said to have invested large sums in acquiring Bermuda-built schooners for sloops of war based upon designs dating to 1609. These small, fast vessels had the advantage of being constructed of Bermuda cedar—highly desirable over traditional oak as the cedar was plentiful, durable, impervious to shipworm, and did not require seasoning. One of the more lighthearted and less plausible explanations for the move, referred to by the *Acadian Recorder*, is based upon local folklore. The Commander-in-Chief of the North America and West Indies Squadron in 1819 was Admiral Edward Griffith. While on station at Halifax, the admiral entertained himself raising pigs in his garden. They were apparently allowed to roam at will, to the chagrin of many, and when requests were received from local citizenry to get rid of the intruders, Griffith packed up and moved operations to Bermuda.

The Halifax dockyard received a new lease on life in the 1860s when the American Civil War saw it refurbished to accommodate a large squadron of British warships intent upon thwarting any aggressive acts directed toward its interests. Halifax was elevated to a prestigious level in 1869, when the Duke of Cambridge made it part of his "Maritime Quadrilateral." As one of the four points—Malta, Gibralter, and Bermuda being the others—Halifax qualified for substantial expenditures to build and upgrade all aspects of its defensive capabilities, solidifying its importance into the twentieth century. Until the early 1900s, the duties of the Royal Navy in the North Atlantic remained consistent with policy established in 1819: "showing the flag" to British colonies, monitoring the Newfoundland fishery, keeping a watch on the Americans, and diffusing political unrest in the West Indies and Central America.

1. Ship's company on deck of Flagsship HMS *Blake*, Halifax c.1895.

2. NORTH DOCKYARD GATE FROM UPPER WATER STREET, LEADING TO NAVAL HOSPITAL AND VICTUALING YARD, 1883.

The North Dockyard Gate was built in 1809. A similar entrance known as the Main or South Gate opening onto Dockyard Lane (later Artz Street) was of an earlier period, dating to 1770. A stone wall enclosing the yard boundaries was erected in 1769 and originally featured a cat-walk for defenders to fire from in the event of attack. Several bell posts (like the one featured here) were placed throughout the yard, to be rung in the event of emergency. The Intercolonial Railway linking Halifax with Truro (opened 1858) ran close to the yard, as can be seen in this photo. In 1883, vibrations from locomotives and rail cars caused structural damage, requiring portions of the South Gate entrance and dockyard wall to be rebuilt.

3. HM DOCKYARD, HALIFAX, C.1870. THE VESSEL IS *PYRAMUS*, CAPTURED BY ADMIRAL NELSON AT THE BATTLE OF COPENHAGEN. WHILE MOORED AT HALIFAX FROM 1832 TO 1879, *PYRAMUS* SERVED AS A PRISON HULK, RECEIVING SHIP, AND FLOATING HOSPITAL, THEN WAS BROKEN UP FOR ITS COPPER FASTENINGS.

Copper was literally worth its weight in gold during the era of wooden ships. Legend contends "a vest pocket full of copper nails was an equivalent for a gill of rum in any of the numerous grog-shops outside and contiguous the dockyard." Men were commonly observed scrounging for the valuable commodity in parts of the naval yard where vessels were repaired and broken up. A most interesting character from that time period was a man known only as "Old Copper Nails." As the name implies, he had a "wonderful fondness for those articles" and generally carried one or two pounds in his pockets. One day the eccentric gentleman was hired for a menial job in naval stores. To his amazement, the room contained open kegs of copper! Upon leaving the dockyard sometime later it was evident that Old Copper Nails was having difficulty walking and displayed a decidedly suspicious persona. Upon closer inspection, guards discovered that he had secreted away fifty pounds of nails throughout his clothing. Barred from ever stepping foot in the dockyard again, Old Copper Nails died shortly thereafter from what some say was a broken heart.

the attention of then Commander-in-Chief Prince Edward, Duke of Kent. The man was summoned into Edward's presence to explain himself. Standing firm upon religious conviction, he reiterated a willingness to work on Sunday for king and country but declined to be reimbursed. A royal order was immediately given for the fervently patriotic but religious individual to receive increased pay every weekday and never again be required to work on Sunday.

The long-service award for years of employment at the dockyard surely must go to Samuel Sellon, who began in 1776 apprenticing to the master shipwright. He worked seventy-five years in that vocation, passing away in 1851 at the age of eighty-seven. Hundreds of civilians were dependent upon the dockyard for their livelihood, especially during times of war when employment was high and the hours of work long. On many occasions, men were required to work on Sunday, which proved unpopular but lucrative as double pay was then given. One man, although he worked on the Sabbath, refused to accept his pay; such an irregularity confounded the book-keepers who brought the matter to

5. ADMIRALTY HOUSE, 1928. THE GRAND OLD MANSION IS MAINTAINED TODAY AS THE MARITIME COMMAND MUSEUM, WHICH HOUSES A TREASURE TROVE OF ARTIFACTS, PHOTOGRAPHS, AND DOCUMENTS PERTAINING TO CANADA'S NAVAL HERITAGE.

A residence befitting the admiral on station was imperative, and in October 1814 the building of Admiralty House commenced. As dockyard construction workers neared completion of the basement level, word arrived from England that changes be made to the structural plans, with wood replacing the stone exterior. Rear-Admiral Edward Griffith, in charge of the project, ignored the order and simply modified the stone design by omitting two proposed wings. Initially financed with a grant of £3,000 from the British Admiralty, cost overruns incurred from ornate plaster ceilings, mahogany woodwork, and marble fireplaces necessitated a further £1500 being appropriated from the Nova Scotia House of Assembly. Shortly after Admiralty House was completed, naval headquarters was transferred to Bermuda, but the mansion remained the admiral's summer residence until sold in 1905 as part of the Canadian takeover of the dockyard. Admiralty House served as a naval hospital in World War One, but severe damages incurred during the 1917 Halifax Explosion necessitated its evacuation pending repairs. In 1925, the Royal Canadian Navy assumed responsibility for Admiralty House, incorporating it into HMCS Stadacona.

6. 1878 CITY ATLAS OF HALIFAX SHOWING ADMIRALTY HOUSE, WELLINGTON ARMY BARRACKS, AND EXTENT OF DOCKYARD. NOTE POWDER MAGAZINES AT WELLINGTON BARRACKS AND DOCKYARD.

The safe storage of gunpowder was of long standing concern for military officials and citizens alike. The first magazines were established aboard vessels anchored in the harbour. As previously noted, British forces built a magazine on George's Island within the first year of Halifax's founding. This magazine was considered too dangerous, however, as it was located outside the Fort Charlotte ramparts and directly under its guns, making for a "giant firecracker in the heart of the anchorage." In 1784, a wooden barrack at Fort Clarence was used to hold seven thousand barrels of powder "til proper magazines may be built." Fort George had a small magazine by 1795, but a large central facility was needed; finally, in 1807, a five-acre lot in the north end of Halifax was acquired for a "Magazine Field." While some powder was still being stored in 1812 aboard the floating magazine *Inflexible* and at Fort Massey, the Magazine Field near Wellington Barracks was the central repository. On August 15, 1857, it blew up. The September 2, 1857 *Canadian News & British American Intelligencer* reported the explosion: "By a telegraph despatch which had been received from Canada, we learn that the powder magazine, containing the whole stock of powder in Halifax, exploded with a terrific concussion shortly after midnight on the 14th ult. One man was killed and fifteen others were seriously injured. Five houses were demolished and several damaged. The Government magazines and the new barracks were much shattered, and nearly all the windows in the northern part of the city were broken. The damage is estimated at $100,000. The magazine is supposed to have been fired by an incendiary. The excitement was intense. Many persons were thrown from their beds, and others, bewildered, rushed to the streets for safety, believing an earthquake had occurred." A large, replacement "bomb-proof" ironstone magazine was built in 1863-64 with additions made in 1872-73 when the entire works were banked with earth. And in 1872, a small arms magazine was erected at the dockyard, between two older masonry naval magazines.

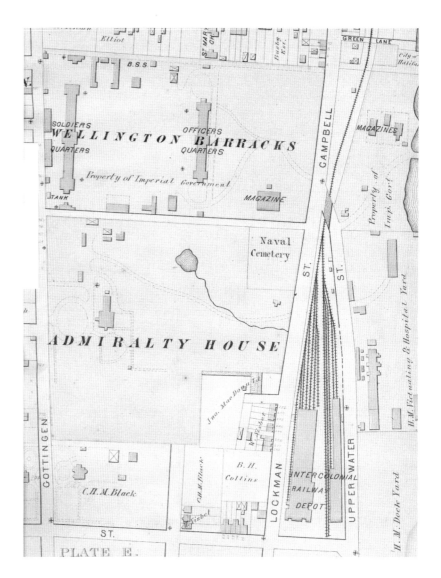

7. OLD NAVAL HOSPITAL C.1925.

The original hospital grounds, established in 1783, included a naval hospital, morgue (known as the Dead House), lunatic cells, wharf, guard house, and porter's or warden's residence. Its greatest claim to fame occurred in the War of 1812, when survivors from the naval engagement off Boston Harbour between HMS *Shannon* and USS *Chesapeake* were treated here. The hospital burned in 1819; alternative medical treatment was provided for within the dockyard, but details for the next forty years are vague as to what this treatment entailed. The arrival of yellow fever aboard four of Her Majesty's warships from the West Indies in 1861 magnified the need for a new naval hospital. Construction of this three-storey brick infirmary began in 1863 on the original hospital site, and a small building near the harbour was erected to serve as a fever ward for quarantined seamen. The hospital was used as the Royal Naval College of Canada in 1910 for the newly formed Royal Canadian Navy; it saw duty in later years as naval barracks, then HMCS Scotian (the headquarters for Naval Reserves).

8. NAVAL CEMETERY C.1880.

In 1894, the naval hospital grounds and cemetery encompassed approximately four acres of land. The oldest headstone then bearing any discernible markings was that of seaman Frederick Scales from HMS *Vernon*, the stone dated 1808. Early cemetery history is sketchy, as prior to 1860 there was "no regular or systematic record of interments." Vice-Admiral Sir Alexander Milne initiated a register of deaths in 1860 and divided the cemetery into thirty numbered sections. A detailed record of each interment—including name of deceased, age, place of birth, vessel served upon, date, location and cause of death, and burial section number—was thereafter forwarded quarterly to the Medical Director, General Admiralty, England. Little in the way of cemetery maintenance was done until 1871, when Vice-Admiral E. G. Fanshawe budgeted for a caretaker in the annual naval estimates. The triangular topped stone is the Shannon Monument, marking the burial place of five British sailors who died at the naval hospital in 1813 from wounds received aboard HMS *Shannon*. Twelve others from USS *Chesapeake* are thought to be buried in the cemetery as well; a memorial in their honour was erected in 1966.

9. COMMISSIONER'S RESIDENCE C.1882.

The Commissioner of the Navy was in charge of HM Dockyard from its inception in 1759 to its reduction in 1819, when many services were moved to Bermuda. The first commissioner's residence was built circa 1761, then, in 1784, torn down or refurbished into the one featured here. The Georgian building measured fifty by fifty feet, having identical front and back designs, with the exception of a verandah along the rear, which faced the harbour. Extensive renovations were undertaken in 1799 to accommodate Prince Edward, who used it as his winter residence in 1800 when serving as Commander-in-Chief of His Majesty's Forces in North America. Eight fireplaces heated the grand building, which included a main-level ballroom. Following the change in command to Bermuda, the residence was used as the Superintendent's House and Officers' Barracks. Vacated in 1905 when the Royal Navy left Halifax, the venerable structure was reduced to ash in a 1909 November fire.

10. OFFICIAL RESIDENCES ONE, TWO, THREE c.1882.

A number of houses were built within the dockyard for the use of naval and civilian employees. Most were nondescript one- and two-storey dwellings lived in by such persons as the Boatswain of the Yard, Foreman of the Works, Foreman of the Shipwrights, Commissioner's Clerk, Messenger, Policeman, Store Porter, Storehouseman First and Second Class, and Barrack Keeper. A triplex erected in 1815 at the Victualling Yard housed the Surgeon, Agent, and Dispenser from the Royal Navy Hospital. The most grandiose was another triplex built circa 1791 at the south gate entrance to the yard. Blandly known as Official Residences One, Two, Three, these served as living quarters for the Naval Officer, Master Shipwright, and Master Attendant. In the late 1800s, the Chief Clerk, Naval Store-keeper, and Chief Engineer lived here. During World War One, these structures were converted to the Pay Office, Electrical Foreman's Office, and Naval Stores. After being vacated in the 1920s, Official Residences One, Two, Three fell into disrepair and were torn down in 1930.

11. SAIL LOFT WITH
CLOCK TOWER, EARLY
1900s. THIRTY-THREE
BUILDINGS COMPRISED
HM DOCKYARD BY 1820,
MANY OF WHICH SERVICED
THE MAINTENANCE NEEDS
OF THE ROYAL NAVY.
MOST, IF NOT ALL, HAD
BEEN DEMOLISHED BY THE
END OF WORLD WAR TWO.

The Sail Loft, or Hawser Stores (later called Storehouse Number One), was built in 1769 of ironstone and wood; sails were stored in the upper floor, with cables, rope, oil, and paint kept below. A prominent feature was the clock at the building's south end, hand crafted by Aynesth Thwaites of London, England in 1767 and erected atop the Sail Loft in 1772. In 1823, James Deckmann was appointed the first "keeper of the government clocks" in Halifax, which by 1828 included military clocks at Fort George, the Ordnance Yard, and HM Dockyard. When Hawser Stores was demolished in 1941, the clock was saved and, in 1943, placed atop the newly completed naval fire station. It remained there until 1993, when the fire station succumbed to modern expansion. In 1996, the Royal Canadian Navy presented the two-hundred-year-old timepiece to Halifax Regional Municipality, which then erected a small tower for the clock at the ferry terminal near to where the original settlers landed in 1749. The clock is claimed to be the last architectural feature remaining from the days of HM Dockyard.

12. WATCH HOUSE AT LANDING STAGE ON WHARF #3, c.1880. VISIBLE TO IMMEDIATE RIGHT IS THE STERN OF VICE-ADMIRAL McCLINTOCK'S FLAGSHIP HMS *NORTHAMPTON*, WITH A GUNBOAT OR CORVETTE IN THE DISTANCE.

The Landing Stage was, as the name implies, an arrival and departure point for admirals and lesser naval brass as well as for visitors of note, including many of royal personage. Louis Phillipe, Duc d'Orleans and future king of France called at Halifax in 1799; his son Prince de Joinville came in 1841. King George III's party-hardy son Prince William Henry (later King William IV) left a lasting impression upon Halifax society during his four stop-overs with the Royal Navy between 1786 and 1788. His brother Prince Edward was stationed in Halifax twice with His Majesty's Imperial troops in the 1790s, and another sibling—Augustus, Duke of Sussex—made Halifax a port of call in 1839. Queen Victoria's nineteen-year-old son Albert Edward, Prince of Wales and future King Edward VII, visited in 1860 as part of his world tour, which triggered a celebration seldom seen in the garrison town. Prince Alfred and Prince Arthur followed their brother in 1861 and 1869, as did sister Princess Louise in 1878 as wife of the Marquis of Lorne, Governor-General of Canada.

13. ROYAL NAVY'S NORTH AMERICA AND WEST INDIES SQUADRON IN HALIFAX HARBOUR, C.1865. RARE PHOTO TAKEN FROM NAVAL HOSPITAL GROUNDS DEPICTS HMS *ABOUKIN, WENDAY, NILE, HERO,* AND *AGAMEMNON.*

The size of the North America and West Indies Squadron at Halifax was dictated by the vagrancies of war and peace. During the Napoleonic Wars, sixteen men-of-war were on station in 1797, the largest being the 74-gun HMS *Resolution*. Numbers swelled to 104 in 1814 as the War of 1812 was in full swing. Included then were all manner of vessels, from the 80-gun flagship HMS *Tonnant* down to the 8-gun HMS *Cockchafer* and numerous smaller auxiliary ships, three being the *Halifax*, the *Indian*, and the *Emelous*, all built in the dockyard. While the entire fleet would not have been in port at one time, the pressure upon local resources to feed and entertain up to fifteen thousand sailors can be imagined. In 1821, only six men-of-war were in Halifax, but this increased to thirty-three in 1839, and forty-three in 1841, following the Upper Canada Rebellion. The squadron averaged fifteen warships in the 1850s, a number that doubled the following decade with the American Civil War and Fenian Raids. By 1901, thirteen remained on station.

14. HMS *INDUS* c.1860.

The 78-gun *Indus* was Vice-Admiral Sir Houston Stewart's flagship during his Halifax posting as Commander-in-Chief of the North America and West Indies Squadron from 1856 to 1860. A third-rated ship of the line, the *Indus* mounted guns on two deck levels and was manned by upwards of 650 men. Ships of the line were the equivalent of latter-day battleships, a first-rated man-of-war carrying a hundred or more guns and a crew of possibly 850. By comparison, the smaller frigate had a flush gun deck mounting between twenty-four and forty-four cannons. HMS *Indus* was the last flagship on the Halifax station propelled solely by sails.

15. HMS *NORTHAMPTON*.

HMS *Northampton*, a Nelson Class armoured cruiser launched in 1876, served as Vice-Admiral Sir F. L. McClintock's flagship in 1880 when he commanded the North America and West Indies Squadron. The sail-and steam-driven new-age warship relegated wooden men-of-war (such as *Indus*) to the scrap heap. While the first armed steam warship to call at Halifax was the 4-gun HMS *Rhodomanthus* in 1835, the first ironclad ship (iron sheathing over a wooden hull) to arrive on station was HMS *Favourite* in 1867, a steam screw-driven 21-gun corvette capable of speeds of forty miles an hour.

France built the world's first armoured warship, *Gloire*, a 5,630-ton ironclad battleship launched in August 1860. Forced to play catch-up, Britain began laying keels at a vigourous pace, and in 1861 HMS *Warrior* slid down the ways; this prototype, iron-hulled, 9,210-ton warship dwarfed and out-performed anything then afloat. Charles Dickens called *Warrior* "a black vicious ugly customer as ever I saw, whale-like in size, and with as terrible a row of incisors [guns] as ever closed on a French frigate."

16. Coaling Wharf At HM Dockyard c.1912.

Using baskets and wheelbarrows, sailors endure the time-consuming, back-breaking drudgery of loading coal bunkers aboard *HMCS Niobe* at the naval dockyard. This was no mean feat, as the ship had a storage capacity of two thousand tons. The advent of steam-driven warships gave rise to the logistical problem of fueling boilers. With the vast coal reserves of Pictou County and Cape Breton Island at its disposal, Halifax played a vital role as a refueling station, beginning with the Royal Navy in the mid 1800s and continuing through two world wars for the Allied merchant and naval forces. "Imperial policy makers," writes historian Roger Sarty, "always recognized the special importance of the commodious Nova Scotia port, located close by the North Atlantic shipping routes that were the heart of Britain's trading economy. Indeed, the advent of steam-powered merchant and war ships, utterly dependent upon secure refueling places, had increased the need for defended ports."

17. UPPER FORWARD DECK OF HMS *BELLEROPHON*, HALIFAX HARBOUR, C.1891. LAUNCHED ON MAY 26, 1865, *BELLEROPHON* SERVED AT HALIFAX FROM 1875 TO 1879 AND 1891 TO 1892. CONVERTED TO A TRAINING VESSEL IN 1904 AND RENAMED *INDUS III*, IT WAS SOLD FOR SCRAP IN 1922.

access to fresh meat, fish, fruit, and vegetables. Sea rations, on the other hand, were described as "sparse" and "sickeningly monotonous." Breakfast consisted of a pint of milkless cocoa or chocolate served with biscuit known as "hardtack," which was infamous for being infested with weevils and maggots; according to sea humor, "the only fresh meat we got was in the biscuit." A smart man first tapped the biscuit on a table to knock out "the little browned carcasses." Others didn't bother, choosing instead to crawl into a dark corner "so as not to see what you were eating." Dinner at noon was a pound of salted beef and some flour one day, salt pork and pease soup the next, "in endless alternation." Supper at 4:30 p.m. included plain tea and hardtack. That was it for the day's food intake until 6:30 a.m. the next morning. Naval officers ate relatively well, often pooling monies to purchase fresh produce, including meat "on the hoof," which was brought live on board. Servants prepared meals for the officers' mess in various ways, while seamen boiled everything. A knife and fork wasn't issued to the lower deck crews until 1904.

While naval technology produced startling advances in late nineteenth century warships, living conditions of crews did not keep pace. A sailor's life during the Victorian and Edwardian eras remained largely unchanged from 1837 to 1907. Meals in port were certainly edible, with

18. CREW OF UNIDENTIFIED BRITISH WARSHIP IN HALIFAX, 1894.

Uniform designs changed several times from 1632, when "slops"—nondescript, loose fitting clothing—were introduced to the navy. No "official" clothing was authorized until 1857, when the blue serge blouse pictured here became standard. Why blue was the universal navy colour remains a matter of conjecture. One source credits King George II, who in 1748 was so taken by the Duchess of Bedford's blue riding costume with brass buttons that he ordered the colour be adopted by Royal Navy officers in place of the traditional red then being worn.

Rum and the navy have been inextricably linked, but, historically, a gallon of beer a day per man was the standard naval issue; this was later supplemented per diem with a half pint of "grog": rum mixed with two parts water. The potency of rum is said to have been determined using a magnifying glass and the sun to heat a small amount of the alcohol mixed with gunpowder. If just the gunpowder burned, it was good rum; if everything ignited, it was too potent; if nothing burned, the rum was too watered down and the purser responsible disciplined.

19. ROYAL MARINES MARCH THROUGH HM DOCKYARD AT HALIFAX.

A regiment of Royal Marines was stationed in Halifax from 1876 to 1878. Recruiting practices, pay, terms of service, uniform, and training mirrored the army, but marines were the amphibious assault force of the Royal Navy and, as such, fell under its command. Founded in 1664, the Royal Marines had grown to a force of thirty thousand men at the close of the Napoleonic Wars. Many warships carried a complement as part of the crew, yet the marines lived apart and were "not to be diverted by the ordinary duties of the ship." They were, however, responsible for certain ship and shore assignments, including guard duty, suppressing mutinies, enforcing regulations, overseeing punishments, and maintaining a vigilant watch for deserting seamen. Of the 705 men and boys who comprised the ship's complement of HMS *Warrior* in 1860, 118 were Royal Marines.

Royal Marines, H.M. Dockyad
Coronation Day

Notman Studio
9999

20. HMS *TRIBUNE* FIELD-GUN CREW AT FORT GEORGE. THE ROYAL NAVY PLAYED A ROLE IN THE DEFENCE OF BRITISH NORTH AMERICA BOTH AT SEA AND ON LAND.

In the War of 1812, a famous march by British "tars" in defence of Canada originated in Halifax. Two hundred and ten sailors, with a captain and two lieutenants, left Halifax on January 22, 1814 aboard the brig HMS *Fantome*, bound for Saint John, New Brunswick. Breaking into three groups of seventy upon arrival, the men sleighed to Fredericton, rested briefly, then continued over the frozen Saint John River to a bar-rack and depot at Presque Isle. En route, one man froze to death and another lost two toes from frostbite. At Presque Isle, sleighs were exchanged for snowshoes and toboggans. With provisions securely stowed, a trek of nine hundred miles to Kingston began, with four men dragging one toboggan. A good day of travel covered fifteen to twenty miles. The sailors persevered through blinding snowstorms, chest-high drifts, and debilitating fatigue to reach Quebec City on February 28th. The remainder of the grueling march was less severe than their trek through the wilds of New Brunswick and Quebec, but "still the sailors had to endure considerable hardship until they reached Kingston."

21. VICE-ADMIRAL SIR A. L. DOUGLAS, KCB.

Vice-Admiral Sir A. L. Douglas was the last commander of the North America and West Indies Squadron prior to Britain relinquishing HM Dockyard to the Dominion Government. The down-sized fleet at that time consisted of only six warships—the 11,000 ton flagship *Ariadne* with *Charybdis, Tribune, Retribution, Calypso,* and *Fantome.* Douglas'

departure marked the end of an era dating back to 1749, when John Rous was appointed senior naval officer in Nova Scotia. Since that time, more than fifty commodores, admirals, rear-admirals, and vice-admirals had commanded the Halifax station. Of course, many others of note passed through the harbour portals, including such recognizable persons as Vice-Admiral Edward Boscawen, of Louisbourg fame, and Captain James Cooke, who honed his mapping and navigational skills for future Antarctic and Pacific explorations while serving at Halifax during the Seven Years' War.

Seven Nova Scotians, five hailing from Halifax, attained the rank of admiral in the Royal Navy. An eighth, Ransford (Pasha) Bucknam from Halls Harbour became an admiral in the Turkish Navy circa 1900. Phillips Cosby and nephew William Wolseley, both of Annapolis Royal, joined the Royal Navy in the mid 1700s and fought in naval engagements around the globe. Brothers Philip and George Westphal, from Preston, both sailed with Horatio Nelson—Philip at Copenhagen in 1801 and George Augustus at the Battle of Trafalgar in 1805 on board Nelson's flagship *Victory*. Severely wounded himself during the course of action, Westphal was laid beside the dying Nelson below decks. The admiral's jacket was placed under Westphal's head for a pillow, and he later retained the buttons from it as a memento. George Westphal would go on to lose a hand in the Battle of New Orleans. Provo Wallis attained fame while serving aboard *Shannon* in its fabled battle with Chesapeake in the War of 1812. Twenty-two year old Wallis assumed command from *Shannon's* wounded captain and brought both vessels safely into Halifax. Admiral Wallis, "The Father Of The British Fleet" remained on the naval active list for eighty-eight years, living to the age of 101, the first Admiral of the Flag List to attain the century mark. George Watts fought in the War of 1812, capturing more than thirty enemy vessels; he was also wounded seventeen times during his career with the Royal Navy. Edward Belcher (grandson of Jonathan Belcher, Nova Scotia's first chief justice) was a renowned explorer, twice knighted for circumnavigating the globe and pioneering Arctic expeditions in search of the North-West Passage and the lost Franklin expedition. His exploits are thought to have been the basis for the fictional Horatio Hornblower adventure novels.

CHAPTER 3

MANNING THE RAMPARTS

The first soldiers to step ashore at Chebucto in the summer of 1749 comprised two small companies numbering only a hundred men. The expedition to settle Halifax being predominately volunteer, these were not crack regiment of the line infantry but discharged officers and privates, enticed to sign on with promises of land grants that ranged from eighty to six hundred acres, depending on rank. Help was not far off, however, as transports soon brought Hopson's 29th and Warburton's 45th Regiments of Foot from Louisbourg, where they had been garrisoned since its capture in 1745 and just recently ordered to withdraw according to the terms of the Treaty of Aix-la-Chapelle, which returned the fortress to French control. Battle-hardened reinforcements also arrived in Philip's 40th Regiment of Foot from Fort Anne and in John Gorham's Mohawk Rangers, whose feared and controversial guerrilla warfare tactics against French and Indian allies in the previous three years had single-handedly kept Acadie in British hands.

Militia played an integral role in the defence of Halifax from its earliest days. On December 10, 1749, all male settlers between the ages of sixteen and sixty were mustered on the Grand Parade and ordered to report for militia duty with a musket, two spare flints, and twelve charges of powder and ball. This was not the first Nova Scotia militia; that distinction belongs to Canso, where traders and fishermen formed militia companies between 1710 and 1748 for the purpose of warding off "occasional forays" by French and Indian attackers. Militia were indispensable in times of crisis. In the spring of 1775, for example, only thirty-six "effective men" remained at Halifax when all available Imperial troops were transferred to Boston. More than a thousand militia from around the province were ordered to fill the void, four hundred sent from Lunenburg alone. During the Napoleonic Wars, a militia company at Annapolis marched the 135 miles to Halifax in thirty-five hours, served four weeks, then returned home. For the War of 1812, militia

units throughout Nova Scotia safe-guarded coastal communities against American privateers. The Halifax militia and its military contribution to queen and country is discussed in detail later in this chapter.

During the reign of Queen Victoria (1837-1901), fifty of her first sixty years on the throne are said to have been marked by armed conflict somewhere in the world. This comes as no surprise, considering the sun never set on the British Empire, which encompassed West Africa, South Africa, Australia, Hong Kong, India, Malta, the Ionian Islands, Gibraltar, the West Indies, and British North America. In 1837, one hundred thousand men served in the British army at home and abroad; twenty thousand alone (which included four cavalry regiments) were posted to India. In 1856, the army was comprised of ninety-nine regiments of the line; by 1878, there were a hundred and nine, of which nine were Scottish. In 1897, the British army had grown to a permanent force of 195,000 men, with another 78,000 in reserve.

Until the mid 1700s, British infantry regiments were named for their commanding officers, which often led to confusion as some officers had the same last name. But in 1751, by Royal Warrant, regiments were thereafter numbered according to seniority; it later became common, circa 1881, for regiments also to bear the name of the county from where their members were recruited—for example, the 16th Bedfordshire Regiment of Foot.

Historians have claimed that every Imperial regiment was in Halifax at some point in the garrison town's storied past. And the May 15, 1920 *Acadian Recorder* lists 436 regiments at Halifax between just 1783 and 1896—this in addition to the companies and batteries of Royal Engineers and Royal Artillery who spent more than a hundred and fifty years manning the ramparts. Historian George Mullane, who penned the article, went on to claim that "Almost every British general who since arrived to high eminence served on duty in this city."

1. GENERAL SIR PATRICK MACDOUGALL (CENTRE RIGHT), COMMANDER-IN-CHIEF OF BRITISH NORTH AMERICA, WITH SUBORDINATE OFFICERS OF THE 101ST REGIMENT, HALIFAX, 1882.

2. PRINCE EDWARD (1767-1820), COMMANDER-IN-CHIEF OF HIS MAJESTY'S FORCES IN NORTH AMERICA, C.1800.

Prince Edward, fourth son of King George III and father of Queen Victoria, left an indelible mark upon the military and social structure of Halifax, which remains to this day. Edward joined the British Army at the age of seventeen, first coming to Canada when his regiment was stationed in 1791 at Quebec. Transferred to the West Indies in 1793, he won accolades for bravery during action at Martinique, St. Lucia, and Guadalupe. A year later, with England and France again at war, Edward arrived in Halifax as commander-in-chief of military forces in Nova Scotia. What he found was a series of crumbling fortifications left from the American Revolution. Historian Thomas Raddall writes that Edward had three faults: "He had too great a sense of his own importance, he had no sense of the value of money, and he had not a spark of humanity in dealing with his soldiers." The Prince immediately set about living up to his reputation. As patron of the arts, Grand Master of the Masonic Order, and promoter of social life in general, his stay has been referred to as the "Duke's Time" and the "Golden Age of Halifax." Employment soared, as Fort George and surrounding batteries were refurbished and strengthened. When completed, Halifax was claimed to be the most heavily fortified town outside of Europe. Edward continued to drain coffers to the chagrin of King and Parliament, building his telegraph, laying plans for a garrison clock and round church, and erecting a couple of grand residences for he and his French mistress. After suffering a serious thigh injury when thrown from his horse, Edward left temporarily for England in 1799 to receive medical treatment, then returned in 1800 as newly titled Duke of Kent and Commander-in-Chief of His Majesty's Forces in North America. His Royal Highness laid the cornerstone for a Masonic Hall and was honoured when the name of St. John's Island (Isle-St.-Jean) was changed to "Prince Edward Island." Popular with the citizenry, Edward was loathed by his soldiers for being a martinet who spared neither the noose nor lash. In 1800, he departed Halifax, for the last time, to assume the governorship of Gibraltar. His appointment in 1802 came with a stern economic warning from his father: "Now Sir, when you go to Gibraltar, do not make such a trade of it as when you went to Halifax." Recalled to England in 1803 for excessive cruelty to his men, Edward put aside his mistress of twenty-seven years (who later died in a convent) and entered a marriage of convenience to sire an heir to the throne. He died a year after Victoria's birth in 1819 from complications of a cold attributed to wet feet.

3. DUKE OF WELLINGTON'S WEST RIDING REGIMENT, C.1890. BATTALIONS OF THE WEST RIDING SERVED AT HALIFAX FROM 1853 TO 1856 AND 1888 TO 1891.

The number of infantry regiments garrisoning Halifax at a single time fluctuated over the years. Three was the average number during decades of nearly continuous war in the mid-eighteenth to early-nineteenth centuries. From the end of the Crimean War in 1856 until 1883, two regiments were the norm, after which only one regiment generally remained on station, until the last Imperial forces withdrew in 1905-06. A regiment's strength depended upon the posting and current world events. In 1893, about one thousand men comprised a regiment serving in India, Egypt, or the Mediterranean; eight hundred and ninety was average for most other colonial stations, with eight hundred forming a regimental home guard. Halifax was most often "below strength" in the late 1800s, a regiment then counting between six hundred and seven hundred rank-and-file troops. A tour of duty averaged two and one-half years, though some lasted five years or more, others less than one.

4. CORPORALS OF THE 2ND BATTALION, PRINCE OF WALES LEINSTER REGIMENT POSE AT WELLINGTON BARRACKS DRESSED IN TRADITIONAL WINTER GARB. THE LEINSTER REGIMENT SERVED AT HALIFAX FROM 1897 TO 1900.

Understanding military command structure and terminology can be difficult for the layperson, a case in point being that "regiment" and "battalion" often were used interchangeably. A regiment is a symbolic, administrative term denoting "the home of its members and enshrines their loyalty and traditions," while a battalion is "the tactical or functional unit of the regiment." When at war, a regiment could be bolstered by any number of battalions; conversely, a regiment in times of peace generally constituted only one battalion, meaning both were one and the same. A colonel was the "honorary" commander of a regiment. Between 1856 and 1872, most regiments were comprised of one battalion commanded by a lieutenant-colonel. A battalion was generally made up of eight or ten companies of about one hundred men each. A company, in turn, was commanded by a captain or major and two subalterns, with additional officers including an adjutant, paymaster, instructor of musketry, quarter master, and surgeon. Non-commissioned officers (NCOs) were led by a sergeant-major who usually had one sergeant and one corporal under his command for every twenty rank-and-file troops.

5. OFFICERS OF THE KING'S ROYAL RIFLES, WELLINGTON BARRACKS. THIS SENIOR RIFLE CORPS OF THE BRITISH ARMY SERVED AT HALIFAX ON SIX OCCASIONS: 1758-60, 1786-87, 1803-05, 1814-24, 1846-47, AND 1871-77.

British soldiers were nicknamed Tommy or Tommy Atkins, the origin of which has several accounts. One source credits the War Office, who in 1815 placed the name "Tommy Atkins" in the infantry and cavalry *Soldier's Book* beside the signature space, to assist illiterate men in signing their name, i.e. *Tommy Atkins, his X mark*. This was not the first reference to the moniker, however: correspondence from Jamaica to the Home Office, regarding a mutiny there in 1743, described how "...ye Marines and Tommy Atkins behaved splendidly." A later and widely accepted version cites the Duke of Wellington with initiating "Tommy" in 1843 when Commander-in-Chief of the British Army. Recalling an inspirational act of courage from a British soldier named Tommy Atkins at the Battle of Boxtel in 1794, Wellington is said to have used the Atkins name as an example on new military documents submitted to him for approval. A fourth account, submitted in 1900 by army chaplain Reverend E. J. Hardy, claims that "Tommy Atkins" originat-ed with the Indian Mutiny of 1857. At the Battle of Lucknow, a soldier of the 32nd Regiment of Foot steadfastly refused to leave his post in the face of certain death and was eventually killed. "His name happened to be Tommy Atkins," the chaplain writes, "and so throughout the Mutiny Campaign, when a daring deed was done, the doer was said to be 'a regular Tommy Atkins.'" However the name came about, Rudyard Kipling immortalized its use with the poem "Tommy" in his 1892 collection of *Barrack-Room Ballads*. The British soldier was universally known as Tommy throughout the Boer War and two world wars, even having a small portable army stove and the highly flammable Sherman tanks of World War Two named after him: "Tommy Cookers."

6. 97TH REGIMENT COLOURS. "A MOTH-EATEN RAG, ON A WORM-EATEN POLE. / IT DOES NOT LOOK LIKELY TO STIR A MAN'S SOUL. / TIS THE DEEDS THAT WERE DONE 'NEATH THE MOTH-EATEN RAG. / WHEN THE POLE WAS A STAFF, AND THE RAG WAS A FLAG." (— SIR EDWARD HAMLEY)

The 97th Regiment, which garrisoned Halifax from 1848 to 1853 and 1876 to 1880, was presented with new colours on November 15, 1880 by Lady MacDougall, wife of Lieutenant-General Sir Patrick MacDougall, Commander-in-Chief of British North America. The carrying of regimental colours into battle dates back five thousand years, their purpose through the ages being to identify individual military units and to serve as a rallying point in the maelstrom of combat. For the British Army, it was 1743 when a Royal Warrant proclaimed that each regiment would henceforth carry two flags or colours. The King's or Queen's Colour (right) pledged a soldier's allegiance to the monarchy and country, while the Regimental Colour (left) was a symbol of tradition and of the duty each member owed to his respective regiment. Regulations introduced in 1747 dictated the design of colours: "The King's or First Colour of every Regiment or Battalion to be the Great Union. The Second Colour to be the colour of the Facings of the Regiment with the Union in the upper canton. In the centre of each Colour is to be painted or embroidered in gold Roman characters the number of the Rank of the Regiment within a wreath of Roses and Thistles on the same stalk." In 1784, it became customary for "battle honours"—the names of distinctive campaigns in which a regiment fought—to be placed onto their colours. The two flags together, known as the Regimental Colours, were always carried into battle until 1881, when the practice was stopped. Despite their worn or fragile condition, colours were never repaired. Instead, they were deposited or "laid up" (generally in a church or public building) in a solemn ceremony, when a replacement set of colours were presented. Several Halifax buildings—including St. Paul's Church, King's College Chapel, and the Provincial Archives—serve as repositories for regimental colours.

7. PRIVATE BURNS, 78TH HIGHLANDERS, DRESSED IN RED DOUBLET, CLAN MACKENZIE TARTAN, RED-AND-WHITE-CHECKERED HOSE STOCKINGS, AND FEATHER BONNET, C.1871.

Canada has a rich heritage of Scottish military service dating from 1757 when Highland regiments were first incorporated into the British Army. Several Highland regiments garrisoned Halifax, including Fraser's Highlanders, Montgomerie's Highlanders, the Royal Scots, Royal Highlanders (Black Watch), and Sutherland Highlanders. Many veterans of these regiments accepted land grants at the end of their service, rather than return to Scotland, and formed the nucleus of militia units in the 1800s.

The 78th Highland Regiment "Ross-shire Buffs" arrived in 1869 for a two-year posting and moved into Fort George; this was the first Highland regiment to garrison Halifax since the Black Watch left in 1852. In the regiment's eighty-eight years of existence—from its inception in 1793 to its merger in 1881 with the 72nd Duke of Albany's own Highlanders (forming the 2nd Battalion Seaforth Highlanders)—the Ross-shire Buffs served in a dozen foreign countries, winning numerous battle honours and a regimental Victoria Cross. They were named "Ross-shire Buffs" as most of the men came from Clan MacKenzie lands in Ross-shire, and because their regimental facings on cuffs and collar were buff coloured. Only seven Highland regiments wore kilts, and even among those, few cared for the garment, complaining that it was "unfit for the cold, severe winters and hot summers."

One of the most noted of the Highland Regiments to garrison Halifax was the 93rd Sutherland Highlanders. This storied old regiment of Crimea and India fame apparently took exception to the wearing of traditional garb, as recounted in the September 19, 1914 *Acadian Recorder*:

"The men of the 93rd, as a rule, disliked the kilt. Just before the Crimean War, their complement was 850 and they were 50 below strength, a position which many of the privates attributed to disapproval of the uniform. Sergeants, on recruiting service, wore trousers constantly excepting Sundays so that it frequently happened that recruits saw the kilt for the first time on joining the regiment."

8. SERGEANT CAMPBELL, 78TH HIGHLANDERS, DRESSED IN "TREWS" OR TROUSERS SEWN BY REGIMENTAL TAILORS FROM OLD KILTS C.1871.

8. SERGEANT CAMPBELL, 78TH HIGHLANDERS, DRESSED IN "TREWS" OR TROUSERS SEWN BY REGIMENTAL TAILORS FROM OLD KILTS C.1871.

September 19, 1914 *Acadian Recorder* (cont'd):
"A corporal, although he could count ten years service, and had two good conduct badges on his arm, bought himself out by a payment of 6 pounds, chiefly on account of the kilt, against the use of which he openly expressed himself…. The men complained that in damp, cold weather, the exposure consequent on wearing the kilt, caused severe pains, commencing at the knee and ascending. They also complained that their uniform was unlike the highland dress of former times, when the kilt was not made of a thin, fancy tartan but was of a warm, thick and durable texture, manufactured from the wool of their native sheep by the women of Scotland who also knitted for them substantial gray worsted stockings, which reached to the knee. As the kilt was made more voluminous and was wrapped round the body, scarcely any portion of their body was exposed.

"In March 1854, the 93rd were in Turkey and displayed the same spirit of not caring a "tinker's dam" for anybody…. The Turks looked at them with a mixture of awe and admiration. They admired their high stature, their broad chests, their muscular limbs, their martial bearing and the natural ease of their movements…. But what most struck the Turks, who in the matter of trousers were accustomed to go to any extent, was the fact that those formidable soldiers actually wore no pantaloons. An Englishman who knew Turkish, and who had been holding some conversation with the natives, was applied to on the point, 'Were those fine soldiers indeed trouserless?' He translated the question to one of the highlanders, who, pulling up his kilt and slapping his brawny thigh, exclaimed that there was blood enough in that to keep him warm even without trousers. The Turk sighed and said: 'If we had such soldiers we should not want help against the Russians'; and upon the Englishman's asking him whether it would not be advisable to propagate the species in this country, the old Turk sighed again, saying, 'It would be done whether we like it or not.'"

9. HALIFAX GARRISON ARTILLERY BAND, 1895. THE FIRST ROYAL ARTILLERY BAND WAS ORGANIZED IN 1762 AT MINDUN, MAKING IT BRITAIN'S OLDEST ORCHESTRA.

A regiment's reputation was based nearly as much on the quality and quantity of music produced by its band as by the battle honours won. In 1799, the Duke of Kent recruited the best musicians from other Halifax regiments for his 7th Royal Fusiliers' Band. Military bands played for public concerts, garden parties, balls, dinners, theatrical productions, sleigh rides, ferry excursions, and skating parties—such as that described in the February 19,1867 *Halifax Reporter*: "Yesterday Oathill [Lake] was enlivened by the strains of music, the 4th [King's Own Royal Lancaster Regiment] band being posted in the woods near the north end of the lake, adding materially to the enjoyment of the large number present." On Sunday evenings, bands "were stationed at the door of their respective colonels and the public promenaded in the vicinity." Regimental bands also performed for a litany of official duties, including church parades, funerals, public holidays, victory celebrations, visits by dignitaries, royal birth- days and weddings, troop arrivals and departures, grand revues and route marches, even punishment parades and executions. Winter temperatures occasionally wreaked havoc, freezing moisture in wind instruments, which resulted in "a horrible cacophony of discords which usually irritated the C.O."

10. REGIMENTAL PIPERS OF THE 78TH HIGHLANDERS DRESSED IN GREEN UNIFORMS, A CONTRAST TO THE STANDARD RED, WHITE, AND BUFF COLOURS.

Regimental bands in the mid 1800s were comprised of a corps of twenty-one drummers, fifers, and buglers led by a drum major. In addition, Highland regiments had a pipe major and five pipers. Early bands served a tactical purpose that outweighed any social importance. Regiments used the fife and drum to instill discipline and precision when training in battlefield manoeuvres, a sometimes frustrating task for soldiers who did not know their left from right and often stuck a piece of straw into one boot to distinguish their "straw foot." An assortment of bugle calls and pipe tunes were also used in everyday routine to muster men for reveille, meals, parade, fatigue parties, retreat, and lights out. Featured in this photo is Pipe Major Ronald MacKenzie and an unidentified piper from the 78th Highlanders. MacKenzie had won a dirk (knife), gold medal, and set of pipes in a prestigious competition the year before he came to Halifax and was "long regarded as one of the best pipers of his day."

The history of the bagpipe can be traced to ancient Egypt. Roman Legion infantry carried pipes into battle, with cavalry using the more traditional trumpet. Although the basic operating principle of the bagpipe remained unchanged, it took many forms around the world. How the pipes came to be introduced to Scotland is a matter of conjecture, some historians crediting the Romans, others Irish emigrants or native artisans. However they arrived, the pipes were perfected by the Scots, with Lowland and Highland pipers earning reputations for distinctive airs. Following the defeat of Bonnie Prince Charlie in 1746 at the Battle of Culloden, the victorious British subjugated vanquished Scots, outlawing many customs and traditions including kilts and bagpipes, the latter considered an instrument of war. The fierceness and tenacity of the Scottish soldier was legendary, as was his history for mercenary service, and, in 1757, advisors to King George II convinced His Majesty to employ Highlanders in the British Army. Pipes and kilts returned to favour and the shrill, penetrating notes, radiating to distances of ten miles, once more led Scottish soldiers onto battlefields of the world, under the banner of the Union Jack.

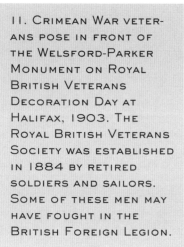

11. CRIMEAN WAR VETERANS POSE IN FRONT OF THE WELSFORD-PARKER MONUMENT ON ROYAL BRITISH VETERANS DECORATION DAY AT HALIFAX, 1903. THE ROYAL BRITISH VETERANS SOCIETY WAS ESTABLISHED IN 1884 BY RETIRED SOLDIERS AND SAILORS. SOME OF THESE MEN MAY HAVE FOUGHT IN THE BRITISH FOREIGN LEGION.

Only the 76th Regiment garrisoned Halifax in 1855, when the majority of troops left for the Crimean War. A controversy arose that year over the recruitment of Canadian and American citizens to fight the Russians. The British Foreign Legion established headquarters at the Melville Island Naval Prison in Halifax; similar recruiting arrangements were also made in Ontario. A bounty of thirty dollars was paid each "able-bodied" recruit, aged nineteen to forty, who signed up for three years. He was then paid a monthly salary of eight dollars, "with clothing, quarters, and other advantages to which British soldiers are enti-

tled." Convincing a buddy to volunteer brought a bonus of four dollars. The British also established a recruiting office at New York, which contravened the Foreign Enlistment Act signed in 1818 by Britain and the United States. This resulted in much sabre rattling and threats of war by the Americans. Nova Scotia political icon Joseph Howe was in New York at the time and actively recruited on behalf of the British, which caused such an outcry he was forced to skulk about the streets with carriage curtains drawn to avoid detection.

12. SERGEANT STEVENS OF THE 16TH BEDFORDSHIRE REGIMENT WAS GARRISONED IN HALIFAX FROM 1862 TO 1866, IN RESPONSE TO THE TRENT AFFAIR DURING THE AMERICAN CIVIL WAR. DESERTION WAS ESPECIALLY RAMPANT IN THAT TIME, WITH UNION RECRUITERS OFFERING FORTY-THREE CENTS A DAY TO JOIN THE BEST-PAID ARMY IN THE WORLD.

The 1860s was a decade of intense anxiety as Halifax was swept up in events stemming from the American Civil War, followed to a lesser degree by the Fenian Raids. The city was abuzz with Union and Confederate sympathizers debating issues in the press and on the streets. More than fifty-thousand Canadians fought in the Union Army, while another ten thousand signed on under the Confederacy flag. Possibly one thousand Nova Scotians—at least seventy hailing from Halifax—served with Union regiments, primarily those from New England. Britain and the United States exchanged hawkish barbs in 1861 over the Trent Affair, when the Union Navy nearly instigated war by seizing two southern diplomats from a British steamer. In August 1864, the confederate raider CSS *Tallahassee* made its historic stopover in Halifax to refuel coal bunkers, then slipped away through the shallow eastern-harbour passage, under the cover of darkness and fog, to narrowly escape its pursuers. The Civil War was also a time when turn about was fair play, with American recruiters, or "crimps," openly flaunting the Foreign Enlistment Act to approach the very gates of Halifax barracks, with inducements to desert the British army. "The American war," according to historian Greg Marquis, "offered higher pay, slacker discipline, improved chances of promotion, and the very real possibility of action"—all benefits non-existent to the Imperial Halifax garrison. Despite the stiff fines and imprisonment that a crimp faced if caught, and harsher treatment still for a captured deserter (see Chapter 6), the recruiting business was brisk. This was especially so when the North introduced conscription in 1863 yet permitted conscripts to provide substitutes. Deserters filled the bill nicely, and wealthy families shelled out "astonishing" bounties (up to seven hundred dollars) for others to stand in for loved ones. Not only did Halifax provide a wealth of disenchanted, well-trained candidates, it was a bustling seaport town, which gave prospective deserters ample opportunity for escape. In 1862, an entire guard of twelve soldiers quit their post at the lumber yard, overpowered the sergeant (whom they bound and gagged), and disappeared into the night aboard an American fishing schooner, to parts unknown.

13. IMPERIAL TROOPS ON MANOEUVRES MARCH ALONG
PLEASANT STREET PAST STEEL'S POND, EN ROUTE TO POINT
PLEASANT PARK, C.1890.

Mock attacks upon Halifax were staged for decades and served as much to entertain local citizenry as to test combat readiness. Historian George Mullane recounted one such spectacle in the November 25, 1916 *Acadian Recorder*:

"On a beautiful day in August, 1853, a fleet of boats, manned with sailors and marines, closed in on the shore in front of Freshwater bridge.

This was about three o'clock in the afternoon. Shortly afterwards, the men of the flagship and squadron, numbering 300, headed by the band of HMS *Leander*, and a corps of drums and fifes, marched through the city, taking up a line of march through Pleasant Street to Point Pleasant. The gathering of troops and sailors indicated that a grand shamfight was planned, and the object of the attacking party was to get possession of forts along the sea front. The troops engaged in this object comprised the Royal Artillery, sappers and miners, 72nd Highlanders and the 76th Regt."

14. SOLDIERS BLOWING BUGLES LEAD TROOPS IN "SHAMFIGHT" c.1890.

November 25, 1916 *Acadian Recorder* (cont'd):
"About 4 p.m., Lord Elesmere, His Excellency the Lieutenant-Governor, and the Admiral of the fleet, landed at the foot of Inglis Street, under a salute of seventeen guns from the artillery. The attacking party, comprising gun boats, portions of the artillery, marines, sappers, and Highlanders, were soon in motion, and then advanced to Point Pleasant, held by the 76th Regiment and other troops. The scene on the harbor and on the shore was at this time most animated and picturesque. Sail boats, ferry steamers, and small craft of every conceivable shape and size lined the shore from Green Bank south to the vicinity of the Point. Crowds of people also lined the waterfront from Freshwater to the Point. About six o'clock, the mimic siege was over, and the respective bands, followed by the troops, returned to the city, the Marine band playing 'Annie Laurie.'"

15. ROYAL CANADIAN GARRISON ARTILLERY GUNNERS DRILL WITH ARMSTRONG FIELD GUNS ON THE EAST GLACIS OF FORT GEORGE, c.1890.

Despite the fact that Fortress Halifax never fired a shot to repel a hostile attack, there were anxious moments. Such was the case during the Spanish–American War, when a cable arrived from the London War Office directing Imperial troops to ready for possible action. The May 27, 1898 *Halifax Daily Echo* carried this account: "It was a single word which started the feverish sensation of yesterday afternoon. Translated from the cipher into the common English it read 'Mobilize!' Its receipt was followed by one of the most sensational incidents that has ever occurred in Halifax. The men garrisoned in the Citadel were enjoying a good dinner when an orderly carried the famous order to their commander. Five minutes were given the men to finish their meal and it is safe to say that it was despatched with little thought of dyspepsia on the morrow. The boys in red and the black-coated Artillerymen were looking forward to a happy half-holiday— Thursday afternoon being always so observed in garrison circles—but military orders wait not and they all had to go."

16. TROOPS MASSED ALONG NORTHEAST GLACIS.

May 27, 1898 *Halifax Daily Echo* (cont'd):
"In ten minutes the garrison was on fire with excitement. In ten minutes more the force, uniformed and armed, were in motion, and the citadel and barrack gates were opening and bodies of troops were beginning to issue from them. Officers and military messengers were hurrying and scurrying from one part of the garrison to another. Magazines and storehouses in which were vast quantities of munitions of war for use in case of emergency were thrown wide open and nearly a hundred men were passing out shot and shell and powder, which moved from hand to hand with clock-work regularity and rapidity and were deposited with expeditious care into military waggons [sic] which stood outside to receive them. Twenty minutes from the time at which the order went forth from the brigade office, hundreds of British troops, fully officered and fully equipped for action marched through the city streets...on their way to all points about the harbor where are located the defences of the Gibraltar of British North America."

17. BRITISH FORCES PREPARE TO EMBARK, POSSIBLY AT POINT PLEASANT.

May 27, 1898 *Halifax Daily Echo* (cont'd):
"The troops which left the various quarters included the whole force of artillery excepting a handful of men, nearly all of the Royal Engineers and about one-half of the Leinster regiment. From the South Barracks, the Wellington Barracks and the Citadel most of them marched quickly to the Queen's Wharf, where they embarked for York Redoubt, MacNab's Island, George's Island, and Fort Clarence. Those who did not go by steamer went on foot to Point Pleasant to man the batteries there. One day's provisions and munitions of all descriptions were carried by the soldiers. The heavy shots, shells and projectiles of all kinds loaded on the waggons [sic] at the army centres were transferred to the Queen's Wharf, from which point part was conveyed to the forts and parts placed in store for transportation later. Orders were also given to the army contractors for further food supplies."

17. British forces prepare to embark, possibly at Point Pleasant.

18. STEAMER FERRIES TROOPS NEAR POINT PLEASANT.

May 27, 1898 *Halifax Daily Echo* (cont'd):
"Excited crowds commenced to gather about the Citadel and barracks' gates and wild rumors as to the motive for the sudden movement were soon in circulation.... At 9 o'clock last night the forces that went out in the afternoon began to return from the forts and by 10 o'clock most of them had been landed at the Queen's Wharf. The citizens did not get properly over the "war scare" for some hours, while many of the militiamen expected every minute to receive orders to "go into barracks." Soldiers as well as citizens were disinclined to believe the report that the movement was only a test to see in what time, with unexpected notice, the guns at the different forts could be manned and ready for business. One man said it might be a practice movement all right but he had never heard of or seen such a test before."

19. OFFICERS OF THE SYDNEY MINES VOLUNTEER RIFLES, 2ND COMPANY, 4TH REGIMENT, JULY 1859. UNIFORMS WERE PROVIDED BY THE GENERAL MINING COMPANY, PROPRIETORS OF THE LOCAL COLLIERIES.

1749, militia duty had been compulsory, but in 1859 a movement began to organize a new force comprised strictly of volunteers. Cape Breton had for many years mustered the most regiments in the province under the old system; in 1859, a corps of 171 men from Sydney Mines stepped to the fore as the first volunteer militia unit in Nova Scotia.

Interest in militia service waned after 1815 with the end of the Napoleonic Wars and the War of 1812. A provincial force that in 1813 had numbered twenty-six battalions of foot and two companies of artillery was reduced in 1820 to one active regiment for each county (with the exception of Halifax, which retained two). On paper, the Nova Scotia militia in the 1830s still embodied twenty-six thousand officers and men, but the true state of affairs is seen in an 1844 Act that cancelled all musters, drill, and training unless so ordered. Spurred on perhaps by the Crimean War (1854-56), a renewed fervour for the militia swept Nova Scotia in the 1850s. Since its inception in

20. & 21. WILLIS RIDDICK STOWE WAINWRIGHT POSES (LEFT) IN HIS SERGEANT'S CHEBUCTO GREYS MILITIA UNIFORM, 1860, THEN AS CAPTAIN AND ADJUTANT, 1ST BRIGADE, HALIFAX MILITIA ARTILLERY, 1865.

By the summer of 1860, the province boasted thirty companies of 2,300 volunteers. Eleven of these companies were in Halifax, six having been formed in December 1859 into rifle companies totalling eight hundred men—the Chebucto Greys, Scottish Rifles, Mayflower Rifles, Halifax Rifles, Irish Volunteer Rifles, and Dartmouth Rifles. In May 1860, these six, under the command of William Chearnley of the Chebucto Greys, formed the Halifax Volunteer Battalion. At least fourteen Militia Acts were passed between 1753 and 1844 in an effort to address continual problems and concerns arising with the old compulsory service. A new Act in 1862, containing 133 clauses, placed the volunteer force (if called out) under the Mutiny Act and Articles of War, effectively making it subject to all the laws of the regular British Army, with the exception of corporal punishment. Under the old system, drills were held only once every three months with one muster every six months. Militia officers now were required to hold, each year, twenty-eight drills (of three hours duration each), and five days parade drill (of four hours each) devoted to company and battalion movements.

22. OFFICERS OF THE 63RD HALIFAX VOLUNTEER BATTALION, 1882

A number of army drill sergeants were freed up from the garrison to act as instructors. In addition to regular training of regiments, thirty-eight militia adjutants were required to spend sixty days of specialized drill training in Halifax. A significant day of recognition for militia occurred in 1862, when a military review included the Windsor, Halifax, and Truro volunteer companies on parade with Imperial troops. In 1864, there were 56,111 volunteers of all ranks organized into 110 regiments. By 1865, militia artillery brigades had been organized at Halifax, Pictou, Digby, Annapolis, and Sydney Mines. Five regiments of foot, totalling 3,250 men, were converted at Halifax into artillery units to support Royal Artillery gunners in manning the ordnance. Total provincial militia expenditure for 1865 was $81,578, smashing all previous records; if you included artillery, volunteer militia numbers now totalled 59,379 men. General Hastings Doyle, in charge of British troops at Halifax, wrote that the militia "deserve the greatest possible credit for the spirited manner in which they have responded to the call upon them for their services."

23. 63RD REGIMENT HALIFAX RIFLES GATHER IN 1910, ON FIELD NEAR MORRIS STREET AND TOWER ROAD, TO CELEBRATE FIFTIETH ANNIVERSARY.

Over time, the six founding rifle companies of the Halifax Volunteer Battalion faded away, but the battalion itself evolved—first into the 63rd Halifax Volunteer Battalion Rifles (1869), then into the 63rd Regiment Halifax Rifles (1900), and finally into the Halifax Rifles (1920), a moniker its members carried proudly until the regiment was disbanded, to the chagrin of many, in 1965. Regardless of whether service was compulsory or voluntary, the Nova Scotia militia made a valuable contribution to home and national defence from its inception in 1749 to 1867, when the responsibility for militia passed from provincial to Dominion jurisdiction. The Halifax Rifles left a rich military legacy, earning battle honours in the Riel Rebellion of 1885, the Boer War, and two world wars. Its ranks were filled with a litany of political heavyweights, including Joseph Howe, Sir Charles Tupper and son Sir Charles Hibbert Tupper, James Johnstone, and Angus L. MacDonald.

24. "H" COMPANY, HALIFAX PROVISIONAL BATTALION, 1885. A FORCE OF 2,900 SOLDIERS FROM EASTERN CANADA WERE SENT TO HELP 2,000 TROOPS FROM THE WEST DURING LOUIS RIEL'S REBELLION.

A Halifax Provisional Battalion of militia—the Princess Louise Fusiliers, 63rd Halifax Volunteer Battalion Rifles and the Halifax Garrison Artillery—was sent west in 1885, to assist the federal government in quelling the Louis Riel-led North–West Rebellion. As part of a larger Canadian contingent made up of seventy-five similar units from across the country, the Halifax battalion was stationed at Medicine Hat and Swift Current in a predominately garrison-duty role. Those at Medicine Hat, while far removed from actual combat, did have skirmishes of a different nature to contend with. Bivouacked close to the Halifax militia were the Rocky Mountain Rangers, a rough-and-tumble cavalry group of cowboys and ranchers from Alberta, dubbed the "Tough Men" by townsfolk. Bored with uneventful mounted patrols, the Rangers took great pleasure in riding through the Halifax encampment, tearing down tents and throwing verbal taunts. William Tupper, a Halifax militia man, wrote home that Rangers "go through town firing revolvers and swearing like fiends." While the Albertans were eventually ordered to camp farther away, the two groups settled matters in a gentlemanly fashion by competing in spirited contests of target shooting, cricket, baseball, and tug-of-war.

The Princess Louise Fusiliers provided three of the militia companies comprising the 1885 Halifax Provisional Battalion. With roots dating back to 1749, the Princess Louise Fusiliers received official status on June 18, 1869, when the Halifax Volunteer Battalion of Infantry was organized. Five months later, it was re-designated the 66th Halifax Volunteer Battalion of Infantry, which in turn was renamed the 66th Battalion Princess Louise Fusiliers on November 14, 1879—in honour of Queen Victoria's fourth daughter, whose husband (the Marquess of Lorne) became Governor General of Canada in 1878. On May 8, 1900, yet another change resulted in the 66th Regiment Princess Louise Fusiliers, one of four Canadian Army regiments over the years to be named for Princess Louise. This regiment provided troops for the Canadian Contingent during the Boer War, with more Fusilier volunteers serving in the South African campaign than any other Canadian militia regiment. The Princess Louise Fusiliers won many battle honours in both world wars, including the Somme, Arras, Amiens, Liri Valley, Melfa Crossing, Gothic Line, Coriano, Lamone Crossing, Misano Ridge, Delfzijl Pocket, Italy 1944-45, and Northwest Europe 1945.

26. "SOLDIERS OF THE QUEEN": CANADIAN BOER WAR VETERANS AT HALIFAX, C.1902. SLOGANS OF "WHERE'S THE COWARD THAT WOULD NOT DARE TO FIGHT FOR SUCH A QUEEN" FUELED DEBATE IN CANADA, CAUSING A RIFT BETWEEN ENGLISH-CANADIANS WHO SUPPORTED THE WAR AND FRENCH-CANADIANS, WHO LARGELY OPPOSED IT.

The South African War (or Boer War) of 1899-1902 has been called Canada's "last colonial war." An uneasy peace existed for many years between the British possessions of Cape Colony and Natal and the northern independent republics of the Orange Free State and Transvaal, populated by settlers of Dutch ancestry known as Boers (farmers). The discovery of gold in the Transvaal in 1886 was the spark that ignited long-simmering bitterness into full-blown conflict. For thirteen years, the suspicious Boers had refused to grant political rights to the uitlanders, foreigners of largely British extent who came seeking riches. Such treatment was unacceptable to Britain, and in 1899 the South African garrison was strengthened in preparation of defending its subjects. When the British ignored a Transvaal government ultimatum to desist from sending reinforcements, the Boers declared war on October 11, 1899. In Canada—a "self-governing member state of the British Empire"—patriotism reached a feverish pitch, prompting Prime Minister Sir Wilfred Laurier to order a small volunteer force raised and sent to South Africa in support of the Mother Country.

27. 2ND CANADIAN MOUNTED RIFLES PARADE DOWN BELL ROAD IN HALIFAX, PRIOR TO EMBARKING FOR THE BOER WAR, 1900.

The Canadian contingent arrived in South Africa on November 29, 1899. The Second (Special Service) Battalion, Royal Canadian Regiment (RCR) was comprised of eight 125-man companies representing regions across Canada. The Boers proved to be a more formidable opponent than expected—in one battle alone, the British lost 1,139 to only 29 Boer fatalities. Between January and March 1900, a second Canadian contingent was sent, made up of the 1st and 2nd Canadian Mounted Rifles (CMR), whose members were drawn largely from the regular army force RCR and the North West Mounted Police. The Boers had taken to horseback, launching highly successful mounted commando attacks, and the British hoped the Canadians could counter the threat. The second contingent also included three batteries of Royal Canadian Field Artillery, with thirty-six twelve-pounder field guns. Between April 1900 and March 1901, these were followed by an independently financed unit, Strathcona's Horse, and by 1,248 Canadians for the South African Constabulary. Five more Canadian battalions were sent in early 1902, but only one saw action before peace was negotiated in May of that year.

28. SIX COMPANIES OF THE ROYAL CANADIAN REGIMENT, UNDER THE COMMAND OF LT.-COL. R. L. WADMORE, FORM UP IN QUARTER COLUMN ON PARADE GROUND IN FRONT OF WELLINGTON BARRACKS OFFICERS' QUARTERS, c.1906.

Britain sent 450,000 troops to South Africa during the Boer War. Canada contributed 7,368, including small numbers of medical, nursing, and postal personnel. An additional 1,004 troops with the 3rd (Special Service) Battalion, Royal Canadian Regiment, were stationed in Halifax for three years, which freed up the British regiment doing garrison duty for overseas service. The Royal Canadian Regiment (RCR) was organized in 1883 to train Canadian militia. The regiment garrisoned Fort George from 1897 to 1931, providing the first and last Canadian troops in the fortress. Canada's oldest regular-force infantry regiment, the RCR's garnered fifty-four battle honours for distinguished service in the North–West Rebellion, the Boer War, both world wars, and the Korean War. In the past half-century, the Royal Canadian Regiment has more than upheld its motto *Pro Patria* ("For Country"), policing civil unrest at home and helping to fulfill Canada's multi-national peacekeeping and military commitments world wide.

29. BOER WAR VICTORY PARADE PASSES GRAND PARADE ON
BARRINGTON STREET, HALIFAX, 1902.

Canadian troops returned to a heroes' welcome of cheering crowds, decorated archways, Union Jacks, and accolades. Under the command of British authorities while in South Africa, Canadians distinguished themselves on many fronts—at the capture of the Transvaal capital Pretoria, the relief of General Robert Baden-Powell's besieged forces at Mafeking, and the battles of Wolve Spruit and Hart's River. Canadians earned three Victoria Crosses (the most for a single battle excepting Vimy) in a bloody stand at Leliefontein, where they were outnumbered three-to-one by superior Boer forces. But Canada's crowning achievement came at Paardeberg Drift, where the Royal Canadian Regiment helped to hand the Boers their first defeat of the war, with a cost to the RCR of eighteen dead and sixty-three wounded, the highest loss for a Canadian unit in the conflict. Following Paardeberg, Commander-in-Chief Lord Frederick Roberts declared that "Canadian now stands for bravery, dash, and courage." The final Boer War tally stood at 89 Canadians killed in action, 252 wounded, and 135 dead from disease.

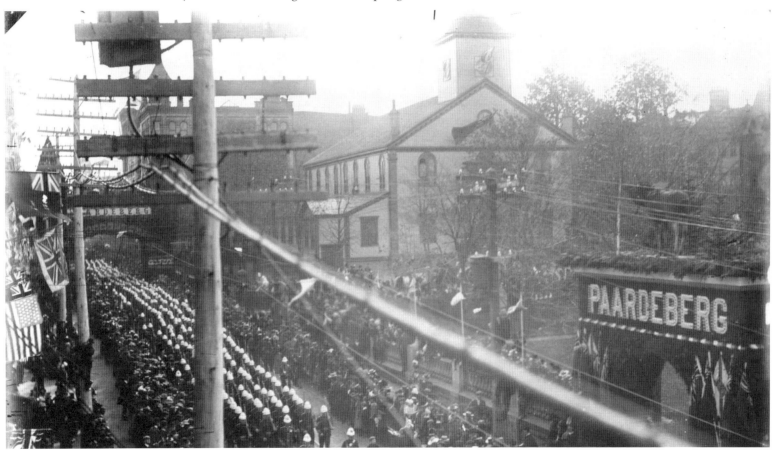

29. BOER WAR VICTORY PARADE PASSES GRAND PARADE ON BARRINGTON STREET, HALIFAX, 1902.

30. GENERAL WILLIAM FENWICK WILLIAMS, THE HERO OF KARS.

Just as several Nova Scotians rose to the highest ranks of the Royal Navy, a number also served with distinction in the British army. In 1868, William Fenwick Williams became the first Canadian soldier to attain the British rank of full general. Born at Annapolis Royal in 1800, Williams achieved fame in the Crimean War as commander of a Turkish army garrison at the fortress of Kars. In the face of overwhelming Russian forces, Williams held out for months, delaying the enemy until the Caucasus offensive was abandoned. Captured and held prisoner for a short time by the Russians, the highly decorated Williams was hailed as the "Hero of Kars" upon his release, returning to Halifax in 1859 as Commander-in-Chief of British North American forces. In 1865, he was appointed Lieutenant-Governor of Nova Scotia, a post he held for two years. Williams then returned to England and later served as Governor of Gibraltar before retiring from the army in 1877; he died a bachelor in London in 1883.

Lt.-Col. John Inglis from Halifax was commander of the 32nd Regiment in India at the time of the 1857 Indian Mutiny. Despite being outnumbered five to one by sepoy mutineers, Inglis successfully defended the lightly forti-

fied compound at Lucknow for eighty-seven days, holding out under horrendous conditions until reinforced. For this the "Hero of Lucknow" was knighted, promoted to major-general, and had a Halifax street named in his honour. Inglis died of fever at the age of forty-seven, a result, some think, of his India ordeal. Taking part in the relief of Lucknow was William Hall from Horton Bluff, Nova Scotia; his "conspicuous valour" made him the first Black man and first Canadian to win the Victoria Cross.

Other Haligonians besides Inglis achieved fame and glory. John Beckworth, the "Hero of Waterloo," lost a leg in the famous battle; Thomas "Tiger Tom" Willshire defeated the Khan of Kelat in 1839 in Afghanistan; William Cochran fought beside the Duke of Wellington in the Peninsular Wars against Napoleon. A story in himself was Captain William Stairs—soldier, explorer, and adventurer—who won world acclaim for several African exploits, one of the most notable being his accompaniment of Henry Morton Stanley during the Emin Pasha Relief Expedition in 1886-1889; Stairs died at the age of twenty-eight from repeated bouts of malaria.

CHAPTER 4

ROYAL COUPLE

The Royal Engineers and Royal Artillery were inseparable when it came to defending the home front, guarding colonial outposts or supporting infantry on campaign, a fact borne out in that they shared a common motto: *Ubique*, meaning "everywhere." Both corps maintained a Halifax presence for 150 years.

Military engineers have been around since medieval siege warfare, when combatants dug trenches to undermine and collapse defences. The French were Canada's first engineers, building fortifications in Acadie and Quebec in the seventeenth century. Britain organized its Royal Engineers in 1716, then established a Royal Military Academy in 1741 at Woolich, England to train both engineer and artillery officers. A separate School of Military Engineering was opened in 1812 at Chatham for engineers and artificers. While most engineer officers graduated from Woolich, all went through the specialized training at Chatham. The Royal Engineers were an officer's unit of the British army and commanded the rank-and-file of the engineering corps, known as Royal Sappers and Miners. Officer numbers were small, promotion slow, and postings generally longer than for infantry regiments. Royal Engineers, being "scientific specialists" were (according to Parks Canada historians), "on a different footing" than the other elements of the British Army which was reflected in their unique ranking system—Chief Engineer, Director, Engineer in Ordinary, Engineer Extra-Ordinary, Sub-Engineer, Practitioner Engineer.

French explorer Jacques Cartier was the first to make use of artillery in Canada in 1534, when his ship's crew fired cannons to drive off a flotilla of Indian war canoes at *Baie des Chaleurs*. This initiation to artillery warfare no doubt had a profound effect upon the attackers' psyche, but it would pale in comparison to the second siege of Louisbourg in 1758, when British ordnance—comprised of eighty-eight cannons, six howitzers, and fifty-two mortars—pounded the French garrison into

submission during a thirty-eight-day bombardment. The history of guns begins in the thirteenth century, but it was not until 1346 that Britain first used them at the Battle of Crecy; "official" gunners date to 1485, with Trains of Artillery first appearing on campaign in 1544. In keeping with the army policy applied to temporary infantry regiments raised in times of crisis, "trains" were disbanded at the conclusion of hostilities. But as a result of the Jacobite Rebellion of 1715—when fighting was over before guns could even be brought into play—King George I ordered by Royal Warrant the raising of two permanent companies of artillery in 1716 (the same year that engineers were organized), to be headquartered at the Woolwich Royal Arsenal. The title of "Royal Artillery" was bestowed in 1720, and within two years the corps had grown to four companies. With the onset of the Industrial Revolution in the 1740s, which spurred a technological explosion in the field of ordnance, Royal Artillery numbers swelled to thirty-five thousand men by the 1800s, making it the largest single regiment in the British Army.

In addition to Ubique, the Royal Artillery had a second motto, *Quo Fas et Gloria Ducunt*, meaning "Whither Right and Glory Lead." In 1832, King William IV of England granted gunners the right to wear an insignia, featuring royal arms over a cannon, incorporating both mottoes. In lieu of individual unit battle honours, Ubique served as the regiment's universal battle honour, signifying service in all campaigns waged by the British army. Infantrymen rallied to their regimental "colours" or flags (see Chapter 3) but the Royal Artillery rallied to their guns. This unique honour was granted by Queen Victoria following the Crimean War, a tradition that Canadians continued in 1870 as outlined in *Regulation and Orders for the Active Militia of the Dominion of Canada*: "A Battery of Artillery with its guns is equivalent to a Battalion with its colours, and is to be saluted accordingly."

Until 1855, Britain had two distinct military forces: the infantry and cavalry, under authority of the Horse Guards; and the Royal Engineers and Royal Artillery, controlled by the Board of Ordnance. The debacle of the Crimean War (1853-1856)—in which 17,580 of the 22,182 dead British succumbed to disease—led to a complete restructuring of the army chain of command. Such drastic measures were largely due to William Howard Russell, considered the"father of the modern war correspondent," whose graphic accounts for *The Times* reported gross military mismanagement and incompetence in the Crimea. The early nineteenth-century British Army administration has been described as "complicated, confusing, and contradictory"; there were eleven separate governing bodies (some professional, others political) "which either independently or in co-operation ruled the army." Following the post-Crimean reforms, only two remained, the Horse Guards and War Department—the latter having complete command of all Britain's land forces, including the Royal Artillery and Royal Engineers. Nomenclature also changed, with battalions, troops, and companies of artillery thereafter known as "brigades" and "batteries." All battalions had once headquartered at Woolwich, but after 1859, each brigade's head of command was removed to the country in which the majority of its batteries were stationed.

The Royal Artillery was made up of three distinct parts. Horse Artillery worked in conjunction with the cavalry, Field Artillery supported infantry regiments, and Garrison Artillery manned and maintained all guns within a fortification. Unlike Royal Engineers, the Royal Artillery officer ranks mirrored those of the army, ranging in descending order from General to Lieutenant, then to non-commissioned officers (sergeants, corporals). Most artillery officers were recruited from the upper class; however, contrary to their infantry and cavalry counterparts who had the luxury of a "purchase system" to secure commissions, advancement through the artillery (and engineer) officer ranks was based solely upon qualifications and years of service. While this may have slowed promotion, it increased the career chances of aspiring middle-class recruits. Artillery officers generally received their commission only after completing a two-or three-year program of intensive training at the Woolich Royal Military Academy. Considered a "scientific corps" like their engineer counterparts, potential artillery officers faced certain criteria for admission; the age for acceptance was raised to twenty-one from eighteen, with each candidate required to pass an entrance exam.

The time-honoured practice of infantry and cavalry officers purchasing commissions was instituted in 1720 by Royal Warrant. Prices depended on rank and were often inflated. A 2nd Lieutenant might sell for as little as £450, while a Captain could bring £6,000, and a regimental colonel £40,000 (a full £30,000 above the going rate); cavalry commissions were sometimes a hundred percent above regulation, at £14,000. This corrupt system lined the pockets of those empowered to recommend promotions, while dooming some to a life of impoverishment—men who could ill afford such expenditures but felt pressured to conform. Little wonder that officers were drawn from the wealthy upper class who joined the army predominately for reasons of family tradition, to seek adventure and to enhance social status. In short, they only met the officer criteria of being "gentlemen first and soldiers second." A story is told of one officer who received his commission the day he was born, rising to the rank of company commander by the age of thirteen, while still in school. Another account relates how a young lad about to be caned by the school headmaster was reprieved when it was learned the boy owned a commission, and the schoolmaster could not raise a hand against one of His Majesty's officers. Not all commissions were purchased; sons of poor officers who died while serving were automatically eligible, as were sons or brothers of officers in favour with the Commander-in-Chief. Prior to the Crimean War, an average of sixty commissions a year were given away. The war itself turned into a patronage plum, being Britain's first military campaign in forty years. Between 1853 and 1859, there was a long line at the trough, with 2,825 first commissions handed out. To progress through the system, an officer paid the difference between his present rank and the next; a certain length of service was needed, however, before doing so—two years for a captain, six for a major. Few made the army their life's vocation, usually selling off their commission at the rank of captain. Officers who purchased their commission could leave the army at any time, but those granted commissions had to serve twenty years before selling out. Retired officers were kept on the books at half-pay.

The public outcry for reform intensified as a result of the Crimean War and the Indian Mutiny of 1857, with shortcomings of the purchase system laid bare, exposing a complete lack of knowledge and competency on the part of most officers. Edward Cardwell handled the army make-over between 1868 and 1874, making numerous changes, one of the most significant being the abolition of the purchase system in 1871, after which time officers were "driven to the cruel necessity of deserving" promotions. Prior to Cardwell's reformation, the commanding army officer of the Halifax garrison could ask for but never demand compliance from the Royal Engineer and Royal Artillery officers. As Carol Whitfield points out in *Tommy Atkins: The British Soldier in Canada 1759-1870*, such bureaucratic pettiness rarely manifested itself. "Most of the tension between the army and ordnance existed in London where the two administrations quarrelled over responsibilities and failures. At the local stations their junior officers usually co-operated. They were forced to do so by the social conventions of the time: as officers serving the Crown, sharing the same accommodation and frequently members of the same mess, it became extremely awkward socially if their working relationship was vituperative."

1. Royal Engineers build an addition to Wellington ("C") Magazine, Halifax, 1873.

2. SAPPERS AT WORK IN THE ROYAL ENGINEERS YARD, 1873. "SAPPER" (A TERM STILL USED TODAY TO DENOTE A MILITARY ENGINEER) CAME FROM THE DAYS OF SIEGE WARFARE, WHEN SHALLOW TRENCHES, OR SAPS, WERE DUG TO PROVIDE COVER FROM ENEMY FIRE FOR TROOPS MOVING HEAVY GUNS TO FORWARD LINES.

The first engineer associated with Halifax was John Brewse, whose services Edward Cornwallis borrowed from the garrison at Placentia, Newfoundland in 1749 to lay out the town and oversee the design and building of rudimentary defences. Early colonial policy dictated that engineering departments be organized on an ad hoc basis, leaving Halifax from 1749 to 1763 with only three or four Royal Engineer officers to oversee a labour force comprised mainly of unskilled, lethargic workers drawn from the infantry regiments and the general population, as well as Acadians before their deportation in 1755. During the wars with Napoleonic France, Britain organized the Royal Military Artificers, a name changed in 1813 to the Royal Sappers and Miners. Made up of trade specialists—including carpenters, masons, bricklayers, smithies, wheelers and coopers—sappers were held in higher esteem than the rank-and-file infantry, thereby entitling them to preferential treatment such as better pay and food and no regulatory restrictions on marriage, the latter being a privilege not easily obtained by either the Royal Artillery or Army.

3. STRENGTHENING HALIFAX DEFENCES, LATE 1800s. PHOTO THOUGHT TO BE OF EITHER IVES POINT OR YORK REDOUBT.

By the early 1800s, groundwork for an engineering department had been established at Halifax, with three elements: Royal Engineer Officers, Royal Sappers and Miners, and civilian personnel. The Commanding Royal Engineer (CRE) was in overall charge of both the military and civil side of operations. Until 1870, there was also a CRE for the New Brunswick command, but he was subordinate to his Halifax counterpart. A CRE's duties were myriad—meting out discipline to officers and sappers; inspecting defences and "buildings of every description belonging to His Majesty's Ordnance"; overseeing all military lands; submitting financial estimates and progress reports for new construction, repairs and maintenance; monitoring goods and services supplied by local contractors. Junior officers were responsible for "regular garrison duties of an engineering nature." There were never a great number of Royal Engineer officers at Halifax, far less, certainly, than those of the Royal Artillery. Following the War of 1812, Royal Sappers & Miners returned to England, leaving only two officers behind, a move consistent with Imperial neglect of Halifax in times of peace.

4. ROYAL ENGINEERS WOULD HAVE BUILT THIS TRAMWAY AND OVERSEEN THE ADVANCE PREPARATIONS NECESSARY TO HAUL AN 18-TON RIFLED MUZZLE LOADER UP THE CLIFFS TO YORK REDOUBT, c.1873.

In 1825, Gustavus Nicholls arrived in Halifax as the new CRE in charge of initiating the rebuilding program that would culminate with the completion of the fourth citadel. Such an undertaking required expertise; in 1829, three Royal Engineer officers and sixty men of the Royal Sappers and Miners arrived, bolstered by an additional sixty-four artificers from the Royal Staff Corps (the army equivalent of rank-and-file engineering specialists). Additional labour was available from the infantry regiments of the garrison as well as from civil workers and contractors.

Generally speaking, the Royal Sappers and Miners were not versed in the finer points of infantry manoeuvers, a shortcoming apparently accepted in the interests of national defence. "The drill and discipline of the Companies stationed abroad at this time appear to have left much to be desired, owing perhaps to the small importance attached to soldiery appearance and achievements as compared with the Works." Drills were eventually implemented, "which enabled them to march creditably with the Line on Sunday Garrison parades. Although not very tight and tidy soldiers they were valuable artificers and good workmen."

Following the post-Crimea takeover of the Royal Engineers and the Royal Sappers and Miners by the War Department, the two were merged in 1856 into the Corps of Royal Engineers, forming companies which specialized in building bridges and organizing field supply trains in times of war. By 1871, "static companies" of engineers were re-designated as submarine mining and fortress companies to be stationed at key defences in England and abroad. In 1893, the Corps of Royal Engineers included 974 officers and 6,848 men serving in bridging, telegraph, and coast battalions as well as in field, fortress, survey, railway, submarine mining, and depot companies.

The Corps of Royal Engineers were much more than designers and builders of fortifications, roads, and bridges; they led the way in technological advances during the Victorian era. Engineers pioneered underwater diving techniques in 1839, introduced battlefield telegraphy during the Crimean War, were among the world's first combat photographers, and perfected the use of cast and wrought iron in the construction of slipways for naval dockyards. Engineers were also Britain's first aviators, forming a hot-air balloon unit in 1878—Air Battalion Royal Engineers—forerunner of the Royal Air Force.

5. OFFICERS' MESS AT ROYAL ENGINEERS CAMP, MCNAB'S ISLAND, C.1904. THE EXACT PURPOSE OF THE CAMP IS NOT KNOWN, BUT IT COULD HAVE BILLETED ENGINEERS ASSIGNED TO SUMMER WORK DETAILS ON THE ISLAND'S DEFENCES, OR PERHAPS FOR TRAINING AND RECREATIONAL PURPOSES.

Mining Company—with a total complement of approximately 152 men and ten officers. Duties remained largely unchanged from the previous twenty years, with the Fortress Company responsible for the upgrading and maintenance of fortifications and all associated structures and properties, and the Submarine Mining Company handling the technical side of signalling, electricity, telegraphy, and harbour mine fields.

Because of its mercantile and strategic importance, Halifax was one of nineteen stations throughout the British Empire selected in 1851 to receive the first meteorological instruments. Armed with barometers, thermometers, and wind and rain gauges, the Royal Engineers assumed the role of weathermen for the next twenty-five years, when it then became a civilian responsibility. In 1863, Britain organized a select group of engineers into the Submarine Mining Service, which in the early 1870s became responsible for the defence of Halifax Harbour, deploying electrically detonated mines. This highly specialized work remained under Royal Engineer control until taken over in 1905 by the Royal Navy. In the early 1890s, two companies of Royal Engineers garrisoned Halifax—a Fortress Company and Submarine

who moved to Halifax in the mid 1860s after a successful stint building railways in New Brunswick. He and son Samuel Manners were responsible for the massive forty-year building and re-construction of Fortress Halifax, including Cambridge Battery; Ives Point Battery; Forts Clarence, Charlotte, Ogilvie, McNab, and Hugonin; York Redoubt; Prince of Wales Tower; Glacis and North Barracks; Wellington Magazine; and Garrison Hospital.

The contracting of civilian labor was a contentious issue for many years, the feeling among military authorities being that workmanship was often shoddy and the costs inordinately high. A case in point was the building of Wellington Barracks. In June 1852, Peters, Blaiklock, and Peters of Quebec were hired to build a new brick barracks in the north of town on Gottingen Street. By 1856, their accepted tender bid of £43,271 had risen to £52,943, with cost overruns. When work was finally completed in 1860, eight years after beginning, the company "do not seem to have received any further military contracts," writes historian Harry Piers. The principal military contractor from that point on was John Brookfield, a Yorkshireman

97

7. KING'S QUARRY, PURCELL'S COVE.

One need only take note of the images in this book to gain an appreciation for the tons of granite, ironstone, and slate that went into the building of Fortress Halifax. The principal source was the King's Quarry in Purcell's Cove, which comprised some two hundred acres controlled by "said offices of the commanding Royal Engineers for the use of His Majesty." In 1815, Lieutenant-Colonel Wright of the Royal Engineers reported that he "had recourse to a very fine Granite Stone from a Quarry in what is called the Northwest Arm and which is procured on the most economical principles being brought from thence by the vessels and boats belonging to the Department manned by the military, after being quarried by detachments of the Royal Sappers & Miners assisted by Troops of the Line...." Bricks, too, were needed, but in 1825 the Inspector General of Fortifications recommended they be sent out from England as ship's ballast because "the Bricks here are of a very inferior quality." Local product had apparently improved by 1852, as Wellington Brickworks at Eastern Passage in Dartmouth was then filling military contracts.

Canada learned many lessons from the Boer War, one being the value of engineers to a military campaign. After the General Officer Commanding Canadian Militia recommended a permanent force of military engineers, the Canadian Engineering Corps was officially established in November 1903; King Edward VII granted the prefix "Royal" in 1904. Within two years, when Britain withdrew the last of the garrison from Halifax, the Royal Canadian Engineering Corps assumed the duties of its Imperial counterpart. A school for engineers was established at Fort George in 1903 and operated until World War Two. The Royal Canadian Engineering Corps maintained contact with its traditional British roots when King George VI became the Corps' Colonel-in-Chief in 1938, a role perpetuated today by his daughter Queen Elizabeth II. Military engineering remained the key role of the Corps, while communications was turned over to the Royal Canadian Corps of Signals. More than forty thousand Canadian engineers served in World War One; the First Canadian Division Engineers was formed in 1939, with eighteen thousand sappers shipped overseas by the end of World War Two.

9. MAJOR BAKER, OFFICERS, AND SERGEANTS OF 98TH
COMPANY, ROYAL GARRISON ARTILLERY, C.1904.

An artillery command comprised a "district," one of which was headquartered in Halifax and included the "lower provinces of North America"—Nova Scotia, New Brunswick, and Newfoundland (Bermuda was added in 1863 but "struck off" in 1868). A colonel, as district commander, was expected to be "responsible for the discipline, efficiency, and general good order of all under his command [and] to exercise careful and complete supervision over all the armament and material in his district." A lieutenant colonel commanded the Halifax garrison artillery, which was a brigade divided into batteries or companies, each containing five officers and 116 non-commissioned officers and enlisted men. Captains were in charge of batteries, with subaltern officers (lieutenants)—assisted by sergeants and corporals—handling the daily operations, drills, and inspections; support services were provided by adjuncts and quartermasters. Artillery officers performed a myriad of duties, which included sitting on boards of inquiry, convening court-martials, and inspecting the military prison.

Marriage was only permitted after ten years of service and even then begrudgingly: "It is impossible to point out in too strong terms the general inconvenience that arises and the evil consequences entailed upon individuals in a regiment encumbered with women. Poverty and loss of independence is the lot of the married soldier."

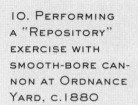

10. PERFORMING A "REPOSITORY" EXERCISE WITH SMOOTH-BORE CANNON AT ORDNANCE YARD, C.1880

Like engineers, artillerymen enjoyed certain advantages over the regular army—better wages and clothing, short route marches, and little equipment to carry, reasonably good food and lodgings, more leisure time, increased opportunity for advancement, and fewer transfers. Efficiency was thought to improve if batteries were "wedded" to defensive positions, so postings were on average longer, three to five years, often rotating between Halifax, Quebec, and the West Indies. Rank-and-file gunners came predominately from the working class, many having fathers in the Royal Artillery. Terms of enlistment mirrored the army but minimum standards were higher—eighteen years of age and five feet seven inches tall, the exception being seventeen-year-old "growing lads," who could be an inch shorter. Recruits also underwent eye and medical examinations; glasses were forbidden, as keen eyesight was essential. It was imperative for a recruit in 1860 to have "perfect use of his eyes and ears, the full power of motion of the joints and limbs, [be] free from varicose veins of the legs [and] inveterate cutaneous [skin] eruptions."

11. Artillerymen with 10-inch rifled muzzle loader, c.1885. Note the antiquated smooth-bore cannon at right foreground in photo.

The number of Royal Artillery garrisoned at Halifax rarely exceeded three batteries of 350 men in total. In 1864, there were more than four hundred pieces of ordnance in Halifax. With each of the heaviest guns requiring a crew of at least ten to operate, there were never sufficient numbers of artillery personnel to man and maintain all the armament. To alleviate the shortfall, Royal Artillery officers spent a great deal of time training local militia and soldiers from the regiments on station in the art of gunnery. This worked well until Confederation in 1867, after which the new Dominion Government stonewalled Imperial forces in training militia gunners, a stance taken, some believe, for nationalistic reasons, while others claim it was due to lack of interest or financial commitment to military matters. Whatever the reason, a lack of trained artillerymen significantly curtailed defensive capability. In 1890, only twenty-two of sixty-five rifled muzzle loaders could be manned. Beginning in 1887, the Halifax Defence Scheme was implemented, whereby defenders' responsibilities were annually reviewed and prioritized in case of attack.

12. ROYAL
GARRISON
ARTILLERY
FIRING
ARMSTRONG
FIELD GUNS,
C.1900.

The Royal Artillery was governed by two sets of statutes: *Queen's Regulations for the Army* and *Standing Orders for the Royal Regiment of Artillery*. The number one priority was "the protection and maintenance of ordnance, the efficient operation of all guns, and the manufacture and care of ammunition and powder." An artilleryman's day was a "monotonous" routine of continuous gun drills. While such training was essential, it was time consuming, intensive, and vigorous, thereby excusing him from some of the more mundane chores of garrison life. One of these was garrison sentry duty, which fell to the infantry regi-ments—although gunners mounted guard at Artillery Park and, in an emergency, sent regimental guards to some forts. Another perk was exemption from fatigue and work parties. The Royal Artillery did have some specific responsibilities, such as manning the Fort George signal station, mustering piquets in the event of riots or fires, supplying garrison police, firing salutes on special occasions, standing ceremonial guard for the opening and closing of the Nova Scotia Legislature, and parading military convicts to transport ships bound for penal colonies.

13. YORK REDOUBT MAIN POWDER MAGAZINE, 1873.

A large central magazine was located in north-end Halifax, but smaller, on-site magazines were an integral component of fortifications—such as the one pictured here at York Redoubt. Note the ventilators in the roof, which allowed for free circulation of air that, in turn, helped preserve the powder. Arched masonry roofs were often covered with thick layers of dirt to protect against shelling. Artillerymen were responsible for making up powder charges for the guns. Since this was an exact science requiring not only skill but also proper facilities, laboratories for the manufacture of ammunition were provided at key installations. There were two types of magazines: an expense magazine for pre-made ammunition, within easy access of the guns, and a storage magazine for powder located (if possible) in a more isolated area. Expense magazines were the responsibility of the Royal Artillery, while jurisdiction for storage magazines was shared by the Artillery, Ordnance Storekeeper, and Royal Engineers. It was understood, however, that the Commander Royal Artillery was in overall charge of magazines, with the supervision of ammunition and powder assigned to the Inspector of Warlike Stores and Firemaster.

An army's uniform was nationalistic in colour, the British wearing red tunics, the French blue, and the Russians green. When Britain raised its first permanent army in 1645, it adopted red, which had been the colour of Henry VIII's Yeoman of the Guard (the Beefeaters). The highly visible scarlet of musket days remained the colour of choice until the late 1800s, when the advent of more accurate, high-powdered, rapid-fire rifles necessitated not only a change in battlefield tactics but also better camouflage, so the British introduced khaki uniforms.

In the days of the "redcoat," officers' uniforms were a much finer weave of wool than those of the rank-and-file, which were made of melton or serge. While Royal Engineers wore the traditional red tunic, the Royal Artillery were distinctive in that they dressed completely in midnight blue, with red stripes on the pants—the reason given was that the dark colour hid dirt and grime that came from working around guns and powder.

15. ROYAL CANADIAN ARTILLERY ON MANOEUVRES, C.1910.

When Britain removed the majority of its forces from Canada in 1871, Canadian authorities were forced to address the issue of home defence. Two permanent batteries of Garrison Artillery (A and B) were raised and assigned to Kingston, Ontario and Quebec City. Although there had long been volunteer militia artillery, these two batteries that comprised the Royal Regiment of Canadian Artillery marked the beginning of a Permanent (Regular Force) Army in Canada. When the remaining British forces pulled out in 1905-06, there were the original A and B batteries and five additional companies of Garrison Artillery in the Canadian Permanent Force to take their place. In 1905, the Royal Canadian Horse Artillery was organized and equipped with thirteen-pounder field guns. Thirty-eight thousand Canadian artillerymen shipped overseas in World War One, with another six thousand assigned to depots, coastal batteries, and gunnery schools; eighty-nine thousand served in the Royal Canadian Artillery in World War Two.

Horses played a vital role in military campaigns into the early twentieth century. After the Boer War, the Blue Cross Hospital was initiated in England, "when the great need of helping the sufferings of the soldier's dearest companion, the horse, was brought to the attention of the war office." A number of these animal hospitals, under the auspices of the Royal Army Veterinary Corps, were built in parks and unused open spaces. In World War One, according to the September 14, 1914 *Acadian Recorder*, "The value of the dumb animal is almost equal with that of a human life and deserves equal protection from the enemy as it is being transported across the ocean to take part in the defence of the empire." Horses awaiting embarkation at Halifax were staged at the exhibition grounds under the "skillful eye" of a Dr. Gough. The newspaper called upon Haligonians for their support. "The thoughtfully humane in Canada are now providing bandages and pads for the horses; and it is said that anyone who knows anything of knitting can make these useful articles."

CHAPTER 5

A GARRISON TOWN

Halifax was born a garrison town, forty of its first sixty-six years of existence revolving around armed conflict. The Seven Years' War, the American Revolutionary War, the Napoleonic Wars, and the War of 1812 were all times of progression and recession, with employment and fortunes soaring and falling with the comings and goings of Imperial forces. In 1758, twenty-two thousand army and navy personnel descended upon Halifax in preparation for the second siege of Louisbourg, temporarily outnumbering the civilian population six to one. The following year, thousands more arrived for the conquest of Quebec. The evacuation of British forces from Boston in March 1776 brought a wave of redcoats to Halifax, where, three months later, twenty-thousand men embarked to attack New York. In the American Civil War, nearly fifteen thousand soldiers were transported to Canada in 1861-62, at a cost of £1 million; the British spent another million to house and feed them from 1862 to 63, with seven regiments garrisoned at Halifax. "When the troops and fleet on some occasions invaded the town by thousands," wrote George William Hill, an Anglican clergyman, "their consumption almost created a famine in the land...." W. M. Brown recalled in his memoirs, "The army and navy on the station were very important. They were patrons of the place. Great deference was paid to them; shopkeepers found them their best customers."

Nineteenth-century historian Thomas Beamish Akins describes Halifax:

"At the first settlement, it had been found necessary to occupy not only every elevated position in the vicinity but also large spaces around the town as at first laid out for the purposes of defence and other military objects. After the necessity for those defences had ceased, it frequently occurred that the military commanders would lay claim to the grounds as military property, and in this way obstacles had continually arisen to the extension of the town, a grievance which has continued to be felt until the present time [circa 1890]. Those whose duty it was to plan and lay out the town appear to have been guided more with a view to the construction of a military encampment than that of a town for the accommodation of an increasing population."

At the town's core was Fort George, its east-facing ramparts overlooking a military infrastructure of barracks, a garrison clock, chapel, hospital, grand parade, and artillery park, all nestled on a narrow strip of land only four blocks wide. The strip ran down the hill to join with clusters of nondescript harbour-front warehouses, fuel yards, ironstone armouries, and wharves specifically designated on early city maps as Property of the Imperial Government. Another side of Halifax emerged through the years: the slow but steady metamorphosis from a rough and tumble eighteenth-century frontier town to a "dynamic centre for trade" as a prosperous seaport in the early to mid nineteenth century. In 1808, the population stood at eight thousand; immigration increased it to twenty thousand by 1851, a number that would double within fifty years. An industrial base was nurtured by steamship lines, deep-water terminals, and a railway. In 1890, Halifax became the first city in North America to be lit entirely by electricity. Socially, culturally, economically, and politically, Halifax forged an identity separate from—yet very much dependent upon—the military. Even as residences and businesses broke free of the old parameters of the stockaded town, Halifax lived in the shadow of its Imperial founders and protectors until the day they departed.

1. Residence of Anthony Sutton Beswick, Asst. Commissary General of Ordinance, 158 Barrington Street, c.1879. Today the building is a popular eatery and pub known as The Henry House.

2. Royal Canadian Regiment changing guard at Wellington Barracks, c.1900.

Acadian Recorder: "In consequence of an attempt to set fire to the town in several places the previous night, the Governor ordered the Town Major to patrol Water Street and the principal streets of the town nightly until further orders. The night patrols were to consist of one captain, 5 subalterns, 7 sergeants, 9 corporals, 4 drummers and 107 men. The patrols were to report to the officers commanding the Main and Dockyard guards every two hours. All persons found on the street after 10 o'clock not being able to give a satisfactory account of themselves to the officer commanding patrols, were to be arrested and taken to the main guard house."

Sentries were a common sight about the streets of Halifax. In 1875, as many as 120 soldiers were deployed daily to stand guard at Government House, King's Wharf, Bellevue, Province House, ordinance gate, commissariat office, fuel yard, storekeeper's house, dockyard gate and grounds, naval and military hospitals, powder magazines, lumber yards, and various barracks. An emergency often necessitated the deployment of piquets as happened in 1801 and recounted in the December 26, 1916

3. PROVINCE HOUSE, HOLLIS STREET, 1890s; HOME OF THE
NOVA SCOTIA LEGISLATURE AND CANADA'S OLDEST SEAT OF
GOVERNMENT. THREE MILITARY GOVERNORS DIED IN THE FIRST
GOVERNMENT HOUSE: MAJOR-GENERAL CHARLES LAWRENCE,
1760; MAJOR MONTAGUE WILMOT, 1766; MAJOR-GENERAL
JOHN PARR, 1791.

The first governor's house, erected in 1749 on Hollis Street for Colonel Edward Cornwallis, was a plain, hastily built "cottage" only a stone's throw from where the founding settlers landed. Born of urgency, it was replaced in 1758 by a decidedly more ostentatious structure enclosed within a palisaded compound which also included several smaller buildings for government offices. This remained the governor's official residence until 1805, when then-Lieutenant Governor John Wentworth (the title of Governor was replaced by Lieutenant Governor after the American Revolution) built a newer "government house" farther south along Hollis Street. Wentworth offered the then-vacated governor's grounds as a much needed permanent site for the House of Assembly and new law courts. After many delays, construction began on Province House in 1811 and took eight years to complete. With a final price tag of £52,000, it was, in typical bureaucratic fashion, a mere £32,000 over budget! Home today of the Nova Scotia Legislature, Province House has been described as an "architectural gem, one of the finest examples of Palladian style in North America."

When Edward Cornwallis arrived at Chebucto, he carried orders from London "to summon and call General Assemblys [sic] of the Freeholders and Planters within your Government according to the usage of the rest of our colonies and plantations in America." The governor chose to ignore the edict and on July 12, 1749 organized a six-member civil government comprised of experienced military men. Thomas Raddall writes, "Soldiers all, they regarded with a profound distrust any civilian pretensions towards government." Pressure for change mounted, however, with a steady influx of New Englanders bent upon self-government. After nine years, a General Assembly was finally convened in October 1758, a first for representative government not only in Canada but in the British Empire. But the military still held sway in matters of law making and taxation for another ninety years, with governors over-ruling or dissolving assemblies they disapproved of. Led by Joseph Howe, reformers pressed for change, ultimately winning responsible government in 1848, another first for Canadian politics. "A landmark in the constitutional evolution of Canada, more history has been made within these four walls than in all other legislatures combined."

4. PORTRAITS OF PAST GOVERNORS, MILITARY HEROES, AND ROYALTY ADORN THE WALLS OF RED CHAMBER IN PROVINCE HOUSE. THE OAK TABLE PICTURED HERE, AROUND WHICH THE FIRST CIVIL GOVERNMENT CONVENED ON BOARD THE TRANSPORT HMS *BEAUFORT* AT HALIFAX, CAN BE SEEN THERE TODAY.

5. GOVERNMENT HOUSE, BARRINGTON STREET, HOME TO NOVA SCOTIA'S LIEUTENANT-GOVERNOR AND CANADA'S OLDEST EXECUTIVE RESIDENCE.

John Wentworth was Governor of New Hampshire before the American Revolution. A staunch Loyalist, he and Lady Francis escaped to Nova Scotia with the wave of refugees who fled before the victorious rebels in 1783. Wentworth was appointed Surveyor General of the King's Woods, but the couple were accustomed to a grander lifestyle. When the Lieutenant-Governor's post became available with the sudden death of John Parr in 1791, John Wentworth was named his successor. Much of the credit for his patronage appointment lies with forty-one-year-old Lady Francis, whose royal tryst with young Prince William Henry from 1786-89 had Halifax tongues wagging whenever His Highness dropped anchor in port with the Royal Navy. In reference to their affair, and to husband John's apparent acceptance of it, one prominent citizen wrote, "While her husband stretches his surveyor's chain in the forest, she measures the length of a grown man's affection." Although the Lieutenant-Governor's salary was paid by the Imperial Government, the Nova Scotia Assembly was on the hook for his residence and its maintenance. One of Wentworth's most ambitious and enduring projects was the building of a new Government House more befitting the prestige of his title. Its construction caused considerable anguish in the Assembly, outstripping the projected budget of £10,500 by twice that amount—three times if furniture and continual additions and repairs are factored in. The cornerstone was laid in 1800, with work still going on when the Wentworths moved in five years later; craftsmen were just putting on the finishing touches in 1808 when John was unceremoniously dismissed from his post. In financial straits, the Wentworths returned to England, where Francis took sick and died in 1813, a year after John had returned to Halifax to escape irate creditors. His death elicited little more than passing notice: "On Saturday. 8th of April 1820, Sir John Wentworth died in his 84th year. He administered the government of this province for many years and was Surveyor of His Majesty's woods in British North America." A Halifax memorial plaque to Wentworth states somewhat unflatteringly that Government House "was built to gratify his own sense of prosperity and that of his glamorous wife."

In the late 1700s, it became fashionable for the upper class to build estates on the outskirts of Halifax, "well away from the squalor of the town while keeping it well within reach." After the arrival in 1794 of Prince Edward with French mistress Julie St. Laurent, the couple were frequently entertained at Sir John and Lady Francis Wentworth's country home along the shores of Bedford Basin. Ever the gracious hosts, the Wentworths offered their retreat for Edward's exclusive use during his military tenure at Halifax. The Duke of Kent readily accepted, and commenced extensive renovations to the house and its expansive grounds. A heart-shaped pond was built and named in Julie's honour. Secluded trails, magnificent gardens, strategically placed wind chimes, and gazebos all added to the ambience. The rotunda featured here was erected on a hill along the basin shore and served as the "music room," where garrison bands played in concert. On-site barracks housed a company of soldiers to ensure security and privacy, and a signaling mast—part of the military telegraph system—kept Edward in touch with daily affairs; if needed, he could be at Halifax within the hour. Edward named his love nest "Prince's Lodge" and remained there until his departure in 1800, at which time the Wentworths resumed occupancy. Upon John's death in 1820, the estate fell into disrepair and was pretty much in ruins by 1870 when sold at auction and divided into building lots. The rotunda is all that remains of Prince's Lodge. Having survived a hundred and fifty years of neglect and harsh weather, the Provincial Government saved the building in 1959; today, Prince's Lodge is a registered heritage property.

7. "BELLEVUE": COMMANDING GENERAL'S RESIDENCE (1801-1906), SPRING GARDEN ROAD, c.1865.

In 1800, Edward built a new town house he named "Bellevue" at the corner of Spring Garden Road and Queen Street. This remained the official residence for commanders of the Halifax garrison until the end of the British military era in 1905-06. Fire gutted the structure in March 1885, but it was rebuilt within two years. Teas, banquets, and balls at Bellevue were the highlight of social registers. The *Halifax Daily Echo* reported in October 1896: "On Wednesday evening General and Mrs. Montgomery Moore gave a very delightful dance, the first for which cards were sent out last week. Dancing began at nine and was kept up till two, though carriages were ordered at half-past one…. A very large navy element was there from the several ships now in port and they added very much to the prettiness of the dance, for there is not anything much smarter in a ball room than full dress uniform…." Used as an army mess from 1907 to 1920, nothing remains today of the grand old building, which was demolished in 1955 and replaced with a parking lot.

8. 1878 Halifax City Atlas showing Bellevue, Governor's Grounds, Royal Artillery Park, and South Barracks. Abermarle Street, now Market Street, was a lively section of town known for its brothels and drinking dens.

8. 1878 Halifax City Atlas showing Bellevue, Governor's Grounds, Royal Artillery Park, and South Barracks. Abermarle Street, now Market Street, was a lively section of town known for its brothels and drinking dens.

The once-spacious grounds of Government House, known as the Governor's Grounds or South Farm, crossed Barrington Street (originally Pleasant Street) and took in much of what today constitutes the Sexton Campus of Dalhousie University. The Military Office And Drill Shed were used for training militia. This map gives a clear picture of the military compound, which included Royal Artillery Park and South Barracks. Note how Brunswick Street (originally Barrack Street) had not as yet been cut through to connect with Spring Garden Road. South Barracks was built in 1786 for infantry regiments, then enlarged in 1802 to accommodate 549 men; it was torn down circa 1946. Wedged between Royal Artillery Park and South Barracks was a narrow strip of property known as the Royal Engineers Square, which contained a work yard and small barracks built in 1804 for Royal Sappers and Miners, the rank-and-file of the Royal Engineers. Able to accommodate only forty men, the overflow went to South Barracks, with engineer officers billeting in Royal Artillery Park.

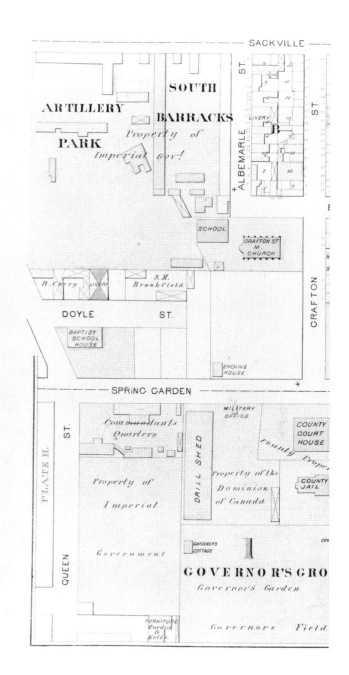

9. ROYAL ARTILLERY PARK, SACKVILLE STREET.

Royal Artillery Park, as it looked in 1928, facing east across parade ground. Buildings visible in the photo are (L-R) guard room and cells at entrance to grounds, stables, brick barracks, commanding officer's quarters, enlisted men's barracks, and headquarter offices. The Royal Artillery were originally housed in a series of forts and barracks, including a one-and-a-half -storey, eighty foot by twenty-five foot Artillery Barracks on the southwest section of the Grand Parade from circa 1760-83, where gunners trained and stored field-guns. In 1801, the Commanding Royal Engineer, Captain William Fenwick, prepared plans and estimates for an expansive Royal Artillery Park to be built across from Fort George on land bounded by Sackville, Queen, and Abermarle Streets. Construction began in 1802 and continued throughout the War of 1812, with additional buildings erected at various times until 1901-03. For more than a hundred years, this was the home of the Royal Artillery. Although many of the original buildings were torn down in 1946, the Canadian Department of National Defence maintains the site today as an operational facility and historical landmark.

Enclosed by a ten-foot-high fence, Royal Artillery Park included—in addition to the aforementioned buildings—a hospital with surgery; a nurses' room; a kitchen; four wards for twenty-four patients; various quarters for field officers, captains, and subalterns; an officers' mess and additional quarters; a cookhouse; an ordnance laboratory; a library; and storehouses for horse harness and field guns. The two-storey house featured here served as the Commanding Royal Engineer's residence in 1813 and was built on the site of Cornwallis Fort, one of the original five stockaded bastions; the residence was demolished in 1900. The other prominent building is the rear of the Royal Artillery Commander's residence, which still stands today. The Royal Engineers Square and South Barracks would be to the far right of the photo. By the late nineteenth century, many barracks were falling into decay, and a number of Royal Engineer officers took up residency at their own expense near the Royal Engineers Square. Thirty-eight homes have been identified throughout south-end Halifax in connection with Royal Engineers between 1880 and 1906, most being within the area bounded by Morris, Queen, South Park, and Sackville Streets.

11. ROYAL ARTILLERY OFFICERS' QUARTERS, BUILT C.1812; PHOTO TAKEN 1880. NOTE FIRE HYDRANT.

For nearly a century, Halifax depended on public wells for drinking water. Artillery Park and Fort George had wells, but military contracts were often tendered to supply water directly to the various infantry barracks. The first city water pipes (and fire hydrants) were installed in 1848, and none too soon, as attested to in this account from the July 24, 1847 *Acadian Recorder*:

"The body of a soldier, belonging to the 89th Regiment, was discovered in the garrison well on the road to the Exercising Ground yesterday afternoon. Some persons who would have used the water were prevented by its rancidity, and the mere taste of it was enough to sicken any person; but as the well was never much resorted to…none supposed on discovering the badness of the water of late that it was affected by any other than ordinary causes. However, a lad happened to drop a bucket in the well, and having procured a hook, in grappling for the bucket brought up a soldier's forage cap with the number 89 in brass figures affixed to it. The corpse was then discovered, and has been recognized to be the body of a man, who unaccountably disappeared about Christmas last."

12. ENLISTED MEN'S BARRACKS, ROYAL ARTILLERY PARK, 1880.

An enlisted men's barracks was built at Artillery Park in 1803 to hold three hundred men. As this was insufficient to house the entire artillery garrison, men were housed in the additional space in surrounding barracks. Verandahs typically were incorporated into barrack designs to provide shade in the summer and shelter from winter's snow. Despite their pleasing outward appearance, barracks and officers quarters at Artillery Park were described as drafty and "much exposed to the weather." While rank-and-file artillerymen and single officers had little choice but to shiver and endure, married officers often rented private accommodations "at great personal expense." New, "finer" officers' quarters were erected in 1901-03.

13. ROYAL ARTILLERY AND ROYAL ENGINEERS MESS, 1880.

A westerly expansion of Artillery Park in 1812 resulted in a section of Queen Street being reshaped into a 310-foot sweeping curve between Sackville Street and Spring Garden Road. The grounds were enlarged to build this officers' mess and quarters (completed 1814-16) for the Royal Artillery and Royal Engineers. Today, the mess remains operational and, together with the commanding officer's quarters (of 1804-05) and Cambridge Military Library (of 1885-86) forges a heritage link with Halifax's military past.

14. OFFICERS' QUARTERS, WELLINGTON BARRACKS, 1870.

The principal barracks for regiments garrisoning Halifax were North and South Barracks, Glacis Barracks, Wellington Barracks, Fort Charlotte, and Fort George. Limited space was also available at Fort Clarence, York Redoubt, and Prince of Wales Tower. Wellington Barracks was in the north end of town, along Gottingen Street, on sixteen acres known as the Magazine or Ordnance Field (present-day Stadacona); it was claimed to be the first military building in Halifax constructed entirely of brick. The barracks consisted of two large blocks, with accommodations for 597 men. The grounds also held a forty-bed hospital and three smaller buildings for married quarters housing forty-four men. Strategically placed sentry towers guarded the expansive compound, which was encircled by a fourteen-foot-high ironstone wall. Wellington Barracks was heavily damaged in the 1917 Halifax Explosion but repaired and taken over by the Royal Canadian Navy in World War Two when incorporated into HMCS Stadacona. It was demolished in the late 1940s, with a section of wall and front gate left standing as a memento.

15. SOUTH BARRACKS, CORNER OF SACKVILLE AND BRUNSWICK STREETS, WITH HALIFAX COUNTY ACADEMY IN DISTANCE, C.1920.

The lure of nightly adventure often outweighed the penalty for breaking curfew. Lieutenant Frederick Harris Vieth, who was stationed at Halifax from 1856 to 1860 with the 63rd West Suffolk Regiment, recounts this tale:

"The back of the old South Barracks, facing as it did on the public street, offered a chance to anyone bold enough to risk being seen by the sentry, to break out. If he could evade discovery in sneaking from his room and slipping down the verandah stairs, he had but to climb an adjoining fence when all was quiet and dropping down find himself in the street. This was not altogether an easy matter. None but an athlete could perform the feat and even after it was accomplished, unless the night was very dark, he was pretty sure of being nabbed by the sentry after all his exertions. The same risk attended his return before daylight—if he was sober enough to try it—and if caught, his acquaintance with a cell for seven days was assured. The penalty did not always prevent the attempt, although it acted as a strong deterrent to its being made at all.

16. OFFICERS' QUARTERS ON COGSWELL STREET WAS BUILT C.1761 ADJACENT TO NORTH BARRACKS, NEAR PRESENT-DAY HALIFAX POLICE DEPARTMENT. AT THE TIME OF THIS 1877 PHOTO, IT HAD BEEN RELEGATED TO BARRACK STORES.

"On the night in question Sergeant Isaac Sallis and another sergeant, having received an invitation to take part in some tempting gaiety in the town, and knowing that leave to be absent from their quarters would, as they had recently enjoyed that privilege, be refused them on this occasion, determined to break out. They made all arrangements for the venture and as men of their own company—the Grenadiers—furnished the barrack guard that night, it is not improbable that the sentry, who was on duty from twelve o'clock until two in the morning, was induced to have his back conveniently turned to the place chosen for their escape at a certain hour agreed upon. They got out all right and were hurrying round the corner of the street when, plump, into the arms of a Staff officer they ran. This officer was very unpopular because of his extreme officiousness, his going out of his way to ferret out little things, trifles in themselves, but which could be magnified into breaches of certain then existing regulations. He had the credit of whispering his discoveries into the ear of the General Commanding, with a view to establishing in that officer's mind a belief in his extreme zeal. This system of espionage became known to both the non-commissioned officers and men, and probably increased neither their respect nor regard. Instead it was rather calculated to engender a desire to retaliate in some way, when a chance offered, where the likelihood of being found out was improbable. His being in the vicinity of the barracks alone and unattended, at midnight, was certainly a surprise to the guilty pair.

17. GLACIS BARRACKS, BUILT C.1866 ON NORTHEAST SLOPE LEADING TO FORT GEORGE, NEAR INTERSECTION OF GOTTINGEN STREET AND RAINNIE DRIVE; PHOTO 1870.

"The night was pitch dark and a heavy fog added to the blackness; but although he was unable to distinguish their features, he evidently could make out that they were wearing uniform, for he cried out "Halt there! What are you doing out at this hour? What are your names and what regiment do you belong to?" and tried to peer into their faces. Sallis recognized his interrogator's voice, having often heard it before and knew no mercy would be shown them if they were discovered to be sergeants out without leave. He was a daring fellow, one not to be cornered without making some effort to extricate himself, and feeling certain it was too dark for the identification of himself and pal to be possible he, without a moment's pause, instead of replying, shot out his fist with full force from the shoulder, and catching his dreaded questioner squarely between the eyes, in quicker time than it takes to tell it, bowled him over into the gutter. It was a lusty blow from the powerful arm of an accomplished pugilist, given with a vim that would have felled an ox, for Sallis was the best of the heavy weights in the Garrison, and with the blow came unconsciousness to his victim.

"The deed being done there was safety only in effacing themselves. The other sergeant prevailed upon Sallis to hurry back with him to the place where they had got over, knowing well if any outcry was raised and a search made, they would be found missing from their rooms and pounced upon. Luck favoured them. Slipping off their shoes when they got inside they reached their rooms undetected, undressed with lightning speed and jumped into their cots. But it was not long before there was a loud knocking at the barrack gate and a tall figure, covered with mud, who gave his name and rank to the sergeant of the guard, was admitted. His face was severely bruised, and he held a handkerchief to his bleeding nose, naturally a very prominent feature, but now swollen to twice its usual size, and the spectacles, which at all times surmounted it, were absent.

18. NORTH BARRACKS WAS BUILT IN 1759 ON PRESENT SITE OF CITADEL HOTEL, AT BRUNSWICK AND COGSWELL STREETS. THE BARRACKS WAS ENLARGED TO A QUADRANGLE WITH A CENTRAL PARADE SQUARE IN 1800, AND HOUSED 1,168 MEN. THE ENTIRE COMPLEX WAS DESTROYED BY FIRE IN 1850 BUT REBUILT IN 1870 AND RENAMED PAVILION MARRIED SOLDIERS' QUARTERS. PHOTO C.1928.

"The subaltern of the day, whose duty it was to sleep in the South Barracks, was hastily awakened, the matter officially made known to him, and orderly sergeants were roused out of bed and ordered to call the roll in every room to see if anyone was absent. This was done in a very short time and each reported "all present." No men were absent excepting those who could be accounted for as being on guard, etc. When this intelligence was conveyed to the assaulted officer he was at a loss to understand it. He felt sure, he said, the men who attacked him had broken out of the South Barracks, or why would he have encountered them where he did? But nobody could explain. The orderly sergeants were positive of the accuracy of their reports and there the matter had to end for the time being. So he took his way out of the gate, boiling with rage, and doubtless inwardly vowing vengeance on his unknown assailants when he discovered them. But that never happened."

19. MARRIED SOLDIERS' QUARTERS, BLOCK A, WELLINGTON BARRACKS, C.1878.

Single and married soldiers shared barrack space until the mid 1800s. A man and his wife or family were allotted a corner of the barrack room away from the rank-and-file with blankets strung up to provide some semblance of privacy. At Fort George in the 1840s, as many as six families shared living space in one casemate. Finally, in 1855, the Barrack Accommodation Committee recommended separate married quarters.

But it wasn't until several years later that the first of these opened at Halifax, with the building of Pavilion Married Quarters, which housed eighty families. Each family was allowed one room measuring sixteen feet square. Pavilion Barracks benefited more than a hundred families then renting slum housing in the city, subsisting on a military living allowance of four cents a day. Interestingly, no provisions whatsoever were made for married army officers who were solely responsible for the shelter and care of their families.

20. GARRISON HOSPITAL, CORNER OF COGSWELL AND GOTTINGEN STREETS, 1876. GARRISON HOSPITAL BECAME OFFICES FOR THE DEPARTMENT OF VETERANS' AFFAIRS IN 1946-47 BUT WAS DEMOLISHED IN 1948-49, TO MAKE ROOM FOR AN APARTMENT BUILDING.

The Army Medical Department was established in 1810 to standardize medical services and to improve the level of care provided British troops. Two types of field operations fell under its jurisdiction: the medical officers of a particular regiment, and the medical staff officers assigned to a hospital or entire garrison. In the late eighteenth and early nineteenth centuries, several small military hospitals were scattered about Halifax at various forts and barracks. In 1806, a General Medical Hospital accommodating 120 patients was established on the north glacis in the town house that Prince Edward had vacated in 1800. An 1835 engineer's report described it being "in a state of great decay and becoming unsafe" and on November 10, 1866 the hospital was razed by fire. An emergency infirmary was then set up at nearby Glacis Barracks. In December 1870, a "fine large, substantial" brick and stucco Garrison Hospital measuring 350 feet by 30 feet (pictured here) opened near the present site of Staples Business Depot on the corner of Cogswell and Gottingen Street.

21. GARRISON HOSPITAL, 1919 (A.K.A. STATION OR COGSWELL STREET HOSPITAL), SAW SERVICE DURING BOTH WORLD WARS. IN 1917, A NEW CAMP HILL MILITARY HOSPITAL WAS BUILT ON THE SOUTHWEST COMMONS.

Halifax was known as the "sanitarium for Bermuda," serving on occasion as an emergency infirmary when yellow fever threatened the island garrison. Halifax, too, had its visitations by dreaded diseases—small pox in 1775, yellow fever in 1835, cholera in 1834 and 1866. Three quarantine hospitals and a disinfection station were built on Lawlor's Island in the harbour, with an infectious disease hospital on Miller's Island in Bedford Basin. Legend contends that small pox saved Halifax from American invasion in 1775, when the American Congress cancelled plans to attack with an army of eighteen thousand troops after learning of the disease spreading through the town. There were few well-trained doctors in Canada until the nineteenth century. Some of the first were regimental surgeons who chose to remain behind and set up practices when their time with the army was finished. Nova Scotia doctor and politician Sir Frederick Borden established a militia medical department in 1896, which became the basis for the Canadian Army Medical Corps.

This photo graphically portrays the commanding position that Fort George held of the southern harbour approaches. A seaborne attacker would have run a gauntlet of shore and island batteries as well as the guns of naval vessels anchored at the inner harbour. The point of land in the distance to the right of the photo is York Redoubt. Directly oppo-site is McNab's Island, a ribbon of beach stretching into the harbour barely visible, where Sherbrooke Tower once stood. Fort Clarence—on the Dartmouth shore to the left of McNab's Island—guarded the eastern channel, with Fort Charlotte on George's Island (centre) anchoring the defences. The expansive compound, centre foreground, comprised (R-L) Royal Artillery Park, Royal Engineers Square, and South Barracks.

23. PANORAMA OF HALIFAX LOOKING NORTHEAST FROM FORT GEORGE TOWARDS DARTMOUTH. IN FAR DISTANCE TO LEFT OUT OF VIEW WAS HM DOCKYARD, C.1886

A large concentration of the military establishment was located within a musket shot of Fort George. The horseshoe cluster of buildings (centre right) is the Pavilion Married Soldiers Barracks. The two-storey, white, elongated building to its left is Glacis Barracks. To the rear of Glacis Barracks (right) you can see the roof of Garrison Chapel on Cogswell Street; the two identical rectangular buildings to its immediate left comprised the Garrison Hospital. (Only footpaths crossed the north glacis in the days before Gottingen was extended southward beyond Cogswell to intercept with Rainnie Drive, when it was cut through in the 1900s.) The saluting battery in the foreground would have been kept busy in early years as signals were fired with the arrival and departure of ships in port. This sometimes caused much ado among the residents of Barrack Street, who complained that concussions broke windows, especially when all twelve guns were fired in a salute. For the past hundred and fifty years, a noon gun has been fired from the Fort George ramparts every day excepting Christmas.

24. GARRISON CLOCK, c.1895. THE ORIGINAL MECHANISM, OPERATIONAL SINCE OCTOBER 20, 1803, CONTINUES TO TICK OFF THE HOURS, ALTHOUGH THE GEORGIAN BUILDING—WHICH SERVED AS THE TIME-KEEPER'S RESIDENCE, A GUARD ROOM, ARMOURY, AND TEMPORARY HOSPITAL—HAS BEEN ALTERED SEVERAL TIMES.

dier-like manner, and understanding that this has arisen from their having been frequently permitted to work for inhabitants of the town, is pleased to order that in future no soldier be permitted to work for anyone unless the commanding officer of his corps will furnish him with a written permit, signed by himself, but those applications must never be made, only in cases of indispensable necessity after this day...." The regulation was rescinded following Edward's departure in 1800.

Prince Edward was a stickler for punctuality and demanded the same of his troops. In 1800, he ordered a turret clock be crafted by London's Royal Clockmaker and erected on the east glacis to assist the garrison with their time keeping. Edward was equally adamant about appearance, being an impeccable dresser himself. Soldiers were often permitted to supplement their meager incomes by working about Halifax during their time off; on November 15, 1796, Edward issued the following order: "His Royal Highness, the Lieutenant-General commanding His Majesty's Army in Nova Scotia, having of late had frequent occasions to observe several soldiers of the garrison appear on the streets in a most slovenly and unsol-

25. ROYAL MILITARY EXERCISING GROUNDS, NORTH COMMON, 1901.

In keeping with European tradition, Chief Surveyor Charles Morris set aside ninety-four hectares of land at Halifax in 1760 for common pasturage and cutting of wood. On the North Common, or Royal Military Exercising Grounds, mock battles were fought, tent encampments pitched, soldiers exercised, and regiments reviewed by local commanders or visiting royalty such as the Duke of York (later King George V), pictured here in 1901. The grounds served a more gruesome purpose as a site for military executions in the nineteenth century (see Chapter 8), replacing a small tract of land to the southwest of Fort George, known as the Garrison Grounds, which had been reserved for that purpose since 1772 and which later became the Wanderers Athletic Ground and Garrison Cricket Field.

26. ARMY & NAVY DEPOT, CORNER OF BUCKINGHAM AND GRANVILLE STREETS, OPPOSITE ORDNANCE YARD, 1871.

James Scott was one of the many Halifax merchants who prospered through catering to the military. A grocer and wine merchant, Scott operated two outlets of his "Army & Navy Depot," the North Branch pictured here with a South Branch conveniently located opposite the commanding general's residence on Spring Garden Road. Not surprisingly, advertisements focused heavily upon liquor: "Finest Old Scotch and Irish Whiskey, Pale and Dark Brandies, Hull and "Old Tom" Gin, Old English Rum, Angostura Bitters, Bass', Alsop's and Edinburgh Ales in pints and quarts, Guinness, Barclay and Perkins. The stock in Both Departments of the above well-known Establishment (one of the oldest in the Lower Provinces) warranted Excellent, having been selected with great care in the best markets of Great Britain and the Continent of Europe." A Halifax citizen wrote in 1915, "Into the old Army & Navy building, in by-gone days, came famous admirals and generals and captains of the army and navy to select rich wines and dainties for the balls and functions to be given on the flagship, at Government House or at Bellevue."

27. COMMISSARIAT OFFICE, BEDFORD ROW, 1873.

The Commissariat was the department of the army in charge of providing food and all daily necessities of the garrison as well as money for the paymaster. The navy counterpart was Commissioner for Victualling, who supplied the Victualling Yard in HM Dockyard. The Commissariat worked in conjunction with various military departments, filling orders, for example, from the Quarter Master General, Barrack Master, and Surgeon General on station, then delivering goods to the Storekeeper General or Ordnance Storekeeper for storage and disbursement. Supplying provisions for the troops and forage for animals remained the Commissariat's responsibility. Another of his duties was submitting newspaper advertisements requesting contract tenders for all manner of local goods, including pale seal oil and cotton wick, boards, shingles, bricks, lime, sand, nails, linseed oil, turpentine, paint, birch brooms, and straw. One asked for bids to supply three thousand pounds of fresh beef daily, "to be of an unexceptionable quality and delivered to the troops in entire quarters with suet...." The Commissariat also provided for garrisons at Annapolis and Windsor, until troops from these outposts were withdrawn during the Crimean War.

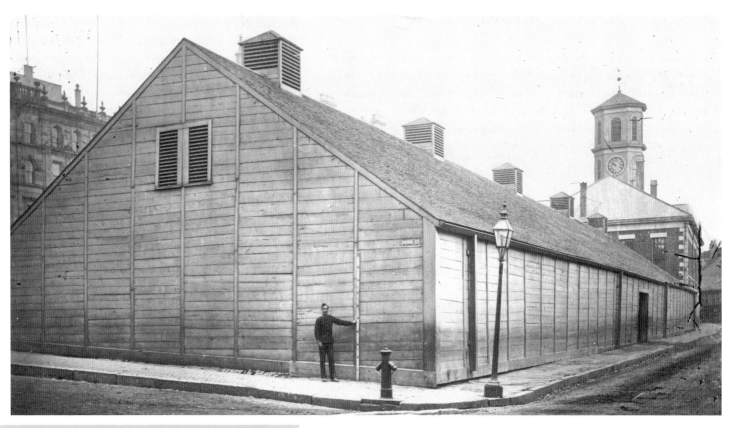

28. FUEL YARDS FOR COAL STORAGE ON NORTHWEST CORNER OF LOWER WATER AND PRINCE STREETS WITH CITY MARKET BUILDING TO RIGHT IN DISTANCE, C.1880. TODAY IT IS THE SITE OF THE DOMINION PUBLIC BUILDING, COMPLETED IN 1929.

The following call for coal and wood tenders was posted in Halifax newspapers on May 8, 1854:

"2,500 Chaldrons of Sydney Screened Coal to be measured according to Law and delivered and piled at the expense of the Contractor, in the Commissariat Fuel Shed at Halifax and in the Fuel Yards at the several Harbour Posts between the 16th of July and 31st October 1854. 2420 Chaldrons to be delivered and piled in Fuel Shed at Halifax; 40 (Chaldrons) in the Fuel Yard at York Redoubt; 25 (Chaldrons) at Sackville; 15 (Chaldrons) at Fort Clarence. The coal is to be of the best quality and each cargo to be accompanied by a Pit Certificate counter-signed by the Collector of Customs. N.B. 100 Chaldrons of the above to be delivered into the Fuel Shed at Halifax in the month of June, if required.

"Fuel wood to be delivered at the following Posts between the 1st June and 30th September 1854, viz. at Annapolis, 112 cords; at Windsor, 36 cords; at Sambro, 40 cords; at Camperdown, 40 cords. The wood to consist of Beech, Black and Yellow Birch, Ash and Maple—to be measured and piled as the Law directs and delivered into the respective Fuel Yards at the expense of the Contracting Parties."

29. "LITTLE FUEL YARDS" AT SOUTHEAST CORNER OF PRINCE STREET AND BEDFORD ROW, 1880. LATER SITE OF BEDFORD ROW FIRE STATION (c.1906), TODAY McKELVIE'S RESTAURANT.

Fuel sometimes was issued sparingly from the Commissariat depot. The winter of 1831 was especially harsh, and the coal allotment for barrack hearths especially sparse. Sergeants from the King's Own, Oxfordshire, and New Irish regiments went to the aid of their men, writing an unsigned letter of complaint to the *Acadian Recorder* in hopes its publication would reach sympathetic ears in England. The ears they reached were far from sympathetic. The Solicitor General paid a less than civil visit to the Editor's office to determine the names of the complainants. Failing this, the Commissariat was sent; he, too, left disgruntled but not before gaining a measure of revenge, ordering the Recorder's editor to cancel publications of all military advertisements. The Editor refused to comply; when the army would not pay its bill, the Lord of the Treasury was asked to intervene but declined. The story goes that no future military business was forthcoming until that particular editor had left the newspaper. "Such was the treatment meted out to an offender against the will of those who were in charge of the militia affairs of the province."

30. A SUBSTANTIAL AREA OF LAND ALONG THE WATERFRONT WAS RESERVED AS "PROPERTY OF THE IMPERIAL GOVERNMENT."

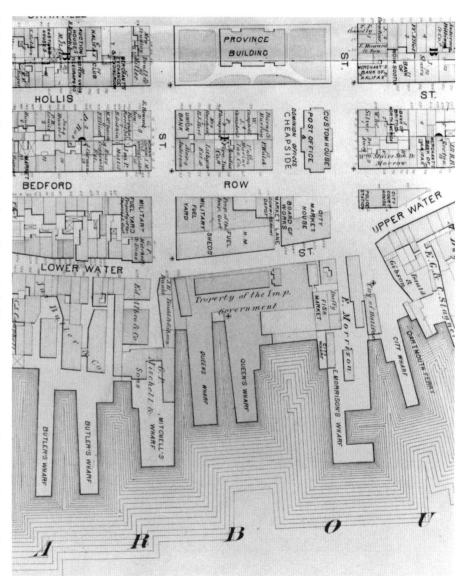

This map from the 1878 Halifax City Atlas shows the Queen's Wharf, Commissariat Office, and Fuel Yards. Today, only the two wharves remain (long since rebuilt but still referred to as Queen's Wharf) near the Maritime Museum of the Atlantic. Note the fish market at Morrison's Wharf and Cheapside off Bedford Row. On weekends, these areas were overflowing with townspeople who came to shop at the farmers' market. W. M. Brown described the scene in his 1895 memoirs *Recollections of Old Halifax*:

"In past days all summer through as regularly as Saturday morning, a mixed company of Eastern Passage, Cow Bay and Chezzetcook farmers, colored people, and a number of the Indian population, had been accustomed to come into town, across the Dartmouth ferry, their wagons laden with farm produce and domestic small wares of various sorts, and ranging themselves along the sidewalks, unobtrusively offering their goods for sale.... Here we can see the regimental mess man, the smart gun-steward from the Dockyard, the caterer for the ships, and the natty private soldier who has just set up housekeeping with a newly made wife from the servant class of the town jostling gentlemen's servants in livery and eager eyed boarding house keepers or even the mistress of some aristocratic mansion, who, in fresh morning gown has thriftily risen early to do her own marketing.

"An old fish market at the entrance of the Market Wharf was always liberally supplied with salmon, cod, halibut, mackerel, herring, lobsters, gaspereaux, and trout. A story is told of a certain naval captain of old days, new to this station who, probably better accustomed to the prices which ruled in Portsmouth or Plymouth than at Halifax, once gave his steward a sovereign [$2.40] to buy lobsters for the cabin dinner. The man returned with a small boat load of the crustaceans in two or three wheelbarrows and presented them to the captain whose surprise can be easily imagined."

31. GUARD HOUSE AT MAIN GATE OF QUEEN'S WHARF, C.1880.

The Queen's Wharf (originally called King's Wharf) was the key military pier for water transport supplying the outlying forts. Lucrative military contracts were available for the hiring of private transports. One advertisement read: "Persons having vessels fit for the conveyance of troops, and who are willing to hire the same to government, on charter to England will leave sealed tenders…expressing therein terms for hire, the name of the vessel and master together with registered tonnage of the vessel, at what wharf she may be laying and when made ready for sea." The Queen's Wharf was also a receiving and storage area for the commissariat; a fuel yard for firewood; an arrival and departure point for regiments, prisoners, and dignitaries; and a terminus for the Royal Mail. The first pair of India rubber boots seen in Halifax arrived at the Queen's Wharf courtesy of Charles Seaver, mail officer of HM Royal Navy, who purchased two pairs in 1828 at Boston for ten dollars. He kept one pair and presented the other as a gift to Admiral Sir Charles Ogle, then commanding the station.

32. QUEEN'S WHARF, SHOWING THE LONG STORE CONTAINING CARPENTER'S SHOP, GENERAL STORES, BOATMAN'S QUARTERS, AND MEAT STORE, 1880.

Commissariat contracts were one of the "chief economic props" in Halifax, with fifty suppliers selling goods and services on a regular basis. One of these was Moir & Son Bakery, who possibly tendered a bid on the following announcement in the December 18, 1858 *Acadian Recorder*:

"The Deputy Commissary General will receive tenders, in duplicate, at this office until noon on Friday the 31st December from all persons desirous of BAKING such quantities of BREAD and BISCUIT as may be required at this Station from 1st April 1859 to 31st March 1860.

"The Bread or Biscuit to be of the best quality and to be baked exclusively from Flour, the produce of the United States or Canada and of the best superfine quality, to be delivered by the Commissariat.

"Bread...to be baked 8 hours previous to delivery; that for troops in 4 lb. Loaves and that for officers and others in 2 lb. Loaves; to be issued daily (Sundays excepted) and to be delivered at the several Barracks and Hospitals and officers quarters at the expense of the Contractor; and the whole to be subject to the approval of the Senior Commissariat officer, or if required, to that of a Board of officers constituted by proper authority whose decision shall be final and binding on all concerned. Bread rejected to be immediately replaced

by the Contractor with Bread of proper quality and should he fail to do so, the Commissariat to have the power of purchasing Bread, at any cost, or of issuing Biscuit in lieu thereof, at the expense of the Contractor.

"The flour in the Commissariat Magazine to be subject to the inspection and approval of the Contractor, and to be delivered to him as required for conveyance to his own Premises, and no other Flour whatever to be used by him in the manufacture of Bread and Biscuit for the Troops; nor is Flour of an inferior quality to be permitted on the premises of the Contractor under a penalty of 20 [pounds] sterling for each offence."

From *Acadian Recorder*, December 18, 1858 (cont'd):
"The Flour to be conveyed by the Contractor to his Premises at his own expense; and all empty barrels may be retained by him, excepting those required for the re-delivery of Biscuit.

"The Contractor to furnish and deliver daily at the Hospital (Sundays excepted) such quantities of Bread as may be required by the Medical officers, and all such Bread to be subject to the approval of the Purveyor, whose decision shall be final. But, it is to be distinctly understood that no Bread once issued to Troops or received at the Hospitals, can on any pretense whatever, be returned to the Contractor. Also, should at any time during the period to be contracted for, Troops be encamped within 10 miles of Halifax, the Contractor to supply them with Bread, or to deliver Flour to be baked into Bread by the Troops themselves at the option of the Senior Commissariat officer; and all and every expense, if any, of such delivery, to be defrayed by the Contractor.

"The Tender must express in words at length, the number of lbs. of Bread and Biscuit, respectively, which will be returned to the Commissariat, for every 100 lbs. of Government Flour which may be

issued, the whole expense of baking being borne by the Contractor; and no Tender will be noticed unless made on the printed forms to be obtained at this office; and they must have the signatures affixed of two persons of unexceptionable responsibility and known property, engaging to become bound, with the Party tendering, in the penal sum of 500 [pounds] sterling, for the due execution and fulfilment of a contract, as above.

"Further information required, may be obtained at the office. Commissariat, Nova Scotia Halifax, 11th December 1858."

34. ENTRANCE TO ORDNANCE YARD, UPPER WATER STREET, C.1933.

A small Ordnance Yard, to house military supplies for the Royal Artillery, was built sometime prior to 1766 on the site of the old North Battery at the foot of Buckingham Street, where the Sheraton Hotel sits today. (Except for a short section, Buckingham Street disappeared in 1957 with the building of Scotia Square). The yard was congested and "very inadequate," a square of only one hundred feet containing six large buildings—a Long Store, Square Store, Armourer's Shop, Bedding Store, Laboratory (for processing gunpowder), and a Victualling Storehouse for the Commissariat. Engineer plans called for expansion onto neighbouring vacant properties. This proved unpopular with military authorities because it resulted in the yard then being divided into two sections with Water Street passing through the centre. By 1809, the original wooden buildings were "fast falling into decay" and alternative housing had to be arranged with private citizens at additional expense. In August of that year, blueprints for new buildings and a re-routing of Water Street were submitted to the Ordnance Board in England for approval. Construction began in 1811, and when completed in 1816, included an Armoury, two new large storehouses, another storehouse for small arms, a Smith and Carpenter's Shop, and a storehouse for gun carriages. All were masonry buildings, constructed of ironstone with freestone trimmings. In 1812, the section of Water Street which bisected the property was "absorbed" into the yard. Water Street was then re-routed at a right-angle to connect onto Hollis Street. The parameters of the yard were defined with a high stone wall. Featured in this photo is the Ordnance Yard Gate built in 1812. The large storehouse in background was designed with sixteen arched doorways to accommodate gun carriages. An octagonal wooden clock tower containing a four faced time piece crafted in 1813 by Jon Thwaites & Co. of Clerkenwell, London, graced the roof for more than a century.

35. Ordnance Yard Armoury c.1879.

Several additions were made to the Ordnance Yard in later years. A Tube and Fuse Store was built in 1885-86, a Shell Store and Oil Store in 1886-87, an Armourer's Shop in 1892, and a guard room at the gate in 1896-97. An article from an 1896 New York newspaper described the yard as "piled all over its broad surface with shot and shell and cannon with long stretches of warehouses." The Ordnance Yard stood for many years after the British left, being taken over by the Royal Canadian Navy during World War Two and converted into the Central Victualling Depot. The original stone wall was retained for a time but—with the exception of one building used as a canteen—the others were razed in favour of "temporary" wartime structures. The French mortars flanking Armoury doorway were brought to Halifax in 1758 following the second siege of Louisbourg. Later displayed at the gates to Fort George, they were removed after World War Two, one taken to Ottawa, the other placed on the grounds of Artillery Park, where it remains today.

36. ROYAL ENGINEERS OFFICE AT LUMBER YARD ON HOLLIS STREET, 1877.

As architects, builders, and keepers of Fortress Halifax, the Royal Engineers needed adequate work space and storage for tools and construction materials. A small lumber yard, including workshops and sheds, was built in the summer of 1761 on a one-acre plot along the northeast glacis, near the present-day Halifax Police Department. In 1797, Prince Edward erected another Royal Engineer workshop nearby, on the south side of Cogswell Street. In the first year of the War of 1812, the lumber yard was moved to the far end of town on a larger three-acre site along the waterfront, near the corner of South and Hollis Streets, a site originally intended as a lime kiln yard. This location was better suited to the engineers' needs as it had a large wharf (built in 1762-63). Twelve new buildings were eventually erected, one being this 90 foot by 30 foot ironstone structure built in 1815, which served as the main office of the Royal Engineers until Imperial forces departed Halifax.

37. ROYAL ENGINEERS LUMBER YARD AND WHARF, 1870.
THE SITE TODAY IS TAKEN UP BY THE WESTIN HOTEL AND OLD
DEEP-WATER PIERS OF THE OCEAN TERMINALS.

At the outbreak of World War One, the lumber yard became embroiled in a political controversy. A $6.5 million project was underway to build the Ocean Terminals, a series of deep-water, thousand-foot-long docks and rail marshalling yards, which would complete the transcontinental railway system. The old Royal Engineers Yard, then under Canadian military control, sat at the northern end of the two-kilometre stretch of shoreline proposed for development. The yard was far from defunct, however, storing building materials as well as electrical and communication cables and equipment. The underwater telephone communication system linking the Halifax defences came ashore at the lumber yard, where it was tested and maintained. Water transport servicing the most seaward coastal defences, still inaccessible by land, also was based at the yard. In addition, the lumber yard served as a headquarters and training school for the Canadian Engineer Corps. A solution was finally reached in 1916, when the engineers moved to a renovated commercial wharf and series of warehouses next to the Queen's Wharf.

38. PRESENTATION OF MEDALS ON GRAND PARADE, LOOKING WEST FROM BARRINGTON STREET, C.1885. THE BUILDINGS IN DISTANCE INCLUDED PRIVATE RESIDENCES AND MOIRS BAKERY, SITE TODAY OF THE WORLD TRADE AND CONVENTION CENTRE.

Initial plans for Halifax in 1749 called for a central "spacious square with an equestrian statue of His Majesty." King George II never materialized and the square became a rectangle, built upon a slope so steep that when troops lined up, the noses of men to the rear were level with the knees of those in front. The Grand Parade, while not owned by the military, was intended initially as a place to muster militia. Prince Edward made many improvements to it from 1794 to 1800. The rough ground was cut down to the level of Barrington Street, steps installed from Argyle Street, and a red, wooden rail fence built around the perimeter with a gate and two turnstiles to allow pedestrians to cross. The Grand Parade became a central assembly point where bonfires were lit to celebrate special occasions, royal proclamations read, medals presented, military band concerts played, and daily guard mounted and inspected at 10 a.m., a tradition that continued until 1856. Allowed to fall into disrepair for many years, the site was improved in 1890, with major restorations in 1977 and 1995, resulting in the showcase Grand Parade of today.

39. DALHOUSIE COLLEGE ON GRAND PARADE, 1870S.

During the War of 1812, Sir John Sherbrooke, Lieutenant-Governor of Nova Scotia, sent a British force into Maine in 1814 to capture the towns of Bangor and Castine, both of which served as safe havens for American privateers terrorizing the eastern seaboard. The occupying forces established Castine as a Port of Entry, collecting customs duty on all exports and imports until war's end. By 1815, monies accrued in the "Castine Fund" amounted to £10,750. These "spoils of war" were returned to Halifax, where then Lieutenant-Governor George Ramsey, 9th Earl of Dalhousie, used the majority of the fund to realize his dream of building a school of higher learning. Dalhousie College was founded in 1818 at the north end of the Grand Parade; it remained there until 1886, when a new five-acre site was chosen on the South Common at the corner of Morris (now University Avenue) and Robie Streets. The original college, pictured here, was dismantled in 1887, its ironstone used to build the inner foundation walls of the new city hall erected on the site.

40. St. Paul's Church, Grand Parade.

At the south extremity of the Grand Parade is St. Paul's Church, the first Anglican church outside Great Britain to be designated a cathedral. Erected in the summer of 1750 from timbers cut in Boston, St. Paul's is the oldest Protestant church in Canada. This late 1800s photo depicts St. Paul's as it looks today, with the front facing north onto the parade. The original design (changed in 1812) had its doors opening south onto Prince Street. Attendance at Divine service was mandatory for all military personnel; a Private Joseph Patterson in 1883 received a thirty-five-day sentence for being absent from church parade. St. Paul's was designated Halifax's first garrison church; occasionally more than one Sunday sermon was required to accommodate the number of troops.

"Sunday presented a gay scene in Halifax in those days," recounted one resident in 1821. "The regiments in garrison, headed by their brass bands playing, marched in full dress amid the ringing of bells and the sound of martial music. The carriage of the Governor (who was then always a General Officer), in full military costume with his aide-de-camp, drove up to the south door of St. Paul's, the whole staff having first assembled under the portico which then ran along the southern end of the Church. His Excellency, followed by a brilliant display of gold lace and feathers, the clank of sabres and spurs, and the shaking of plummed hats of so many officers, many of whom were accompanied by their ladies, on entering the church, presented a most brilliant spectacle. All this was followed by the old Chief Justice in his coach and livery, the carriage of the Admiral, and those of several members of Council. On the sermon in the morning being concluded [which ended punctually, and sometimes abruptly, with the firing of the noon cannon from Fort George], the troops marched back to the barracks and the General and Staff returned to Government House, where they partook of luncheon and were again in requisition by 3 o'clock for the Grand Review of the troops on the Common."

41. INTERIOR OF ST. PAUL'S CHURCH, C.1890.

St. Paul's is said to have the largest number of memorial tablets on its walls of any church in North America. Many honour men of the garrison and naval station. One reads: "Erected to the memory of Captain Henry-Francis Evans, Commander of His Majesty's Ship the *Charles-Town* who was slain on the 25th July 1781 in defending a Convoy against a superior force, and in testimony of his voluntary, generous and successful exertions in protecting the Coast and Commerce of the Province." Captain Evans lies buried beneath the floor of St. Paul's with nineteen other prominent Haligonians. Some were soldier-governors—such as Charles Lawrence and John Parr—while others commanded on station—such as Lieutenant General William Gardiner, garrison commander (d.1806) and Philip Durrell, Vice-Admiral of the Blue and only naval commander-in-chief to die at Halifax (1766). A mysterious character buried below is Baron de Seitz, a Hessian officer (d. 1782) whose lineage it is said cannot be traced in Germany. More recently, in 1929, the bronze Doors of Remembrance were erected at the inner entrance to St. Paul's honouring one hundred parish members who died in World War One.

42. ST. GEORGE'S ANGLICAN CHURCH, BRUNSWICK STREET.

St. George's "Round Church" was built in 1800 to meet the growing demand of Anglicans in north-end Halifax. The church's origins date to 1756, when a house on Brunswick Street was converted by German settlers into the first St. George's or "Little Dutch [Deutsche] Church," which still stands today. The new St. George's became the "evangelical wing of the Church of England" in the nineteenth century and also a second garrison church of sorts. All did not go well, however, between the congregation and the soldiery, as a controversy arose over church pews. One observer wrote that "Salvation was free but the pews in the church were private property [through purchase], and the owners were very jealous of their legal rights." Apparently, soldiers attending St. George's had on numerous occasions plunked themselves down into unoccupied pews. After some time of turning the proverbial other cheek, disgruntled parishioners lodged a formal complaint in 1803 with the commanding officer, which resulted in the following "general order" being issued: "The Pews in St. George's chapel being private property, and the proprietors being objected to the soldiers sitting in them, the non-commissioned officers and soldiers are not to go into any Pew whatever, but are to sit in the galleries and stand in the aisles between the Pews." A second order was issued a short time later. "The Town Major will take care that two sergeants are posted on each side of the organ, before the troops enter the church, with orders that they are not to allow any person to open or otherwise touch it so as to occasion any damage, it having been much damaged last winter from the curiosity of the soldiers."

St. Matthew's Church on Barrington Street served the Presbyterians of the garrison, with soldiers sitting on the right in the gallery, artillerymen and engineers to the left. In the middle stood a sergeant-major with a long pole, which he used to waken those who dozed off from a late night of alcoholic revelry and whose snoring interrupted the service.

43. GARRISON CHAPEL, COGSWELL STREET C.1901, SITE TODAY OF TRINITY CHURCH.

The Church of England was the established church, and it took many turbulent years for the roots of religious tolerance to take hold. Roman Catholics were not allowed to join the British Army until 1799, when losses in the Napoleonic Wars necessitated the acceptance of "anyone willing to bear arms." At the beginning of the nineteenth century, both Roman Catholics and Protestant dissenters in the army were generally permitted to practice their faith. By 1811, Roman Catholics were not to

be punished for missing Sunday parade "when Military Duty does not interfere." It was 1836, however, before Roman Catholic chaplains were introduced, nine years after Presbyterians had become a separate branch of the Army Chaplain's Department.

Prior to 1830, most troops at Halifax attended St. Paul's and St. George's, but from 1830 to 1837, an old building was leased and fitted out as a Garrison Chapel. In October 1844, the cornerstone of a new Garrison Chapel was laid on the north glacis. A newspaper of the time reported, "Within the walls of the sacred edifice about to be erected…the British soldier, though afar from the land of his fathers, may find an altar where he may worship the great and good Being, whose mercy had been the shield of old England in many a time of national peril and difficulty." On June 18, 1847, the first service was held. The wooden chapel, with its fluted Doric columns, measured 100 feet by 60 feet and seated 724, the galleries reserved for officers and their families, the ground floor for non-commissioned officers and enlisted men. When Britain withdrew its garrison in 1905-06, the chapel was purchased by Trinity Church Corporation. Unfortunately on March 5, 1928, fire razed the Garrison Chapel, including all its military memorial tablets.

Parade Garrison Chapel Memorial Service for Queen

Notman Studio 8323

44. Parade along Granville Street marking the visit of the Duke of York, 1901. Photo taken looking north towards Halifax Harbour and Dartmouth.

Events of pomp and circumstance drew large crowds, be it the festive royal visit from a future king, as featured here, or the more sombre occasion on September 29, 1814, when the body of Major-General Robert Ross was interred at Halifax. Ross was felled by a sniper's bullet at the battle for Baltimore only three weeks after leading the British forces that captured the capital city of Washington. Legend contends that Ross's body was conveyed to Halifax in a rum barrel to preserve his remains during the seven-day voyage, and that soldiers and sailors later finished off the remaining rum from the good general's keg. Following is an eye-witness account of the funeral:

"Halifax presented a spectacle of intense interest. The citizens were on foot early to catch a look at the passing pageant; and crowds had come in from the country.... Halifax streets and harbor showed sights that day exceeding any they had witnessed either before or since. Off the dockyard lay the fleets of three admirals—seventeen sail—of the largest size, most of them line-of-battle ships. A hundred transports lay around them."

45. FUNERAL GUARD OF HONOUR, PRINCESS LOUISE FUSILIERS, C.1896.

Eye-witness account (cont'd):

"No display was wanting that would give effect to the spectacle. At an early hour troops were posted, who lined the streets from the king's yard, where the funeral party was to land, to the gate of the cemetery. The deep boom of the minute guns from twenty ships of war, showed that the funeral barge, attended by boats from every ship, had put off from the fleet. Now they ceased, and the great crowd knew the body and escort were on shore.

"Issuing from the gate, came the soldiers of the army, four deep, with reversed arms, stepping solemnly and slowly, the bronzed veterans of many fights—then the massed bands of many regiments filled the air with the sound of mournful martial music—troop after troop in varied regimentals, cavalry, artillery, line soldiers, highlanders, pass, and then the sailors of the fleet—then a splendid concourse of staff officers, in flashing uniforms, scarlet and gold—then an object, on which every eye was riveted—the bier, and on it the coffin of the dead hero, surmounted by his plumed hat and now useless sword. Next came the general's war horse, led in the procession, who seemed to seek his master in the crowd. Then, on crutches, limped to a waiting carriage, the two aids of General Packenham—more soldiers, the firing party of Grenadiers— more music and the cortege was closed by the officers of the fleet and the three admirals.

"The crowd jammed the streets, hardly leaving room for the procession to pass. The head of the procession had reached the grave before the rear was clear of the landing place. The great multitude, which filled every foot of space, were gazing reverently at the coffin. The bier was carried beside the grave. Every tongue was stilled; every eye fixed on it."

46. ST. PAUL'S CEMETERY, CORNER OF BARRINGTON STREET AND SPRING GARDEN ROAD WITH ST. MARY'S ROMAN CATHOLIC CHURCH IN DISTANCE.

Eye-witness account (cont'd):
"Soon the coffin was lowered into the grave; the soldiers stood around with their chins on the butts of their muskets. The officers of the fleets, of the two armies, the admirals and generals, stood at the foot. The two wounded aids were supported beside it. The stillness was profound, when across the graves came the solemn words of the service, "I am the resurrection and the life," deep feelings seemed to hold the throng spell-bound; many sobs were heard; a vagrant leaf from a tree above the grave fell upon the coffin. The aide-de-camp advanced, broke the general's sword, and threw it on the grave; a brief word of command, the firing party presented arms, then the deep hush was broken by the rattle of musketry. All was over. Bayonets glanced in the sunlight, uniforms flashed, the troops reformed, the bands played, the long procession moved out in all the pride of active life, and the brave General Ross was left alone with his glory, sleeping in the quiet Halifax church-yard."

A final footnote for the 1812 War hero: having captured Washington, General Ross gave orders to burn several structures, including the capitol building. Unsuccessful in destroying it completely, whitewash was later used to cover-up the blackened remains. The United States capitol building has been called the White House ever since.

In 1991, St. Paul's "Old Burying Ground" was designated Canada's first national historic cemetery. Founded in 1749 just beyond the settlement's stockade, there are thought to be twelve thousand graves, although only twelve hundred markers remain, that of General Ross's being one of the more prominent. The graveyard was a public burying ground until 1793, when it was turned over to St. Paul's Church, which continued using it for burials until 1844.

47. "THE LAST TRIBUTE
TO A COMRADE'S MEMORY—
THE SIMPLE SLAB WHICH
RECORDED HIS WORTH AND
YEARS AND EXPRESSED THE
HOPE AND BELIEF THAT THE
IMMORTAL SOUL WAS 'RESTING
IN PEACE.'" GRAVE OF
GEO. E. NORGATE, 26TH CO.
ROYAL ENGINEERS, FORT
MASSEY CEMETERY, c.1880.

During the American Revolutionary War, Fort Massey was built circa 1776-78 on what was then known as Windmill Hill, at the intersection of Queen and South Streets. The fort was intended to cover a deep ravine running along Freshwater Brook, through which an attacker could safely pass under the guns of Fort George. Typical of the hastily constructed earthen and logged fortifications of the time, Fort Massey lay "in ruins" by the early 1800s. Fort Massey Cemetery was then opened on the site, which came to be the Halifax garrison burial ground and remains an active Canadian Armed Forces cemetery today.

Historian George Mullane wrote in the August 15, 1914 *Acadian Recorder*, "Soldiers from many regiments, after having gone through many perils on the battlefield, found a last resting place in Fort Massey cemetery." The Commonwealth War Graves Commission, established in 1917, recognized the importance of Fort Massey by erecting a Cross of Sacrifice in the cemetery. The stone cross with a bronze sword affixed designates Fort Massey as one of twenty-five Canadian cemeteries containing a significant number of war dead.

48. INAUGURATION OF THE WELSFORD-PARKER MONUMENT, JULY 17, 1860.

Towering above the grave markers of Halifax's earliest settlers, statesmen, and military heros in St. Paul's Cemetery stands the Welsford-Parker Monument. Built from funds raised through public donations and a provincial government grant, this lion-topped edifice, which faces east onto Barrington Street, was erected in memory of two Nova Scotians killed in 1855 during the Crimean War while leading an assault against the Great Redan at Sebastopol. Captain William Parker of the 77th Regiment received the Victoria Cross posthumously for his valour (his father, Captain Smith Parker from Lawrencetown, Halifax County, served with the 64th Regiment). In 1858, the settlement of River John Village in Pictou County, Nova Scotia was renamed Welsford to honour Major Augustus Welsford of the 97th Regiment. Welsford had been a friend of Dr. Robert Bayard's son of River John Village, an original settler of the area. The 97th Regiment was considered "one of the finest in the British army," serving at the Halifax garri-son from 1849 to 1853. The Welsford-Parker Monument, a "rare Pre-Confederation Canadian war memorial," is the only Crimean War monument in North America.

49. BOER WAR MONUMENT, NORTH YARD OF PROVINCE HOUSE.
"ERECTED BY THE PEOPLE OF NOVA SCOTIA IN HONOR OF THOSE WHO SERVED AND IN MEMORY OF THOSE WHO FELL IN THE SOUTH AFRICAN CAMPAIGN 1899-1902."

50. BOER WAR MEMORIAL FOUNTAIN, HALIFAX PUBLIC GARDENS.
"ERECTED BY THE COMMISSIONERS OF THE PUBLIC GARDENS IN COMMEMORATION OF THE SERVICE OF OUR CITIZEN SOLDIERS IN THE SOUTH AFRICAN CAMPAIGN 1899-1902."

Two memorials were erected in Halifax to honor Canada's Boer War combatants. The figure atop the Boer War fountain (erected in 1903) is said to have been modelled from a photograph taken of a native son in the Canadian Mounted Rifles. Canadian War Museum historian Cameron Pulsifer writes, "Although largely citizen soldiers, Canadians returned from South Africa confident in their ability to function together in full-time and effective military formations. While it was the cause of the British Empire that had first inspired their participation, once in South Africa, Canadians developed a profound sense of distinctiveness from their imperial counterparts that nourished feelings of national pride and a sense of independent military identity. Fighting together in South Africa taught the Canadians a number of valuable lessons. Thereafter, militia training became more realistic and discipline tighter. In addition, Engineers, Signals, Service and Ordnance Corps were added to the order of battle, laying the foundation of a modern army. During the much larger and bloodier conflicts to come in the twentieth century, Canadian soldiers were to fully justify the reputation their forebearers had gained in South Africa."

51. HALIFAX ARMOURY, CUNARD AND NORTH PARK STREETS, c.1899.

The Halifax Armoury, with its "quaint, candle-snuffer turrets" is the most dominant structure (aside from Fort George) remaining from the Imperial era. It was actually built by the Dominion Government's Department of Militia and Defence in response to a lack of proper training facilities in Halifax for the militia. Designed by noted architect Thomas Fuller, whose credits include the centre block of Ottawa's Parliament Buildings, the Halifax Armoury is claimed to be one of only two of this design built in Canada (Toronto's was torn down in the 1960s). Constructed of freestone, granite, and pressed brick, with iron and steel framing, the armoury took three years to complete (1895-98) at a cost of $250,000. More than sixty workmen and nine 40-ton, steam-powered cranes were needed to build the metre-thick walls. On June 27, 1899, five hundred militiamen of the Princess Louise Fusiliers vacated an antiquated drill hall on Spring Garden Road adjacent to Bellevue and marched to their new home. The massive structure (163 feet wide by 303

feet long) included an indoor parade square 100 feet by 250 feet, officers quarters, three armouries, recreation and lecture rooms, band rooms, three rifle ranges, two bowling alleys, and electric lights, the first such building to have electricity designed into its plans. It was here on January 19, 1900, that 1,320 members of the Canadian Contingent Artillery and Mounted Rifles assembled prior to embarking for the Boer War. Twice it was used as shelter in times of crisis: the Halifax Explosion of 1917 and the Bedford Magazine explosion in 1945. The armoury today serves as headquarters for the Princess Louise Fusiliers.

CHAPTER 6

NO LIFE LIKE IT

The "No Life Like It" recruiting slogan of today's Canadian Armed Forces promises a career far different from that faced by the nineteenth century British soldier. A man who accepted the "King's Shilling" prior to 1847 entered a binding agreement to join His Majesty's Service for life; the exception to the rule came during times of war when temporary regiments were raised, then disbanded at the end of hostilities. After 1847, the life sentence was commuted to ten compulsory service years, with voluntary re-enlistment for another eleven years earning a meagre pension. Should one survive to retirement, he was placed on the army reserve list and paid four cents a day. Old soldiers and invalids qualified for one of the military hospitals such as Chelsea or Dublin, where a private with fourteen years service received two shillings a day, and sergeants three shillings, unless, of course, neither could prove a debilitating injury related to combat whereby compensation was reduced to seven or nine cents a day.

Army life was tough to say the least and, by 1867, numbers had decreased so significantly that initial service years were raised to twelve, with an additional nine then required for a pension. In 1870, short service was initiated by virtue of the Army Enlistment Act whereby a man joined the army for twelve years, six on active service, six with reserves. Regiments or battalions prior to circa 1870 were theoretically to spend ten years abroad and five years at home, then sixteen years abroad followed by sixteen years home; in reality, most garrisoned foreign stations for the majority of their service during the nineteenth century. Depleted ranks owing to death, desertion, and retirement were filled through recruitment from regimental depot companies based in Great Britain. The 40th Regiment of Foot could be compared to the biblical Israelites in the wilderness. Organized in 1717 from eight independent companies stationed at Annapolis Royal in Nova Scotia and at Placentia in Newfoundland, it would be forty-seven years before the regiment saw

the shores of England, doing yeoman duty in Nova Scotia, Barbados, Martinique, Havana, and then back to Nova Scotia before setting sail for a ten-year posting in Ireland. The 40th later returned to North America and fought in numerous battles between 1774 and 1815. There was no such thing, then, as a six-month or year-long posting as there is today; one regiment is claimed to have spent 137 years of its 187 years of existence abroad!

History has not been kind to Tommy Atkins, describing him as "generally beloved of two sorts of Companion, in whores and lice, for both these vermin are great admirers of a Scarlet Coat." To be fair, there were few inducements to encourage anyone other than the most desperate to enlist. Soldierly pay for the rank-and-file was one shilling (twelve cents) per day, plus one pence (one cent) beer money. With this a man could be guaranteed of two things: he would always receive his beer money but he would see nothing of his daily wage. By the time "stoppages" were applied against food, replacement costs for clothing and equipment, medicine, toiletries, domestic supplies, barrack damage deposit, and deductions to pay the regimental surgeon, paymaster, and support to the Chelsea military hospital, poor Tommy Atkins was just that, broke and despondent. There were opportunities to earn good conduct badges up to a maximum of five, with each badge increasing daily pay by one pence. Soldiers could also hire out as an officer's servant, mess waiter, or craftsman if skills and army-related duties permitted. If nothing else, this at least gave money enough to drown one's sorrows in the nearest pub. In the long run, most soldiers were left destitute.

There being no rush to join the colours, incentives and somewhat questionable recruiting practices were needed to fill the ranks. By law, a man had first to accept the King's Shilling before he could be considered to have joined the military. How this was accomplished varied. To entice him to willingly step forward, an enlistment bounty was offered, which varied from one pound (about $2.40, a significant sum at that time) in peacetime to ten pounds (about $24.00) when at war. This turned into a dangerous game, with some taking the bounty then running off, only to reappear later at a different place and re-enlist for yet another signing bonus. One man turned the trick forty-seven times before he was caught and hanged. Recruiters were paid fifteen shillings (about $1.80) for each man signed up. Taverns were a favourite hunting ground, where a potential recruit would first be plied to excess with his favourite beverage before a shilling was slipped surreptitiously into his pocket or ale tankard; this latter practice led some tavern keepers to put glass bottoms in their tankards to take away the element of surprise for patrons. One woman recruiter who happened to be married to a regimental colonel was adept at hiding a shilling in her mouth, then passing out a kiss and the coin to the lips of unsuspecting young men. It mattered little how the shilling got onto one's person, as possession was enough. By 1867, the Inspector General of Recruiting had introduced reforms to clean up the system; bounties were done away with, recruiters banned from drinking establishments, advertising had to be truthful, free discharges were granted to anyone who could prove they had been tricked, and the focus shifted to military tattoos and displays for recruiting. Despite these changes, the British Army still faced two serious problems: desertion and alcohol abuse, both of which it helped to create and foster.

"Alcohol provided the only outlet for men whose lives were devoid of variety and comfort," writes Carol Whitfield in *Tommy Atkins: The British Soldier in Canada 1759-1870*. "Furthermore, the men were confronted by an ambivalent official policy. On one hand, they were given alcohol, or the money to buy it, everyday, while on the other, they were flogged for exhibiting its effects." Soldiers in North America from 1759 to 1830 were issued a free gill of rum (four ounces) a day. Originally intended to be given out only to men on active war service or to those assigned to fatigue duty (extra work detail), the rum ration eventually came to apply to everyone. Officers believed that rum hardened men to want and need increasingly larger quantities of strong drink, thereby driving them to spend what little money they had on rum in local grog shops where it was cheap. Five pints of spruce beer (made by boiling spruce and molasses together, then adding yeast) was also issued daily to

each man in Canadian garrisons; in 1783 the practice was stopped. Beer cost more to produce, so the army didn't substitute it for the free rum ration; the decision to stop the practice may also have had something to do with the fact that in 1780, six hundred thousand gallons of the beverage were consumed within six months.

By 1800, the one pence daily beer allowance was added to a soldier's pay, and by 1831, rum in Nova Scotia was only issued "for troops performing exceptional duty." To curb excessive imbibing, the pay policy changed. In 1822, men were paid daily, instead of monthly as before, to cut down on the sudden amount of available cash, which had led to "scenes of waste, profligacy, and debauchery." To counter this, soldiers organized "boozing schools" whereby small groups pooled their money to binge-drink. And the officers seemed to lead by example—on the eve of leaving Halifax to attack Louisbourg, General Wolfe entertained forty-seven officers at a dinner where they polished off 120 bottles of wine and 25 of brandy. The Royal Military Exercising Grounds on the North Commons, too, had its share of exciting times. "Drunkenness and fighting were somewhat conspicuous. Camp Hill was covered with tents, from which strong drinks were distributed and fiddles and bagpipes roused willing dancers, and gross debauchery prevailed after nightfall. When there was a review of troops or militia, tents and tables were plentiful and boys were furnished with a pleasant drink composed partly of rum, peppermint, and aniseed, known as shrub. Dirty slops of porter and beer were freely used, as also stronger drinks."

Prodigious drinking was not reserved solely for the army and navy; it was a societal norm, described by Craig Heron in *Booze in Canada: A History*:

"According to one Nova Scotian, spirits 'were almost universally regarded as little less necessary to man's healthful existence than flesh and bread. Alcohol, it was thought, kept out heat in summer and cold in winter, supplied strength to labour, helped digestion, warded off disease, and did many other marvellous things'.... Men who worked for wages also expected alcohol in their daily work routines, as had their forebears in Europe for centuries.... In many cases the parallel to the modern coffee breaks took place in the late morning and midafternoon, when workers downed their booze."

One Halifax resident had his nineteenth century memoirs published in the July 31, 1915 *Acadian Recorder*:

"The price of rum was from fifty to sixty cents per gallon by the puncheon [a quart of beer sold for one cent, whiskey for six cents]. I well remember a ship chandlery where a puncheon of rum was kept on tap by the door and water and tumbler at hand for all to partake who wished, free of charge. Another person in later days kept a puncheon on draft in his workshop for use of his journeymen and apprentices and those of his friends who might drop in; and, as might be expected, some of his employees and sons have become drunkards…. Ferry-men, who rowed passengers across the harbor before larger vessels were used, were always full of liquor, and shops in the neighborhood of the ferry, on both sides, were mostly only tippling places. Rum selling was considered a very proper calling and the surest road to wealth, for dram-drinking was almost universal. There was a licensed liquor-shop for every hundred inhabitants, old and young, and not a church building or schoolhouse for every thousand. If a man called on another at any time after breakfast for payment of an account, rum and water were brought forth…. It was said in those days "The Churchmen get drunk in the day-time and the Methodists at night." Sir James Kempt loaned ten thousand pounds to the town, accepting as security money derivable from liquor licenses, which was then considered sure and ample."

In 1862, Boston had a population of 180,000 and 1,904 rum shops—an average of one shop for every ninety-four inhabitants. Halifax, with a population of only 25,000, had 340 "rum-poison" shops—one for every seventy-four citizens.

Drunkenness has been credited as "the main parent of all crime in the Army," being the leading cause of infractions as laid down in the Articles of War. Army temperance societies such as the "Soldiers' Total Abstinence Association" and "The Teetotalers" were organized to combat the habit. In one case, members who stayed on the wagon for six months were eligible to wear a patch on their uniform bearing the motto Watch and be Sober; a badge of courage in one respect, it attested to a soldier's "near superhuman resolution and endurance." Well intentioned, these movements had limited impact. Commanders and clergy could take solace in one blessing at least: the quantity of alcohol consumed by North American garrisons paled in comparison to that quaffed by soldiers stationed in India.

During his travels through Canada in 1850, of which he later wrote, John Bigsby noted that "Common soldiers often become thoroughly disgusted with their monotonous, hopeless and often annoying mode of life, [making them] susceptible to any advice which promises a change." If a soldier failed to find solace from the embrace of a rum bottle and prostitute, he was left with only one option: desertion. "Desertion from the British Army in North America was a problem of major proportions and incalculable costs," writes Carol Whitfield. "Nowhere else in the empire did so many men flee the colours so easily, committing 'a crime so disgraceful to the Character of a British soldier.'" Here, again, the army was often its own worst enemy, sparing no effort in its regulation of soldiers below non-commissioned-officer status to a life of servitude. A shilling was "pittance" pay when compared to the four or five shillings per diem that a labourer in Halifax received; the pay discrepancy was even greater for skilled trades, which many soldiers possessed. Army savings banks were not introduced until 1841, the feeling until then being that a poor man was less likely to desert than one with money. Similar thinking prohibited rank-and-file soldiers from owning civilian clothing, a deserter in uniform being easier to spot. Personal possessions of any kind other than military issue were discouraged, it being the 1890s before an army private was issued a barrack box.

Many joined the British military with the sole intent of deserting, hopeful of being garrisoned in Canada, where it was relatively easy to skip out to the United States. Some could be classed as "unruly, incorrigible malcontents" while others were honestly escaping work shortages or starvation at home but were not prepared to take on army life. The Irish, who made up a large proportion of the forces, were especially noted as deserters, using the army as "something of an unofficial and reluctant emigration service." However, Irish (and English) deserters were not especially adept at avoiding capture as they seldom took time to devise a viable escape plan; Scottish soldiers on the other hand proved to be "more cunning, premeditated and were seldom caught."

Location and season determined the likelihood and frequency of deserting. New Brunswick, Quebec, and Ontario were easier provinces to abscond from than Nova Scotia, as all three shared a common border with the United States. May to October were considered the best months to go AWOL, with December and January the worst because of deep snows and half-frozen waterways; activity picked up again in February with colder temperatures but declined during March and April's spring thaws. Deserters leaving Nova Scotia were more likely to stow away upon vessels so look-out posts were set up at St. Margarets Bay, Prospect, Dartmouth, Sackville, and Windsor. When taking meals to the dockyard guard in Halifax, soldiers were prohibited from travelling Water Street to reduce the chances of disappearing onto one of many ships tied up at the wharves.

Steps were taken to close the flood gates but desertion continued. Severe punishments—such as flogging, hard labour, transportation, branding, even death—did little to dissuade soldiers bent upon deserting. Military police were first organized in the 1860s to patrol streets and taverns in search of AWOL soldiers and to maintain the general peace. Descriptions of deserters were given to look-out parties and were widely circulated in newspapers. Some men stole civilian clothing, even dressing as women, to avoid detection, while others deserted in uniform hoping that punishment would be less severe if captured. Bounties of £5 ($12.00) were offered to any civilian turning in a deserter; many civilians, however, helped deserters, perhaps to gain cheap labour or as an act of defiance toward Imperial rule. The Mutiny Act did not permit soldiers to receive the bounty for turning in a deserter but it did force them to garrison look-out posts or track down men. Married men were less likely to run, so concerted efforts were made to increase their numbers in outposts prone to desertion. Toward this end, the Royal Canadian Rifles was organized in 1836 "to counteract the Crime of desertion from the Regiments of the Line on the Frontier." Loyal veteran soldiers with ten to fifteen years service were courted to volunteer by offering incentives such as increased pay, ample opportunity to "profit" from other jobs during leisure time, short-service retirement pensions, and land grants upon discharge. No records exist to determine the success of this regiment in curbing desertion.

Until 1848, the United States and Britain agreed to turn over deserters, but after this date only murderers, robbers, and forgers were extra-dited. Tracking, apprehending, convicting, and punishing deserters was an expensive proposition that most commanders had little interest in pursuing. A couple of widely divergent approaches were taken at Halifax. One officer locked everyone in barracks and ordered hourly roll call while another provided increased opportunities to play sports and built more recreational facilities. In some cases, when faced with the inevitability of desertion, disenchanted men were allowed to purchase their discharge. By 1850, deserters could apply to the Secretary of War and pay £20 ($48.00) to secure a pardon and "protecting certificate." Again, no numbers are known to exist showing how many took advantage of this. However, one thing is certain: despite post-Crimean War reforms, there was no life like it for a man entering the British military—unless, of course, he joined the Royal Navy, which was twice as bad.

1. Cambridge Battery Canteen, Point Pleasant, 1870s. Profits from regimental canteens exceeding £200 ($480) had to be spent on the men and their families.

At the time of this photo, canteens had become "comfortable, respectable gathering places for the troops." The first army canteens were operated by sutlers—civilians licensed by the military to sell food and goods (mostly booze) to the soldiers. Sutlery is said to have originated in North America during the Seven Years' War, with as many as thirty retired soldiers operating as licensed sutlers in 1757 at Fort Beauséjour. By the early 1800s, canteen services were regulated by strict rules, and the garrison commanding officer was authorized to cancel a license for infractions with one week's notice. Canteen hours of operation were 12 noon to 8 p.m. in winter, 9 p.m. in summer. All prices of goods and food for sale had to be prominently displayed. Card playing and gambling were forbidden, and only "sober" soldiers could be served alcohol. Officers were permitted to take drinks from the canteen but the rank-and-file were not. In an attempt to provide "extra benefits" for the men in the early 1860s, civilian services were replaced by regimental canteens that operated in barracks by committees comprised of a canteen sergeant and two assistants, under the supervision of three senior officers. Beer on tap was popular but so, too, were food stuffs and staples such as coffee, tea, sugar, meat, vegetables, rice, oatmeal, and baking powder; married soldiers were appreciative patrons, buying supplies for

in-barracks cooking. Even officers benefitted, as they could now purchase imported treats tariff free for the mess, including pickles, jams, truffles, caviar, sauces, and biscuits. Profits from canteen sales, generated by a twenty percent mark-up, were used to offset some of the regimental expenses traditionally deducted from a soldier's wage—whitewash, brushes, lime, barrack damages. Soldiers' wives and children received mitts and comforters, with monies also used for family picnics and Christmas dinner. Funds also were spent on "any articles for the convenience of the Canteen establishment which are readily removable, and which the Regiment might wish to carry with it from station to station."

2. LIEUTENANT WILMAN, ROYAL IRISH RIFLES, C.1885. THIS REGIMENT GARRISONED HALIFAX ON TWO OCCASIONS, 1834-37 AND 1883-86.

British Army regulations, as noted earlier with the Royal Artillery, did not look favourably upon marriage. Only six percent of an infantry regiment's complement were permitted to marry, the privileged few receiving an extra living allowance to support their wives and families. In addition, women drew one-half of their soldier-husband's rations per day while children up to seven years of age received one-quarter rations, those to the age of fourteen one-third. Wives often worked menial jobs to make ends meet. There were exceptions to the matrimonial rule, one being that all staff sergeants and half of the remaining sergeants could marry. (The Royal Canadian Rifles were exempt from the six-percent rule, with twelve women per one hundred men permitted, in addition to any wives who may have drawn rations in their husband's previous regiment.) Officers, on the other hand, could not wed before reaching their mid-thirties, and even then it was not encouraged, the feeling being that "the purity of the mess was disturbed by marriage [and] it took officers out of the all male warrior clique." According to one source, "the rule of thumb was that subalterns may not marry, captains might marry, majors should marry and lieutenant-colonels must marry."

There were certainly many soldiers while on station who married "off strength" which meant they received no compensation and their spouse was ineligible to transfer with the regiment. When the Royal Irish Rifles left Halifax in 1886, more than three hundred men had married "without leave," resulting in one hundred and twenty desertions in the last year of the regiment's posting. The March 23, 1893 *Daily Echo* announced the arrival of the King's Own Regiment to relieve the Leicestershire Regiment that had served at Halifax since 1891. While the article is somewhat humorous, it evokes compassion for those left behind:

"The troopship Jiunga arrived in port from Bermuda after a very fine run, having left there Monday afternoon at 4 o'clock. The ship disembarked the First Berkshire regiment, which she brought from Malta, at Bermuda Sunday, and the 1st battalion Liverpool (8th), or King's Own regiment, embarked Monday morning. No mishap occurred on the passage and all were well when they arrived. The troops landed and marched to the Wellington barracks through the north gate of the dockyard at 11:30, headed by the band of the Leicestershire regiment (whom they relieved)."

3. A Sergeant Patrick and wife, 78th Highland Regiment, c.1870.

March 23, 1893 *Daily Echo* (cont'd):

"The men of the new regiment are a good looking body composed of 23 officers, 1 staff-sergeant and 888 men, and attached to it are 5 ladies, 23 children, 31 women, 40 children, 2 servants, 2 horses and 6 dogs. [Wives of officers were no doubt classed as 'ladies' with others designated 'women'].

"The Leicestershire regiment embarked on the Jiunga at the dockyard this morning at 11 o'clock. The street in the vicinity of the dockyard gate was a solid mass of humanity. The majority of those present were females, "soldiers girls" who were there to take a long and last look at their departing sweethearts…. The old scenes of weeping and wailing seem to have to a large extent departed, and the maiden has found consolation in the companionship of the King's Own. Thursday and Friday nights were taken up by the Leicestershire men in introducing the new arrivals to their old sweet-hearts, and this doubtless accounts for the lack of tears and heart-breaking sobs formerly witnessed on such occasions.

"When the regiment had entered the dockyard and the heavy gates had swung to behind them, about twenty young women and several older ones gave free vent to their grief and loss, despite the jibes of the congregated hard-hearts…. In the crowd were a number of married women—soldiers' wives—who are left worse than widows. They married "off the strength" and consequently could not accompany their husbands and the chances are only one in a thousand that they will see their husbands again. Some of them were married quite recently and with a full knowledge that they were to be left "grass widows." This is one of the evils of the imperial service at this station which is in need of reform. Somebody tells a story of a woman, who, when the gate closed, shook her fist at it and between her sobs muttered: 'That darn gate has left me a widow seven times!'"

The first army school was established in 1662 at Madras, India. But it was not until 1811, when regimental schools became officially sanctioned, that steps were taken to provide formal education. Even then, girls were not permitted to attend school until 1840, when this was decreed by Royal Warrant from Queen Victoria; the first trained teachers were provided that year as well. Children to the age of fourteen were required to attend a regimental school. Halifax had several—Royal Artillery Park, Fort George, North Barracks, and Wellington Barracks. Classes were held six days a week, with three weeks off for summer vacation. Adults and children attended school together from 9 a.m. until 12 noon, then returned in the afternoon at different times for one-hour instruction. The curriculum emphasized reading, writing, and arithmetic, with two hours a week of religious studies. Each regiment had an army schoolmaster who taught Adult and Grown Children's School, and a civilian schoolmistress who was responsible for the Infant and Industrial School. Infant School was basically a daycare and nursery which freed up mothers to work. When enrollment topped fifty children, permission was granted to hire an assistant; in 1871, eighty-one attended Infant School from the 78th Highland Regiment alone. Students seven or eight years of age and older attended the Adult and Grown Children's school. Girls received training in domestic skills such as sewing, cooking, and scrubbing at the Industrial School during afternoons. If married to a soldier, the schoolmistress qualified for barrack accommodation and related benefits; if single, she received a lodging allowance. Due to the "peculiarity of their position in barracks and the temptations to which they are exposed" the army preferred either married women or "women well advanced in years." The ideal scenario was a husband-and-wife team for schoolmaster and schoolmistress, as this simplified matters when regiments transferred postings and "prevented professional jealousies."

Ninety-seven percent of Royal Engineers in 1857 were educated but only about half of the infantry could read and write, the remaining half either functionally illiterate or barely able to sign their name. In 1849, all recruits were ordered to attend school for two hours daily (even a military prison school was established in 1857, for those with spare time). By the late 1850s, there was open defiance to compulsory attendance and the order was rescinded. One of the reasons for non-compliance might have been the four to eight cents a month deducted from pay for school fees to cover teacher salaries, a practice abolished in 1863. An attempt was made to reintroduce compulsory education in 1884 but this, too, met with failure.

For those who aspired to promotion above lance-corporal, a certain level of education was required by 1850, as written tests were given on drill, duties, and regulations. Additional requirements for sergeant's stripes included ten years of service, a clean record, and recommendation from regimental officers. In the Victorian era, few of the rank-and-file could aspire to commissioned officer status above the rank of quartermaster and lieutenant. Even then, they faced excommunication from the officers' mess, a fate comparable to death in the social context of army life. While the French Army recruited one-third of its officers from the rank-and-file, the British only commissioned between two and fourteen percent from theirs. It mattered little as most men didn't want the associated headaches that came with promotion.

6. Major Ford, 84th Regiment of Foot, 1870. The 84th York and Lancaster Regiment served at Halifax from January-December 1870 and February 1886-October 1888.

Although infantry and cavalry officers lost the benefit of purchasing commissions in 1871, their ranks continued to mirror class distinctions and to be filled by men of privilege, throughout the Victorian era. These officers were generally well educated, having attended the best British schools, including the Royal Military College at Sandhurst and the Staff College (for senior officers) at Camberley. Entrance exams for officer candidates were instituted in 1849 and covered a wide range of topics, including algebra, geometry, Latin, French, spelling, history, and geography; if test results were unfavourable, standards were simply revised downward. Major Ford, pictured here, would have earned seventeen shillings ($2.04) per diem, a king's ransom compared to the shilling a day paid to the rank-and-file but a pittance, really, if one considers that daily mess fees alone could be six shillings. Officers also were responsible for purchasing their own uniforms, which were fitted and sewn by select tailors. This was an expensive outlay, as officer uniforms were made of high quality wool, sometimes doeskin, and several were needed to meet the occasion—dining, dancing, and daily wear. Officers also were expected to buy their own weapons, a sword and pistol being standard fare. Factor in additional pay stoppages (such as monthly or annual library, theatre, and club subscriptions) and it becomes evident why a supplementary income aside from standard army pay (pay described as "more of an honorarium than a salary") was needed to maintain the lifestyle expected of a "gentleman" in Her Majesty's forces. Many officers preferred a posting to India, where they received a better return for their money. The colonies, however, were not all bad. Seven years service qualified one for free passage to Britain, a furlough which could run into months. Another perk afforded the colonial officer was the opportunity to become involved in politics, a privilege not enjoyed by the military in England.

7. INTERIOR OF OFFICERS' QUARTERS, WELLINGTON BARRACKS. VICTORIAN-ERA OFFICERS WERE PERMITTED TO FURNISH THEIR BARRACK ROOMS WITH AMPLE "MEMENTOES AND CREATURE COMFORTS."

Despite the relative comfort depicted here, officers of the Leinster Regiment wintering at Wellington Barracks in the 1890s complained bitterly of broken water pipes, frozen claret from the wine cellar, and inadequate mess arrangements. "In any mess, it is desirable that officers should be able to proceed from their quarters to the mess proper under cover. At Wellington Barracks many of the occupants had first to emerge into the open, walk some twenty yards in front of the building and then enter the mess by the front door. What this meant in a blizzard or the temperature 18 degrees below zero can be imagined." Fastidiousness aside, lodging could be the biggest drain on already taxed finances. Most infantry officers held Halifax barracks in low esteem. Those with the resources rented accommodations in private homes, like their engineer and artillery colleagues. A servant, quite often a private from the regiment, was employed at additional personal expense; as Royal Engineer officers were not permitted to use sappers for servants, they received an allowance as compensation.

The officers' mess was "a haven from campaign and the day's duties [which] provided atmosphere of tradition, companionship and fine dining wherever a regiment was garrisoned." Historian George Mullane wrote extensively about the Halifax military in a regular newspaper column for the *Acadian Recorder* during the early 1900s. In his February 7, 1920 article he presented an entertaining anecdote regarding the rare case of an officer losing his mess privileges.

"The only instance in the Halifax Garrison when an officer was sent to 'Coventry'—that is, excluded from the mess of his regiment, took place in 1803. To fall into disgrace in this manner was as severe a penalty as could be imposed socially upon an officer. The officer who thus suffered at the hands of his mess was Captain Burdett of the 29th Regiment. This officer petitioned the Commander-in-Chief, Lieutenant General

Bowyer for a court of inquiry to take his case into consideration. He stated to the General that he felt himself much aggrieved and injured by the conduct of the officers of his regiment towards him by expelling him from the regimental mess."

9. ROYAL ARTILLERY AND ROYAL ENGINEERS MESS AT ARTILLERY PARK, C.1890. MANY A FENIMORE COOPER TALE WAS UNDOUBTEDLY TOLD AROUND THIS TABLE.

February 7, 1920, *Acadian Recorder* (cont'd):

"The permission of the inquiry was given and a board of officers appointed with Colonel Barnes of the Royal Artillery, as president. The order book does not state the cause of the expulsion from the mess, but from an officer's diary who was on this station in 1803, we learn that a Captain of a sister regiment, while at a grand ball given at the North Barrack in 1803, made disparaging remarks about one of the other regiments then serving in this garrison which was resented by a lady whose husband was surgeon of the regiment thus gratuitously attacked by the officer above mentioned. The lady, a spirited dame, took off her glove before the company and threw it in the face of the offending officer. This so annoyed the Captain, that the next day he sent the lady a very insulting letter which no gentleman should have done. The husband of the lady took the letter to Major White, then in command, who laid it before the Mess Committee with the result that Captain Burdett was excluded from the mess of the 29th Regiment."

10. SOLDIER'S COT AND KIT, CAVALIER CASEMATE, FORT GEORGE, c.1900. FOLDING IRON COTS SUCH AS THIS WERE USED FROM 1820 UNTIL THE EARLY 1900s, AS THEY AFFORDED MORE SPACE.

There were no fancy mess facilities or bunking quarters for the rank-and-file soldier. He slept and ate in cold, damp, poorly lit, unventilated barrack rooms with only three or four feet between cots. At Fort George, twenty-two men shared one casemate prior to1845, after which time numbers dropped to fifteen or sixteen, eventually reaching eleven by the 1870s. Sanitary conditions left much to be desired. Thirty-seven percent of soldiers were hospitalized in the 1860s for health reasons attributed to barrack life. Each morning, men used communal wash tubs that had served as urinals during the night. Little wonder that twenty-five percent of medical problems stemmed from eye infections. By 1900, every barrack room in Halifax was equipped with a stove, which battled indoor winter temperatures that averaged 48°-56° F. Coal was issued between October and April, the daily ration being one bushel per room. By the end of the 1800s, hot water heat was introduced. As for light, in the early years twelve men shared a single candlestick. By the late 1860s, Albertine oil lamps were widely used; these were replaced by kerosene circa 1889, which in turn gave way to gas and, finally, at the end of the nineteenth century, to electricity. Each man was issued an iron cot, two blankets and two sheets, a pillow, a straw mattress or paillasse, an earthenware basin, a set of dishes, and utensils. While blankets were seldom washed, clean sheets were issued monthly and fresh mattress straw quarterly. Above each cot was a shelf for personal items; photos or mementoes could be hung on the whitewashed walls "provided it is done tidily." Meals were taken at small tables, above which hung an iron rack to hold eating utensils and cooking pots. Only two large copper pots were needed—one for meat, the other for vegetables. There were no mess halls for the rank-and-file in the Victorian era (1837-1901), but there were regimental kitchens where food was boiled in mesh bags (to keep group rations separate) then taken back to the barrack room. Each regiment appointed a weekly cook and a daily assistant, who were chosen more for being poor soldiers than for being skilled chefs.

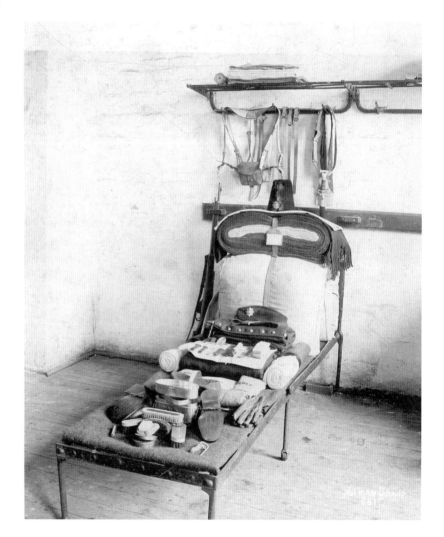

11. ARMY MILK WAGON DELIVERING TO AN UNIDENTIFIED FORT, POSSIBLY AT POINT PLEASANT. THE STATE'S APPROACH TO FOOD RATIONS WAS TO ISSUE THE LEAST POSSIBLE AMOUNT FOR THE CHEAPEST COST WITHOUT INCITING MUTINY.

A soldier's daily diet consisted of one pound of bread, three-quarters of a pound of beef (bone included), potatoes, and tea. For this his pay was deducted seven pence per diem. For many years, he received only two meals a day: breakfast at 7:30 a.m. and dinner at 12:30 p.m. This left a lengthy period of time without food, and eventually he received a third meal at 4:00 p.m. Breakfast consisted of tea and bread, lunch of beef and potatoes, supper of tea and left-over bread from breakfast. Food was always boiled, the meat being derisively nicknamed Harriet Lane in reference to a woman who had been hacked to death by the infamous murderer Henry Wainwright. Two quotes from anonymous sources pretty much sum up army fare: "It takes a great deal of dirt to poison soyers [sic]," and "When a man entered a soldier's life he should have parted with half his stomach." Meals began to improve in 1870 with the establishment of the Army School of Cooking, and in 1873 free rations were introduced.

12. UNIDENTIFIED PRIVATE OF THE 16TH BEDFORDSHIRE REGIMENT, C.1866.

The regimental rank-and-file, whom the Duke of Wellington called "scum of the earth," was filled by out-of-work, uneducated, "lower-class" society. Many recruits came from Ireland, driven to the army by the Irish Potato Famine of 1845-50, which killed more than one million people and cut the island's population in half due to mass emigration. With the rapid growth of the British Empire in the second half of the nineteenth century, the military was overextended trying to meet its commitments. Entrance requirements, based largely upon age and height, had never been overly stringent, especially in times of crisis. Mere boys were taken, as shown by this photo, and height standards varied, changing sixteen times from 1820 to 1859. A recruit in 1861 had to be a minimum 5' 8" tall; by the time of the Boer War in 1900 he was accepted at 5' 3". Upon arrival in North America, an already impoverished soldier had his wage withheld for months to cover the cost of winter clothing, which included mitts, fur cap, and greatcoat; this policy was changed in 1839 with the Winter Clothing Fund. Unlike a commissioned officer, however, he received a free uniform upon enlistment, after which a replacement charge was levied. This uniform was of two kinds: full dress for parades and combat, undress for drills and daily chores. The quality of wool cloth used in uniforms varied from rank-and-file to sergeants and staff sergeants. By 1867, the majority of soldiers' clothing was made by the Royal Army Clothing Factory at Pimlico in London. Uniforms were designed for show, not practicality; their snug fit and tight straps not only impaired movement but adversely affected men's health in much the same way that restrictive corsets felled many Victorian women. Soldiers were provided with a rifle and bayonet. At the time of this photo, the British Army was in the process of converting their then-standard percussion Enfield muzzle loader to the breech-loading Snider-Enfield. Infantry were issued the Long Rifle version, including an eighteen-inch triangular bayonet; rifle regiments and sergeants of infantry regiments received the Short Rifle model with a twenty-three-inch sword bayonet.

13. W. MARSHALL, DRUMMER, 20TH LANCASHIRE FUSILIERS REGIMENT, C.1876-78.

A typical garrison day was one of regimented routine. Reveille sounded at 5:30 a.m from May until September (an hour later, from October to April). One hour was allotted to dress, organize bedding, and wash before marching to the parade ground for thirty minutes of calisthenics and running. Following breakfast, the next two hours were spent in barracks applying spit and polish to boots, buttons, and accoutrements, straightening living spaces, and laying out personal kits for daily inspection. At 10 a.m. it was back to the parade in full marching gear for one hour of battle drill under scrutiny of the regimental sergeant major. Men again returned to barracks and completed remaining chores or, for those so inclined, quaffed a pre-dinner beer in the regimental canteen, which opened at 12 noon. A thirty-minute parade at 2 p.m. officially ended the soldier's day, provided he was not detailed for sentry duty or work parties. Free time until evening Retreat sounded was in all probability spent on Barrack Street or thereabouts searching out cheap gin famous for getting one "drunk for a penny, dead drunk for tuppence [2 cents]." "Beating the Retreat" or "Tattoo" (adapted from Flemish doe den tap toe, meaning "turn off the taps") was a nightly ritual originating in seventeenth century Holland, where drummers walked the streets warning tavern keepers to shut down and soldiers to retire to barracks. A British version was introduced to Halifax. At 9:30 p.m. in summer (8:30 p.m. in winter) the evening cannon was fired from Fort George, signaling the start of tattoo parade. To the regimental beat of drums and the strains of bagpipes and bugles, soldiers returned to their respective barrack grounds, where hymns and God Save The Queen were often sung to the enjoyment of Haligonians, who frequently gathered for the spectacle. After thirty minutes' grace came the tattoo roll-call, with sergeants reading aloud the name of each man in their company. Soldiers failing to reply were reported AWOL to the guard commander, who issued orders to seek out the delinquents. The Last Post was played at 10:00 p.m., followed fifteen minutes later by "lights out."

14. VIEW OF BRUNSWICK STREET FROM FORT GEORGE (ALSO KNOWN AS "BARRACK STREET," "THE HILL," AND "KNOCK-HIM-DOWN STREET"), C.1892.

Less than one month after the founding of Halifax, John Shippey was granted the first license to sell liquor on July 17, 1749. This marked the beginning of a raucous time that lasted nearly two hundred years. In March, 1787, a Halifax judge described the current scene: "The soldiers...lead a life of debauchery...boasting of battles fought, liquor drunk and women ruined; a common litany among uniformed men."

Most taverns were located along Barrack (Brunswick), Albermarle (Market) and Grafton Streets within an area bounded by Buckingham and Sackville Streets. "Here gathered an evil slum of grog sellers, pimps and prostitutes who battened on the desolate soldiery." Barrack Street was by far the most notorious, so named because its south extremity terminated at the South Barracks gate on Sackville Street, its northern course passing at North Barracks on Cogswell Street. Within a matter of only four blocks were brothels and taverns so lewd that Barrack Street was "known through His Majesty's dominions for its evil reputation as the worst haunts of Plymouth or Portsmouth in England."

15. TWO SOLDIERS TAKE A BREAK FROM UNSPECIFIED DUTIES TO QUENCH THEIR THIRST WITH A FEW BEERS, C.1885.

These men may have been relaxing out-of-doors at a regimental canteen more by necessity than choice. "It is not generally known that the whole district bounded by Buckingham, Brunswick [Barrack], Sackville and Argyle Streets have been placed out of bounds," reported the January 14, 1898 *Daily Echo*. "There is a larger number of soldiers than usual in the military hospital at present, which is alleged to be the reason for extending the 'out of bounds limit.' The military authorities will, it is understood, make certain representations to the mayor regarding the houses of the district referred to. A suggestion has been made by a citizen that instead of putting houses or streets out of bounds, the objectionable characters should be put under the ban." No mention was made of whether the soldiers in hospital suffered from bouts of social disease or fist-a-cuffs. Despite the best efforts of temperance societies and clergy, such measures served only as temporary inconveniences for, as one concerned citizen put it, "the dens of iniquity with which this section of our city is infested."

16. SAILORS FROM HMS *RAMBLER* WITH A PROVISION WAGON FULL OF BEER ON WATER STREET. OLANDS AND ALEXANDER KEITH WERE THE PRINCIPAL BREWERS OF BEER FOR THE ARMY AND NAVY.

my oaken towel?') and the soldiers drawing bayonets, and all the queer denizens of those parts diving to cover. Thus, in its earliest days the heart's core of Halifax became sandwiched between two slums, a situation which long remained a reproach and a problem to its citizens."

Barrack Street may have been controlled by the soldiers, but along the harbour front and wharves ran Water Street, and that was the domain of the Royal Navy. More commonly known as "The Beach" (sailor jargon for shore leave), Water Street had its share of dives to rival any on The Hill. One section near the Ordnance Yard was dubbed "Razor Row"— some say because several barbershops there offered close shaves, while others believe razors were the weapon of choice when tempers flared. Historian Thomas Raddall neatly sums up the siutation: "When for a bit of spice the tars went roistering up the hill to Barrack Street, or the redcoats ("lobster-backs") came down to sample the delights of Water Street, there were scuffles and sometimes riots, with the seamen swinging their cudgels (a favourite challenge was 'D'ye want a rub-down with

17. LIEUTENANT H. B. HORSEBURG OF 87TH REGIMENT, c.1875. THE 87TH ROYAL IRISH FUSILIERS SERVED AT HALIFAX FROM 1872 TO 1876.

With a garrison at times of two thousand soldiers and a like number of sailors in port at regular intervals, it is not surprising that stories abound of hijinks committed by men looking to relieve the boredom of daily routine. Newspaper accounts tell of "young officers abroad at night, tearing and misplacing sign boards, breaking windows and engaging in other mischievous pranks." One such act resulted in the following garrison order being issued in 1809: "In consequence of a wanton act committed by a soldier in shooting a horse, the property of John G. Pyke, the Commandant directs that commanding officers of corps will forbid any soldier carrying firearms in the environs of the garrison." Citizens living in the shadow of Fort George complained that soldiers routinely committed "various depredations and acts of irregularity in the enclosures of their grounds" which led to another directive that "any soldier detected in such improper practices in future will be most severely punished." One of the more entertaining accounts involved a Captain Lennox of the 62nd Wiltshire Regiment, who was "in his element when any mad-cap mischief was underway." One evening, the "young blackguard" sought to disrupt a party being held in one of Halifax's most respectable residences. The story has it that Lennox first went to the ordnance yard and secreted away several pounds of gunpowder, which he then placed in a paper bag on the front porch of the house. From there, a powder train was sprinkled across the street and around the corner. Waiting until a lull in the music, Lennox lit the fuse with his cigar, then ran for cover. In the ensuing explosion, "the porch itself was not only shivered to atoms but the whole side of the ball-room was carried away." Fortunately, no one was injured or killed. Such would not have been the fate of Lennox as he was considered the prime suspect and "would have been handled roughly" if captured by the irate homeowner and disgruntled partiers. "As it was he did not appear upon the street for a month afterward; of such material were the wild young sparks."

18. FOUR SOLDIERS IDENTIFIED ONLY AS SERGEANT McMADDEN GROUP.

A love-hate relationship existed between the military and civilian populace for two hundred years. The V-E Day riot of 1945 may be the most widely documented, but there were earlier flare-ups that boiled over into the streets. The first took place in 1838, when a sailor from HM *Dolphin* had money stolen while visiting a house of ill repute on Barrack Street. During an ensuing altercation with the proprietor, the sailor was so "cruelly beaten" with a poker that unsubstantiated rumours about town had him dead. Members of the 93rd Sutherland Highlanders sought retribution, inciting a two-day riot in which several disreputable establishments along Barrack Street were sacked, looted, and wrecked. Military and civic authorities called out piquets to restore law and order, but little was done to quell the disturbance, which caused much ado in the press and fueled already ill feelings among Haligonians toward the raucous interlopers. Nine years later, vigilante justice was again meted out. The May 8, 1847 *Acadian Recorder* reads:

"Yesterday evening a large number of soldiers from the different regiments of the garrison gathered about the house kept by Thomas Morgan at the south corner of Duke and Barrack streets. As it was no secret that the assemblage designed to pull down the house, a notorious one of ill fame, for the purpose of avenging the death of John Wood, a private of the 23rd Fusiliers who disappeared on Monday night last and whose corpse was found in a well on the premises, subsequently many citizens repaired to the scene, in anticipation of enjoying an exciting spectacle.

"Shortly after 7 o'clock, the soldiers commenced the execution of their purpose by breaking the windows, battering the walls, tearing down partitions and casting into the street, along with fragments of boards...The party was employed nearly an hour in battering and wrecking the premises, when the City Marshal, with the Constables, Clerk of the Peace and Deputy Sheriff, appeared, and endeavoured to suppress the tumult, but...being inadequate to cope with the vast numbers of those resisting, they could not enforce order. Some of the Civil force were severely hurt."

19. CREW MEMBERS OF HMS *NORTHAMPTON*. SAILORS AND SOLDIERS WERE TRADITIONAL COMBATANTS ABOUT THE STREETS AND TAVERNS OF HALIFAX, BUT ON RARE OCCASIONS THEY JOINED FORCES.

May 8, 1847 *Acadian Recorder* (cont'd):

"At this period of the commotion a fire was kindled in a pile of the broken boards and rubbish, that was thrown out upon the street, and the flames caught the eves and front beam of the house. As other property was endangered by this crisis, the alarm bells were rung and the [fire]engines promptly put in operation; the original cause of excitement was generally disregarded, until the fire was subdued, and by that time, the soldiers were appeased; they had resumed their customary tone of discipline and retired to the barracks as orderly as though they had never perpetuated the slightest act of misconduct or insubordination….It is quite possible that the suspicions of the soldiers concerning the death of Wood are entirely wrong….There were no marks nor any other appearances of violence on the body….The City authorities, upon inquiry, find that no facts were elicited on the inquest, to give rise to the rumours rife in the city connected with the death of private Wood, 23rd Fusiliers."

A third altercation occurred in 1863 during festive events held to celebrate the Prince of Wales' marriage. The "Greasy Pole Riot" (as it came to be known) began when several citizens tried to prevent a soldier from climbing a forty-five-foot-high greased pole to reach prize money at the top. Relations between the military and townspeople had been at a low ebb for some time, and this set off a three-night orgy of violence with soldiers and sailors running amuck through Barrack Street, tearing apart the Blue Bell Tavern, then laying siege to the city courthouse, where throngs of civilians fended them off. Order was eventually restored, with a number of soldiers imprisoned. A military inquiry determined "for months soldiers frequenting the drinking and other low houses about the neighbourhood of the Citadel have been subject to insult and ill treatment when found alone or in small parties at the hands of Civilians and 'rowdies.' Nor has this been confined to soldiers among whom disturbances sometimes occur but respectable NC officers and Officers passing along who have been pelted with stones and some seriously beaten."

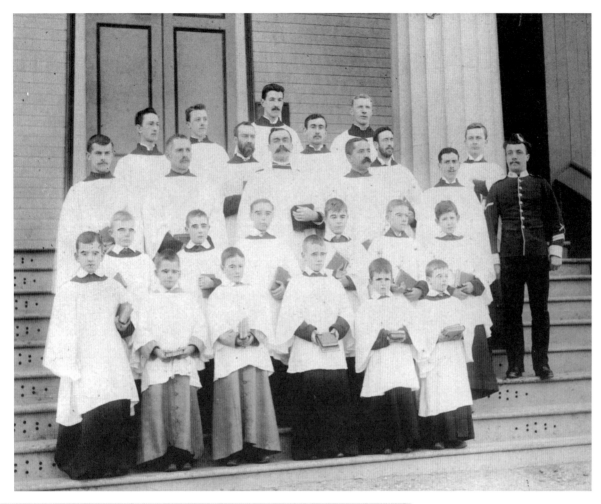

men with drinks until eleven on Saturday night, and on Sunday at noon would be distributing sacramental elements in the church. Church choirs had weekly meeting for practice, when two glasses of punch were provided for each one present. A steward was elected quarterly, usually one who was fond of punch and liked it strong. It was well sweetened, and the beverage, thus disguised, produced a lively effect on the youngsters, who, we may say, were not seasoned. On one occasion these helpers in the church service sallied forth, after practice, into the brightness of a full moon, at a late hour, in very merry mood. One in flowing cloth cloak not unlike a clergyman's gown, headed them in procession. Four others carried a tenor fiddle-case, with handkerchiefs, as children were then borne to burial, and the remainder walked two and two in slow march, all singing as they went:

Poor Johnny's dead, I heard his knell
Bim, bim, bim, bone bell;
The bell doth toll, O may his soul
In Heaven forever dwell.

20. GARRISON CHAPEL CHOIR, C.1890.

In a somewhat lighter vein, it was not only the streets of Halifax that flowed with liquor. Several churches were widely known as "drinking dens." A Halifax resident reminiscing in 1895 recounted how "venerable and religious men obtained a livelihood by vending strong drinks and one, an elder in a church...was engaged serving roaring man-o-war's

After marching a quarter of a mile they met the rector returning home from an evening party, who stood amazed at this exhibition so solemn and yet so ludicrous on the part of his co-workers in the church services, and shortly after took measures to have such lively demonstrations discontinued."

Chapter 7

Rest and Relaxation

The only enemy that soldiers and sailors faced at Halifax was boredom and to help combat it, a wide range of activities were organized. Skating, snowshoeing, curling, hockey, sleigh rides, horse races, polo, cricket, football, baseball, boxing, quoits, and harbour regattas were some of the sports partaken of by the Imperial forces on station. J. McGregor wrote in 1828, "Amusements of Halifax are such as are usual in the other towns in the North American provinces; assemblies, picnics, amateur theatricals, riding, shooting, and fishing form the principal sources of amusement." Another account described how "the whole winter is devoted to a series of pleasures and amusements which we could not partake of with half the zest in England or in Scotland." *The Dominion Illustrated* circa 1878 claimed "the presence of military and naval men gives impetus to all manly sports." Profits from one regimental canteen circa 1880 were used for a variety of sport-related expenses, such as purchasing athletic equipment and awards for regimental competitions, maintaining the cricket field and skittle alley, donating a spotter's telescope for the gun club, and sponsoring a sergeants' mess athletic club.

There were many ways for men to spend their leisure time aside from manly sports. Royal Artillery and Royal Engineer officers promoted interest in physics, zoology, and botany, organizing with civilians to present lectures at the Mechanics Institute and other venues. Seeds were made available for those interested in gardening. George Ramsay, Lieutenant-Governor of Nova Scotia, wrote in 1816, "there is not a Bookseller's shop in Halifax, nor is there an individual possessed of anything that can be called a Library." His Excellency espoused "the great comfort and advantages that might result from the establishment of a Garrison Library" and—wishing to emulate the library at Gibraltar—

allotted £1,000 from the Castine Fund. The Officers' Garrison Library officially opened in 1818, occupying three different sites before finding a permanent home in 1886 at Royal Artillery Park. Halifax's first library, it was described in 1895 as "undoubtedly the most comfortable of all for the readers in Halifax." Another source of entertainment were in-barrack Soldiers' Clubs or Institutes that had their beginnings with temperance movements. Adequate space to accommodate twenty percent of barrack occupants was set aside for a regimental library and librarian's quarters, reading room, recreation room with non-alcoholic refreshment bar, and a small lecture or concert auditorium; an additional two rooms were reserved for a smoker and playing games such as backgammon and chess. These soldier drop-in centres, which cost a monthly subscription of two cents for those wishing to belong, were left open one hour past tattoo to encourage attendance. Lieutenant Frederick Harris Vieth, of the 63rd West Suffolk Regiment wrote: "Dancing and dinner parties, besides invitations to rides, drives, and canoeing jaunts put us under many obligations to our kind entertainers, which later we endeavoured to make some return for in the shape of a series of private theatricals." From 1850 to 1880 there were three thousand performances given in Halifax by forty-one touring groups and fifty amateur groups, mostly from the regiments.

Despite the harshness of Canadian winters, the majority of Imperial troops looked favourably upon a Halifax posting to that in tropical disease-ridden climes. Of course there were always some not enamoured with a two-year stay. "All the officers abuse it [Halifax] & wish to go home," wrote Crofton Thomas Vandeleur in a July 29, 1830 letter. "It is all humbug about the gaiety of the place." In an 1842 comment, Captain

M. M. Hammond concurred: "I still continue to think this the stupidest place in all the world; the people are not the least civil to us, and do not seem to shew [sic] any desire to become acquainted with us; but what can't be cured must be endured. The shooting is now nearly over, and there is no amusement of any sort." These two gentlemen might have been more content with their lot in life if offered the alternative of transfering to the West Indies command where eighty thousand soldiers died of yellow fever from 1794 to 1796, one regiment losing fifteen hundred men.

1. TUG OF WAR TEAM, 98TH COMPANY, ROYAL ARTILLERY, 1904.

Popular among the army and naval ranks were track and field days on the Garrison Grounds or water sports such as swimming and tub races at the dockyard. A case in point occurred on July 8, 1856, when the 76th Regiment hosted a day of games and sports near their temporary summer quarters at Point Pleasant. Newspapers reported, "The affair was under the management of the sergeants of the regiment. There was capital running, leaping of a high order, besides other features of athletic recreation, a great feast for the boys and the climbing of a greasy pole, on the top of which was most temptingly hanging, a pair of boots and a sum of $3. The crowd were also treated to an after-piece— a spirited but unsuccessful chase of a shaved porker, well greased, for the interesting occasion. The band of the 76th was in attendance. The sports took place all around the Prince of Wales Tower. The bivouac at the Point furnished one of the most picturesque scenes imaginable."

2. GARDEN PARTY AT ADMIRALTY HOUSE.

Historian George Mullane writes that Halifax society was "almost exclusively composed of the navy and the military, and few from outside the Admiralty House and the Artillery Park were favoured to a participation with our country's defenders in the pastimes which belong peculiarly to a life in a garrison town....Members of families not, by any means, numerous...entertained the naval and military gentlemen in a style not unlike that which prevailed among the higher classes in England, but there was no familiarity with the masses...."An established "social cleavage" also separated the officers' world from that of the rank-and-file. While working-class rank-and-file chased greased pigs at Point Pleasant or women on Barrack Street, gentry-borne captains and lieutenants spent much of their leisure time pursuing advancement by hobnobbing with visiting generals, admirals, heads of state, and future kings at what local media accounts would lead one to believe were a continuous array of grandiose levees, parties, teas, balls, and banquets.

Norman Studio

3. BRITISH WARSHIP DECORATED FOR "BONNET DANCE," LATE 1800s.

Lieutenant Frederick Harris Vieth described many typical social events in his 1907 memoirs: "Once a week at three o'clock in the afternoon a 'bonnet dance' on board the Flag-Ship 'Boscawen' in the harbor was given, which was always charming. An awning spread completely over the ship sheltered everyone from the sun, while on all sides beneath it the cool breeze off the water had free access, making the dances on deck vastly more agreeable than those in a heated ballroom could possibly be. The popularity of these 'bonnet hops' as they were familiarly called, was unbounded." William Dyott's diary makes reference to a much earlier event staged by Prince William Henry (later King William IV) during one of his sojourns to Halifax aboard a man-of-war in the 1780s. "In the evening his Royal Highness gave a ball on board his ship....The quarter-deck was divided at the mizzen-mast; between it and the main-mast was for dancing, and abaft it for supper, the whole covered in a frame and canvas, and lined with white colours and blue festoons....The whole was by far the most elegant thing I ever saw."

4. CAPTAIN FRANCIS DASHWOOD, 87TH REGIMENT, PERFORMS IN A HALIFAX GARRISON THEATRE PRODUCTION, C.1872.

In his paper "Halifax And The Garrison Theatrical Tradition," Patrick O'Neil writes that officers and enlisted men of the garrison and Royal Navy during the eighteenth and nineteenth centuries "helped lay the foundation of amateur theatrical activity [and] made a substantial contribution to our theatre history." Garrison theatre was popular because it wiled away leisure time, raised money for "humane and charitable purposes" such as poor relief, improved sometimes strained relations between the military and civilian populace, nurtured Old World culture in the colonies, and boosted morale—which subsequently reduced the high rate of desertion prevalent among troops in British North America. There were three categories of garrison theatre—private, public, and subscription. Private performances focused upon after-dinner skits and plays, held in homes of the middle and upper class, with hosts and their civilian and military guests sometimes dressing in elaborate costumes, complete with scenic back-drops. It was fashionable in Britain for wealthy patrons of the performing arts to incorporate a theatre into their homes for such occasions; the first at Halifax was added to Government House in 1836 where, on December 7 a performance "with the aid of Officers of the Garrison, afforded the company the most rational amusement." Private plays were also staged by unmarried officers and men in barracks or the mess. These "regimental evenings at home"—or "Smokers"—helped lessen boredom among the rank-and-file. Similar in-house entertainments were presented on board Royal Navy warships and troop transports. Several public venues in Halifax hosted garrison theatrical productions, in addition to those presented by touring professional acting companies. The Grand Theatre opened on Argyle Street in 1789, Fairbanks Wharf Theatre in 1813, the Garrison Amateur Theatre in 1815-16, the Red Store in 1821, Theatre Royal on Queen Street in 1846, Temperance Hall in 1849, Dockyard Loft Theatre in 1860, and the Academy of Music in 1877.

A third category of theatre, and the most common involving garrison productions, was the subscription theatrical. Admission was strictly regulated, with only "proper people" (military and naval officers and gentry) allowed to purchase a subscription to a series of plays. *The Royal Nova Scotia Gazette* went so far as to advertise a theatre production for January 13, 1795, emphasizing "no children in laps to be admitted" by order of Prince Edward, Commander of His Majesty's forces at Halifax. The August 5, 1848 *Acadian Recorder* made the following announcement:

"The Directors of the Garrison Amateur Theatre have the honor to announce that a Performance will be given on Friday next, the 11th August—being the first night of the Subscription. None but Subscribers will be admitted to any part of the House, except the Pit, for which tickets will be issued at the Bookstores of Messrs. Graham, McKenzie and Fuller. No money will be taken at the Doors. The Subscription list will be closed on the 12th August. The price of admission to a series of six performances, to be given monthly are: Single Ticket: $5.00; Family Ticket to admit two: $8.00; Family Ticket to admit four: $10.00."

Funded and organized by the military, subscription theatre could drain the already taxed financial resources of officers, as it was expected of each man to make a donation dependent upon rank to defray the start-up costs of production. This, however, was the price one paid to partake in the "ambitious displays which drove society." Not until the 1870s were theatres darkened during performances, the emphasis placed as much on being seen and conducting after-hours business as on the on-stage entertainment. The tradition of garrison theatre was continued into the early 1900s, when a troupe of Canadian World War One veterans known as the Dumbells toured communities.

The Officers' Garrison Library, when established in 1818, contained "books of character and value," shipped from England, and "others of light reading and trifling value" purchased in New York. By the 1860s, the library housed thirty thousand volumes with the emphasis on history, travel, military memoirs, and classical French and Italian works. Thousands of these books originated with the valuable Corfu collection, transferred to Halifax when the British evacuated the Island of Corfu in 1864; there had been a garrison library at Messina in 1810 before moving it to Corfu in 1814. Membership in Halifax was open to all officers of the garrison and navy with a subscription of three days pay per year deducted for operating costs; women, mostly officers' wives, were welcome, as were prominent citizens, as honorary members. Strict rules were enforced—failing to sign out a book, for example, carried a fine of twenty shillings. By the 1890s, membership had opened up, with fees set at fifty cents a month. Renamed in 1902 for the Duke of Cambridge, the garrison library served as a focal point of Halifax social life, hosting dances, teas, musicals, and meetings.

7. SKATING PARTY AT ROYAL ARTILLERY PARK RINK, 1890s

The 1st Battalion Royal Irish Fusiliers transferred from Malta to Halifax in June 1872, remaining four years before shipping out to Bermuda. The soldiers benefitted immensely from their stay, learning to skate, toboggan, and snowshoe—"diversions that had not been possible at Malta." The Red Cap Snowshoe Club was organized in 1875 and lasted one hundred years, its all-male membership wearing wool coats and red toques similar to those of Hudson Bay men. Throngs of military personnel and civilians made it a winter ritual to cross the harbour by ferry to skate and play hockey on Lakes Banook, MicMac, Maynard, and Oathill in Dartmouth. Equipment was abundant, with the Dartmouth firm of Starr Manufacturing Company mass-producing their renowned Forbes Acme skate in the 1860s. Newspapers recounted spirited games of hockey, played between officers of the Garrison and Fleet, using sticks carved locally by native Mi'kmaq. The Art Gallery Of Nova Scotia recently acquired a sketch drawn by Lieutenant Henry Buckton Laurence in 1867 showing games of hockey and curling played near Halifax, possibly on Dartmouth's Lake Banook. The lithograph is being touted as proof—in the on-going debate of hockey's origin—that the game started in the Halifax area. Curling also was a favourite winter sport in Halifax by the mid 1800s. It was first introduced in 1824 by Sir Houston Stewart, a captain in the Royal Navy.

The December 7, 1935 *Acadian Recorder* described sleigh rides as a "spectacular custom" that originated—in this area—in the early nineteenth century with the British garrison at Halifax.

"The winter season of 1826-27 in Halifax was remarkable for gaiety. In that year the sleighing of Halifax assumed a new character; in short, "The Sleigh Club" was established. Originating with the naval and military officers, the Acadian Union Club [a later version in the 1850s was the Tandem Club] included all civilians who chose to become members, and there were few who kept aloof. The judges and other great functionaries of the law, the official dignitaries of all degrees, the wealthiest merchants and of course the whole of the garrison, composed a striking assemblage. The laws of the club were simple and easily observed. A president and a vice-president were elected every week whose duties were the first to lead and the latter to bring up the rear of the cortege. Another duty no less pleasing devolved upon the former. On the days of meeting at the general place of rendezvous in front of the Province House, after driving in procession through the town, the club drew up at the president's house or, if that was inconvenient, at a noted pastry cook's where the president stood the treat of ginger nuts and cherry brandy for the whole party. This was the luncheon de rigeur provided on the occasion but if the roads were sufficiently firm this luncheon was dispensed with and the party started for Nine Mile House at the extremity of the [Bedford] Basin."

9. MEMBERS OF 101ST REGIMENT AT WILSON'S INN, ONE OF SEVERAL WATERING HOLES WITHIN COMMUTING DISTANCE OF HALIFAX FOR WINTER SLEIGH PARTIES.

December 7, 1935 *Acadian Recorder* (cont'd):

"It was a sight to warm the frozen and to enliven the dull. First led the way with four bright bays, the kind, hospitable, joyous Colonel Ferguson in the sleigh which he had named the Aurora Borealis conveyance. Each sleigh bore some appropriate designation and the Colonel's, though light and swift was the most capacious in the garrison. Perhaps it seemed to hold more than it really did, as all were welcome to a seat and it was always filled. Seated on a high box the Colonel drove. Beside him sat some young officers whom he had indulged for the day. Beneath was the body of the carriage open to the sky with an enormous bear skin for an apron and wrapped in shawls and sables, the beauties of Halifax were seen dispensing smiles and happiness to all within their view. In the rumble behind were places for two more—one whose delight was to blow the bugle....Then followed a troop of charioteers in tandem, curricle unicorn and single harness—the Reindeer, the Artie Ranger, Esquimaux, Chebucto, Metor [sic], Walrus and the Mic-Mac [sic]. Some 20 or 30 sleighs formed the general cavalcade while a four-in-hand, the Avalanche brought up in the rear of the procession.

"All was mirth and frolic and glee. The single bugle blew and they were off at 12 miles an hour on their track through the snow, with no sound to indicate their flight but the quick harmony of sleigh-bells. On the party sped and soon drew near the haven of their wishes where a famous luncheon was ready, for the inn was noted for good things—hot turkeys, smoking cariboo steaks, reindeer tongue, pickled herrings from Digby, bear hams from Annapolis, cherry brandy, noyau [sic] and Prince Edward Island whisky. Here was enough to satisfy all tastes and appetites. Returning, the order of driving reversed. Homeward the party scurried, discussing enroute the approaching amateur play, the last government ball or some other topic of local interest. Arriving at Dutch Town [north-end Halifax], the sleighs drew off to their separate destinations."

10. EQUITATION WAS ONE OF THE MOST POPULAR SPORTING EVENTS AMONG THE BRITISH GARRISON. PICTURED HERE IS A LIEUTENANT CRICHTON DRESSED IN RIDING FINERY AT ARTILLERY PARK, 1890.

Historian Thomas Raddall credits Governor Lord William Campbell and his "handsome" wife (circa 1764) with setting "a new pace in the gay naval and military society of Halifax" which included the establishment of a race track on the North Common. Thoroughbred horses were imported from Ireland, New York, and Baltimore, "and the spring and autumn race meets at Halifax [known as the Garrison Races] became famous in the colonies." There was one event that stood above all the rest, according to Raddall, a race against time on horseback from Halifax to Windsor. "It was a famous wager and a famous ride and a whole generation of Haligonians talked about the daredevil horseman and his two mounts…." While Raddall makes only passing mention of the event, the July 24, 1915 *Acadian Recorder* carried a detailed account:

"On the morning of the 30th October, 1834, there was unusual commotion on what is now known as Cogswell Street. Just outside the gate posts of the walk leading to the old military hospital—once the town residence of the Duke of Kent—a number of young officers with several soldier grooms, were busy about a horse. In the group of officers was a dashing lad of eighteen of aristocratic mien and features—Lord Robert Vincent Jocelyn, a 2nd Lieutenant in the 1st battalion of the rifle brigade….A notice dated at Halifax 23rd of October 1834 announced that Jocelyn had undertaken a match against time for 75 guineas and before Thursday, October 30th, 1834 would ride from Halifax to Windsor and back in seven hours on two horses and it was further arranged (a byc bct) that he should walk eight miles—both feats to be accomplished in ten hours….The conditions were unfavourable for the challenger had to obtain his horses for the purpose and ride them without preliminary training and moreover, for nearly three days previous to the match, rain had fallen continuously and the Windsor road at best was a hard road to travel. His lordship rode 14 stone, and was quite heavily built. The horses he chose for his purposes were Naughty Tommy and Snap."

11. HALIFAX ARTILLERY OFFICER IN FULL DRESS, 1890.

July 24, 1915 *Acadian Recorder* (cont'd):
"On the morning of October 30th, a fine autumn day, the last allowed him, Jocelyn easily accomplished seven miles on foot in an hour and thirty-two minutes; then having mounted Naughty Tommy, at the word "off" given at quarter to nine o'clock in the forenoon, he started from the north corner of the pavilion barracks at the gate post at the entrance of the road leading to the military hospital. He proceeded along the road across the Common to the old Windsor road, and at last turned in at Mrs. Pence's inn—about 25 miles from Halifax—at the end of an hour and thirty-seven minutes. It was here that he arranged to change horses and where Snap had been previously sent to await him. Jocelyn remained three minutes while he washed his mouth with a little brandy and water, and throwing himself on Snap, who was to do the most arduous part of the undertaking, he set out at a slapping pace for Windsor. Lieut. Fitzherbert, one of the umpires, with relays of horses, accompanied him to Mrs. Wilcox's inn, which was the turning point at Windsor. Here, Fitzherbert was relieved by a Mr. Mellish, doubtless of the Rifles, with fresh horses. Jocelyn knew well the stuff that Snap was made of, and the noble animal accomplished his portion of the work (40 miles) in three hours and three minutes. When once more at Pence's his lordship found that Naughty Tommy was not ready, and so he was obliged to wait six minutes, during which he himself took a stimulant somewhat stiffer than the last. When his horse was ready he went on to Halifax. Between the old Rockingham and Halifax (5 1/2 miles) it is said he had an hour and five minutes to spare, but towards the end, the whip and spurs were freely used. His lordship came in by the Kempt road, and when seen on what is now Cunard Street, near the corner of that street and Kempt Road, he was on foot leading his horse. The winning post was reached at nineteen minutes to four in the afternoon. The riding part of the match was thus won by four minutes and the whole feat was accomplished in nine hours. Snap, it was felt, deserved far more praise for his hardiness than Naughty Tommy."

12. FIVES COURT, 1873.

A "Fives" or racquet ball court was located at the intersection of Cogswell and Gottingen Streets on the present site of the Centennial Swimming Pool. Few details exist other than it measured 63 feet by 31 feet, stood 30 feet high at the front, 15 feet at the back, and was demolished in 1883. Just east of the Fives Court (where the Halifax Police Department is today) stood a large complex consisting of a wooden gymnasium and leisure centre—the Soldiers' or Garrison Institute—which originally served as government offices when built by Prince Edward in 1798. Described as "ramshackle" by 1902, the buildings were torn down to accommodate a wagon yard. A new 120 foot by 55 foot brick military gymnasium was erected in their place where the Fives Court once stood. Eight hundred spectators—including military officials, parliamentarians, and civic leaders—attended opening night festivities on February 28, 1902, which highlighted a full card of boxing matches among the garrison. Unlike the normally boisterous pugilistic audience, those in attendance were noticeably subdued, under orders not to speak during bouts despite "many exciting incidents as were liable to cause an outburst."

13. Naval dory off the Royal Engineers Wharf, 1890s.

In the days before steam, dories similar to the one featured here ferried naval personnel about the harbour, as well as troops and stores from the Queen's Wharf to various forts. From these practical beginnings, spirited regattas came to be staged between the navy and army. The Royal Engineers and Royal Artillery both purchased whaler boats from Amos Stevens of Tancook Island, Nova Scotia in 1893-94 for three hundred dollars each. The inaugural harbour regatta was held in the summer of 1826 to celebrate the visit of Lord Dalhousie; appropriately, an Admiral Lake, who "steered the craft himself," won first prize for sail boats. Such matches became an almost annual event, with a four-mile circular course laid out from the dockyard to George's Island. A number of rowing and sailing clubs developed from this, the most noted being the Royal Nova Scotia Yacht Squadron, North America's oldest yacht club. Founded in 1837, the RNSYS was presented with the Prince of Wales Cup, the club's "most treasured trophy," when avid yachtsman Edward, Prince of Wales and future King of England, visited Halifax in 1860.

14. CANADIAN MILITIA SHOOTING TEAM IN ENGLAND, 1889.

Marksmanship was a focal point of regular army and militia training. From this came the sport of competitive target shooting, which had its formal beginnings in 1859 with the organization of the National Rifle Association of Great Britain. The first NRA matches were staged in 1860 at Wimbledon; Queen Victoria fired the first shot, reportedly scoring a bull's eye. Nova Scotia organized a Colonial Rifle Association in 1861, the first in the British Commonwealth. The inaugural competition was held that year at Windsor, Nova Scotia, with 106 participants. The first-place silver medal was awarded to Private R. C. Kinnear from the militia Chebucto Greys of Halifax. In 1866, the Nova Scotia Rifle Association meet was staged at Bedford, with four hundred shooters in attendance. Lieutenant-Colonel Lyons of the 6th King's Militia won the three-hundred-yard individual shooting event, while the "Mayflowers" from Dartmouth took home the Silver Bugle as overall team champion. Following Confederation in 1867, colonial associations became provincial associations; a year later, the Dominion of Canada Rifle Association formed, with teams of local marksmen participating at international meets.

15. MILITARY CAMP AT BEDFORD RIFLE RANGE, C.1876.

Many trophies of note have been contested during the Nova Scotia Rifle Association's storied 140-year history—the Kennedy Gold Medal dating to 1863, the Laurie Bugle (1883), the Stairs–Borden Trophy (1899), and the Irving Trophy (1904). Bedford Rifle Range was a popular site not only for sport shooting but also for military encampments and training. In 1834, it served a far different purpose. Cholera swept through Halifax in August of that year, claiming twenty-nine fatalities from the Rifle Brigade within three weeks. With many families fleeing the city for the sanctuary of cleaner, country environs, military authorities removed much of the garrison to Bedford, five miles distant. There were only two deaths in the regiment after this, "showing the extent to which the propagation of the scourge was owing to atmospheric influences."

By October 2, officials had deemed it safe to return to town, the disease having run its course, leaving 103 dead.

16. STUDIO PORTRAIT OF UNIDENTIFIED MILITARY SPORTSMEN, c.1885.

Halifax was a sportsman's paradise for the British officers of the garrison and fleet, described in the words of Arthur Silver as "one of the few colonial towns which combine most of the amenities of civilized life with the great charm of being within easy reach of cock cover, snipe marsh, salmon stream or the primeval forest haunts of the moose, caribou and black bear." Hundreds of streams, rivers, and lakes close to Halifax afforded fish for the taking, and "one can always count on a basket being fairly filled by anyone ordinarily skilled in the gentle art." The same was true of snipe and woodcock hunting, with as many as four hundred of each being shot by one man in a season. Moose and caribou were the principal big game animal of the time but generally drew the sportsmen farther afield in quest of a trophy rack of antlers. With ample leisure time, British officers pursued their quarry into the woods and bogs of Hammonds Plains, Stewiacke, Sheet Harbour, Tangier, and Ship Harbour, or onto the barrens of Parrsboro and Amherst.

Some British officers left highly entertaining and informative written accounts of their sporting adventures while garrisoned at Halifax— Campbell Hardy, William Chearnley, Francis Duncan, M. M. Hammond, and Frederick Harris Veith. Captain William Chearnley, 8th Regiment of Foot (later, Lieutenant-Colonel of Halifax Volunteer Battalion, 1865) was an ardent proponent of early game management; in 1853 he was instrumental in organizing Canada's first conservation society, the second oldest in North America. As president of the Game and Inland Fishery Protection Society of Nova Scotia, Chearnley led concerted efforts to protect spawning salmon from nets, dams, and the sawdust siltation that blocked many rivers, and to enact laws to address the dramatic decline in moose numbers, attributed to over-hunting and the use of dogs and snares by settlers. Having limited impact, initially, outside the immediate Halifax area, their pioneering efforts were the seeds that eventually grew into game acts and government regulatory enforcement agencies.

17. ONE OF THE EARLIEST IMAGES OF NOVA SCOTIA MI'KMAQ. THE PHOTO CAPTION READS "NORTH AMERICAN INDIANS, REPRESENTING A SMALL REMNANT STILL LIVING IN NOVA SCOTIA," c.1856.

A century removed from their ancestors' bloody wars with Britain, some of these men possibly guided officers of the Halifax garrison on sporting adventures into the backwoods of Nova Scotia. The services of seasoned Indian guides were in great demand in the mid-to-late 1800s. "The powers of wood-craft in all its branches," writes Campbell Hardy in 1855, "appear in the Indian, to amount to an instinct not belonging to and never capable of being attained by the white man." British officers hired several Mi'kmaq on a regular basis, men considered "capital hands in the woods"—Ned Nolan, Joe Pennall from Chester, Joe Philips from Lunenburg, Pauls from Ship Harbour, Tom Philips and Christopher Paul from Ponhook Lakes, Francis Paul and his son Joe from Musquodoboit, two guides known only as Tom and Louis, and one called

Barbei from Cumberland County, Ol' Bonus and Noel Bonus from the Cobequid Hills, and Glodes from Annapolis. John Williams, a favourite of Campbell Hardy, was presented with a hunting knife by Prince Arthur in September 1869. One of the best was Joe Cope, whom Hardy described as "a merry old fellow withal, having at his command an unlimited number of sporting anecdotes wherewith to enliven the camp in the long evenings." With a certain irony, Joe and his son Jim, a famous guide in his own right, quite possibly were descendants of the feared Mi'kmaw Chief Cope from Shubenacadie, a sworn enemy of the British during the battles for Acadie, who mysteriously disappeared in 1758 and, according to legend, was secretly buried in Halifax's Point Pleasant after being killed in a fight; some claim his ghost haunts the popular park to this day.

18. A RARE IMAGE OF MAJOR-GENERAL CAMPBELL HARDY (IN CIVILIAN CLOTHES) POSING WITH INVALID SOLDIERS FROM THE BOER WAR, MOSTLY CANADIANS, AT MISS LUCY R. HARDY'S (DAUGHTER) CONVALESCENT HOME, DOVER, ENGLAND, c.1901-02.

Captain Campbell Hardy of the Royal Artillery served in Halifax from February 1852 until August 1867, during which time he held the post of Inspector of Warlike Stores and Firemaster in charge of ammunition and powder. In 1866-67, he was also the inspecting field officer for the provincial militia artillery. Hardy was the most noted sportsman of the British officers to have garrisoned Halifax and wrote extensively of his hunting and fishing excursions in the Maritimes. His two-volume *Sporting Adventures in the New World*, published in 1855, is considered the bible of nineteenth century outdoor accounts. Hardy was also an accomplished artist and observant naturalist, publishing *Forest Life in Acadie* in 1869, which is still referenced for early Nova Scotia flora and fauna. A prolific writer, Hardy published six scholarly papers, one being The Beaver in Nova Scotia, for which he built a scale model beaver house in 1863 as an illustration that was displayed at the Paris Industrial Exhibition of 1867. Campbell Hardy retired on full pension in May 1880 with the honorary rank of major-general and moved to Dover, England where he passed away on April 11, 1919.

CHAPTER 8

CRIME AND PUNISHMENT

"Discipline is at the heart of any military body," writes historian Carol Whitfield. "Its presence ensures a well-ordered existence; its absence results in chaos....Each man who accepted the king's shilling submitted himself to military law, a set of rules and regulations which applied only to the military and which defined the limits of its existence." The Articles of War and Mutiny Act were the basis of military law, and while the British navy and army conformed closely in punishments meted out, each service had its unique way of dealing with specific offences.

The navy was governed in the beginning by laws of the sea, which can be traced to the Ordonances [sic] or Usages of the Sea instituted in the thirteenth century by Richard I, known as Richard the Lion-Hearted. These were incorporated in the fifteenth century into the Black Book of the Admiralty, which adhered in part to the ancient rule of "an eye for an eye":

Whoever shall commit murder aboard ship shall be tied to the corpse and thrown into the sea.

If a murder be commited [sic] on land the murderer shall be tied to the corpse and buried alive.

If any man be convicted of drawing a knife for the purpose of stabbing another, or shall have stabbed another so that blood shall flow, he shall lose a hand.

For every crime, the navy had a corresponding punishment, a couple of which bear repeating:

If a robber be convicted of theft, boiling pitch shall be poured over his head and a shower of feathers be shaken over to mark him, and he shall be cast ashore at the first land at which the Fleet shall touch.

Sleeping on watch was considered a serious breach of rules as it endangered the entire ship and crew and a repeat offender faced a rather gruesome fate: slung below the vessel's bowsprit in a covered basket, the man was provided a loaf of bread, a mug of beer, and a knife. He was given the choice of either slowly starving to death or cutting free of the bowsprit to be drowned in his basket cell. From these humble beginnings came the Articles of War in 1661, designed "for the good of all, and to prevent unrest and confusion." A noteworthy punishment for repeated offences of various nature was to bore the tongue with a red hot iron. Excessive swearing resulted in gagging and scraping of the tongue, somewhat surprising considering the stereotypical image one has of blasphemous sailors. Should the ship's cook spoil a meal, he was "cobbed and firked," fancy names for a beating administered with barrel staves or socks filled with sand. "Keel hauling"—while not intended as a death sentence—was nearly always fatal. With hands and legs bound and tied to long ropes manned by the crew, the convicted sailor was pulled underwater from one side of the ship to the other in such a manner that his stomach, chest, and face were dragged across razor sharp barnacles encrusting the keel. If drowning didn't kill, then horrific injuries and trauma finished the job; keel-hauling was abolished in 1720. A new set of laws, *The King's Rules and Admiralty Instructions*, was instituted in 1731. Like its predecessor, this code was long on corporal punishment and short on rehabilitation.

Soldiers, too, were subject to a Mutiny Act and Articles of War. In 1837, there were seventy military crimes listed for which a man could be charged. Fines and prison sentences were imposed for neglecting divine worship. Disobeying an order, being drunk on duty, and spreading false rumours "detrimental to morale" were punished with flogging and prison time; mutiny, desertion, and striking an officer were some of the crimes punishable by death or transportation. The severity of punishment often depended upon whether it was committed in a time of war or peace. Further provisions allowed for double punishments, such as loss of pay and flogging for falsifying records, for habitual drunkenness, and for crimes of self-mutilation to avoid duty or to achieve discharge.

For offences of a lesser nature, commanding officers had certain "discretionary powers" to impose punishments such as barrack confinement (two months maximum in 1836; changed to one in 1857), one week cell time, loss of pay, or hard labour. Punishment drills were also popular. Defaulters drill consisted of two hours of intense parade-ground marching in full gear under the scrutiny of a sergeant. Shot drill was a "useless and monotonous" punishment that compelled a man to move a stack of 24-pound cannon balls individually from one end of the parade ground to the other, pile the balls, then carry them back and re-stack them. "Riding the wooden horse" could be a painful experience. The soldier was stripped naked and forced to sit astride a sharpened wooden rail or plank for hours on end, sometimes with heavy ankle weights attached to increase his discomfort level. A man sentenced to hard labour usually was sent to the military prison, where five hundred tons of granite were kept on hand for stone-breaking exercises to supply the Royal Engineers with crushed rock.

Serious offences warranted the convening of a court-martial before a bench of officers. While the rank-and-file soldier could expect nothing short of the full measure of military law, an officer tried by a tribunal of his peers, regardless of the charge, invariably benefitted from preferential treatment, receiving when necessary the most lenient of punishments. Thomas Raddall tells of a lieutenant found guilty of "rape on a child under the age of ten years" whose sentence was to walk to and fro on the Grand Parade for one hour on a frigid winter day, with a paper pinned to his chest announcing the crime. Conversely, when a citizen by the name of Lathum, a baker, shot and killed a Lieutenant Collins of the Royal Navy while defending his property from a band of drunken sailors, he was expeditiously tried and hanged.

Carol Whitfield writes that just because a man joined His Majesty's forces he "did not necessarily free himself from the rights and constraints of civil law. If he was accused of a crime against a civilian, the military authorities were required to hand him over to the civilian courts." At Halifax, this rarely resulted in prosecution. In 1787, charges against three soldiers accused of slitting a peddler's throat were dropped at the insistence of the governor, who felt it "an exhibition of bad manners" to hang them during the royal visit of Prince William Henry. In the 1791 trial of a sergeant in the 20th Regiment accused of beating a child to death with the hilt of his sword in a fit of rage, the defence argued that the man had ten years' service in His Majesty's forces and "it is far more difficult to get a hardened veteran to take the King's shilling than to get the mother again with child." A British sailor in 1797 fared no worse for murdering the wife of a tavern keeper; he was acquitted on the grounds that "we can't unman His Majesty's Navy." In 1825, Captain Richard Cross of the 81st Regiment was charged with murdering Edward Shey, a former schoolmaster. Based upon questionable testimony from two fellow officers, Cross was not only acquitted but sent upon his way with these words of atonement from the trial judge: "Your reputation is not ruined....You return to an honourable profession an unspotted man and free from suspicion." Another Halifax magistrate saw it differently, lamenting in a letter, "The sound of cannon and a bloody bayonette [sic] have given some military men to seeing life with a cold eye. How easily they justify murder on the grounds that one life is more valuable than another."

Military discipline, by comparison, could be swift and harsh when meted out to its own. Execution and flogging were the extreme of punishments with solitary confinement, branding, and transportation thrown in for good measure. Governor Edward Cornwallis took little time after founding Halifax to instill law and order among the troops with "ruthless shootings and hangings." Execution, of course, was the harshest of punishments but was rarely used except during times of war. In August 1800, eleven soldiers were convicted for acts of mutiny and desertion. Three were hanged while eight were reprieved at the foot of the scaffold. Prior to 1800, army executions were carried out by hanging, the body afterward "Hung in Chains to Detere [sic] others from so great a crime." After 1800, prisoners sentenced to death were shot. The following account of execution on May 7, 1804 appeared in the January 10, 1920 *Acadian Recorder*. Garrison Orders 5th May, 1804:

"Order No. 1—The 7th being the day appointed for the execution of Allan McCluskey, private of the 29th Regiment under sentence of death for desertion, the whole garrison will be under arms at daybreak in the North Barrack Square, dressed as for guard but without powder, and each regiment will have their colors.

"Order No. 2—A guard, consisting of one subaltern, one sergeant, one corporal and twenty-four privates will receive the prisoner from the acting provost marshal and conduct him to the place of execution.

"Order No. 3—The officer commanding the 29th Regiment will fix upon one sergeant, one corporal, and twelve privates as an execution party and its reserve which is to be under the direction of the adjutant of the corps.

"Order No. 4—The acting deputy provost marshal is to attend the prisoner to the place of execution, and he will take care that he is shaved tomorrow evening and that he is clean and properly dressed.

"The troops marched to the exercising ground (North Commons) and formed three sides of a square. The doomed soldier stood with his back to Camp Hill with his coffin beside him—a rough board box. The execution party stood about twenty paces away. The order of General Boyer directed that he be allowed full and ample time so by prayer and repentance he may make his peace with his Maker. The chaplain of the garrison who had attended the man while under sentence, prayed for a while with the doomed man and then retired out of range of the shots. The order to fire was given and the man fell dead, pierced with several bullets. Colonel Barnes gave orders to re-form in marching order. The bands struck a lively march to brighten the depressed spirits of the men and the dead soldier was left with the burial party, and silence fell once more upon the scene."

The Royal Navy had its own way of meting out capital punishment. The condemned was hoisted aloft, usually from the yardarm, to die a slow, agonizing death by strangulation. The body would then be coated in tar to ward off scavenging gulls and hung in chains from gibbets at Black Rock on Point Pleasant or on McNab's Island at the end of the spit of land known as Hangman's or Dead Man's Beach, near Sherbrooke Tower. The corpses would be left to swing until their bones bleached white, a grim warning to all those entering port that His Majesty's laws would be enforced. Naval recruits were hard to come by, so in the event of several sailors being found guilty of a capital offense (which was not uncommon), dice were rolled to determine the unfortunate soul among them who would be strung from the yardarm while his mates, though equally at fault, were spared.

Execution may have been the military's harshest punishment but flogging was by far the cruelest, "administered with more ceremony than the distribution of medals." A punishment parade was usually called for early morning, all ranks mustered to form a square facing inwards to a wooden triangle or crossed halberds. The condemned man was marched into the centre, where charges and sentence were read aloud. He then was stripped to the waist and tied spreadeagle to the frame. A red cloth cap placed upon his head and a buff collar about the neck protected "sensitive parts" from the cat-o'-nine-tails, a lash consisting of nine cords attached to a handle, each cord knotted in three places. With luck, friends of the accused may have secreted him a stiff drink to help numb the excruciating pain to follow. One astonished (and no doubt grateful) prisoner was offered liquor from the barrel of a guard's musket.

Two drummers, mere boys not yet eligible to enlist but qualified apparently to carry out sentence, stood to the side of the triangle and alternated in applying twenty-five "of their best." Should they falter at any point, the weight of a drum major's cane was brought to bear squarely upon their shoulders. Stripped to the waist to better strike "with force and vigour" the lads were bespattered with blood long before completing their gruesome task. A sentence of 1,500 lashes was not uncommon, with several hundred being standard. For example, guards returning drunk to Melville Island Military Prison, having stopped into a favourite watering-hole after escorting prisoners the two miles into town, were welcomed back with five hundred lashes. This seems excessive by any standard, as a man "bled freely" from one hundred lashes; it took only fifty to turn one's back to "jelly," with some men swelling grotesquely and turning "black as mahogany" because the knotted cords were too thick to break skin. Prisoners who fainted under the lash were revived with water.

Upon completion of sentence, the man, if capable, was marched off under guard to hospital for medical treatment, which consisted of cloths soaked in diluted sugar of lead applied to the wounds for upwards of one month, a cure as painful as the cause. The regimental surgeon monitored proceedings closely throughout and should he determine death was imminent at any point, the man was cut down immediately from the frame and taken to hospital until healed sufficiently to complete the punishment; a continuance of sentence was prohibited after 1837. Little wonder that more than one soldier at Halifax committed suicide rather than face such a fate. Not all, however, approached a flogging with trepidation. Frederick Harris Vieth of Halifax recounted the following tale:

"A story was told to me of two bad characters of the 8th King's Regiment who were flogged over and over again for crimes committed, until the number of lashes each had received ran into the thousands; but instead of reforming them the punishment seemed only to make them more depraved, in fact they became incorrigible. At last there was nothing for it but to get rid of them, and both were 'drummed out' of the regiment as being of no use in His Majesty's service. It was said that these two worthies met one day at a tavern and each was bragging about the number of times he had been flogged or as he termed it 'had his back scratched.' One boasted of having received four thousand lashes, while the other could only manage to claim three thousand, six hundred and fifty. But said he, *'av I'd known a flatfoot like you wor ahead o'me I'd have downed the Colonel, and led ye by a hundred and fifty.'*

"On one occasion a soldier took his fifty lashes 'without a murmur' and when sentence had been carried out he pulled down his shirt, adjusted his stock, buttoned up his tunic and saluting the Colonel who stood by, said 'That's a warm breakfast you gave me, your honor this morning,' and again saluting, faced about and was marched away to hospital."

When flogging its sailors, the Royal Navy showed more creativity than the army. "According to the customs of the service," the prisoner was seated in leg irons on the upper deck of his ship, provided rope and given twenty-four hours in which to craft his own cat-o'-nine-tails. When completed, the boatswain cut out all but the best nine strands. Should the accused fail to meet the imposed deadline, the number of lashes were increased proportionally. Sentence was generally carried out at the head of the gangway. Unlike the army, which balked at having rank-and-file troops apply the "cat" to one of their own (opting instead for mere boys), the navy possessed no such qualms. A boatswain's mate had the honour of delivering the lash, twelve at a time before spelling off to a companion. Some captains preferred right- and left-handed boatswain's mates, if possible, so they could alternate, which tended to

better "mangle" the flesh with criss-crossing cuts. Another approach was to flog a man through the fleet; W. M. Brown recalled one such incident in *Recollections Of Old Halifax*: "There were seven ships, and he received a portion of his punishment in each ship. I stood on a wharf and saw the hammock in which he lay hoisted and lowered at each ship, and my heart sickened at the thought of his sufferings. Three days after he died in hospital...." Flogging through the fleet was a special day in Halifax, with throngs of citizens, mostly denizens of the slums and grog shops, taking to the water in rowboats to cheer or jeer proceedings, while drummers from the men-of-war in port beat a slow dirge. An alternative method was to first flog a man at the gangway in the accepted manner with a dozen lashes, then have him run a gauntlet between two rows of sailors armed with short lengths of cord. Just for good measure, until 1811, boatswain's mates hid small whips of knotted ropes inside their hats and carried bamboo canes with which to inflict immediate punishment, should the need or opportunity present itself.

Society's abhorrence of the brutality of flogging led to its gradual demise in the nineteenth century. By 1855, the Army Mutiny Act permitted a maximum fifty lashes for any offense. The Naval Discipline Act of 1866 limited the number to forty-eight, although incarceration was already being substituted for corporal punishment as early as 1847. Flogging was abolished during peacetime in 1868, and on campaign by 1881, but not in military prisons until 1907. However, there were only thirty-two cases of flogging, totaling 1,050 lashes, at the Halifax prison after 1848, the last administered in 1884.

One source claims that sixty to eighty men may have been put to death at Halifax from 1794 to 1809 for crimes of mutiny, desertion, and violence. The navy carried out its last execution in 1860 during the Second Chinese War. The army introduced "transportation" in place of execution in the early nineteenth century. Convicted soldiers were transported to "hardship commands" in unhealthy garrisons (such as the West Indies and East Africa) for "general service," meaning they served until death. Interestingly, twenty-six deserters were transported in 1802 from England to the "back settlements of Canada." Transportation for general service was abolished in 1818, except for the Royal African Corps, where it lasted until 1826. Convicts were still transported but only for periods of between seven and fourteen years to garrisons such as Bermuda, where they lived aboard prison hulks in harbour at night and worked in convict gangs by day. New South Wales was another popular banishment spot, where felons worked with civilians to build public utilities such as roads. Later on, "ticket of leave" was introduced, which involved sending felons to Bermuda to be "reformed," then on to Australia to live supposedly productive lives; conditional pardons or tickets of leave would be granted, thereby restoring all rights of a British subject with the exception of the right to leave Australia; of course, any criminal activity and it was back to jail. Tickets of leave were eventually changed to fourteen years banishment rather than life. The practice of transporting disappeared circa 1868. Branding was a punishment often used in conjunction with transporting, whereby the soldier was first tattooed under the left armpit (using a saddler's needle and gunpowder) with a one-half inch letter D for deserter or BC for bad character; branding was abolished in 1871. Drumming-out punished "incorrigible bad conduct" but was rarely used alone because it encouraged misbehavior to secure discharge; instead, drumming-out was frequently awarded in conjunction with flogging. The soldier, after healing from the lash, was stripped of all uniform badges, buttons, shoulder straps, and facings, then led with a rope around his neck through the regimental line while a band played the "Rogue's March." A boot to the backside helped him out the barracks gate, effectively ending his military career. In 1863, a newspaper happily reported that in addition to drumming out, two privates were deported back to England for an eight-year prison term.

The effect of military discipline was heatedly debated for nearly a hundred years. Some argued that corporal punishment was necessary to ensure that the proportion of blackguards remained obedient, while reformers maintained it served only to debase the victim and the Imperial forces in general. By the late 1800s, discipline focused more on fines and imprisonment, and to some extent prevention and reform, rather than the harsher penalties of earlier times.

Each barracks had a guardhouse providing quarters for the guard of the day, which changed on a twenty-four-hour rotation. Accoutrements were sparse—one water bucket, axe, lantern, and candlestick. Comfort, too, was lacking, as relief men slept in pairs, fully dressed, on wooden platforms without bedding. There was a separate room for the "officer of the day" in charge and an "orderly officer" whose duties were to keep an accurate log book, to pay regular visits to the barracks, and to inspect the guard. A guardhouse had cells where soldiers arrested for drunkenness, curfew violation, fighting, desertion, etc. were detained pending discipline from the commanding officer. Some forts, such as Fort George and Fort Charlotte, designated casemates for defaulters' lockup. Guard cells (sometimes called garrison or barrack cells) were used for soldiers sentenced to periods of incarceration and as temporary holding areas for those awaiting execution, transportation, branding, drumming-out, and flogging. Guardhouses were heated by a stove or fireplace, but cells remained cold. Prisoners were not allowed bedding at any time of year until after 1826, when it was provided for the winter months only.

3. MELVILLE ISLAND MILITARY PRISON, SHOWING STONE BRIDGE CONNECTING IT TO THE MAINLAND, 1929.

The Mutiny Act of 1844 introduced military prisons to the British Army. Thereafter, a sentence of seven to twenty-eight days was served in a guard cell, with longer periods of confinement, up to two years, spent in a District Military Prison. The first military prison in Halifax was at Fort George. Two rooms in the Cavalier building were initially allocated but proved unsatisfactory, which resulted in two casemates being converted into six cells. By 1850, overcrowding had become a problem, with 158 men serving time. Fort George was a poor choice from the outset as it was difficult to isolate prisoners and escapes were common. By 1856, it became apparent that a new facility was needed, and permission was granted by the Admiralty to use Melville Island, a then-unoccupied naval prison on the Northwest Arm. Prior to 1884, only those sentenced to imprisonment by court-martial were sent to Melville Island, but after that date all sentences, regardless of length, were served there.

For many years, naval prisoners were incarcerated aboard floating hulks in the harbour. In 1803-04, the Royal Navy purchased a four-acre island on the Northwest Arm from James Kavanaugh for a naval prison, naming it for Henry Dundas, the Viscount Melville, First Lord of the Admiralty. In 1808, a large wooden prisoner barracks and warden's house were erected, replacing two small buildings that had belonged to Kavanaugh. By 1829, there were ten buildings on site; after the army assumed possession, a stone detention barracks was built in 1884, with additional structures added during World War One. Melville Island Prison served many purposes. More than 1,500 French and Spanish sailors from the Napoleonic Wars were interned there, as were eight thousand Americans during the War of 1812. Eight hundred Black refugees awaiting relocation took up temporary residence in 1814; in 1847, Irish immigrants infected with typhus were quarantined on the island. In the Crimean War, Melville Island billeted the British Foreign Legion, in World War One, it housed German POWs, and in World War Two it served as a general troop barracks and ammunition depot.

5. INTERIOR OF CHAPEL, MELVILLE ISLAND PRISON, 1929.

For many years, prisoners were permitted to attend Sunday church service at the Garrison Chapel on Cogswell Street. The Secretary of War disagreed, however, with their leaving prison property and, as the garrison chaplain was paid £73 annually to perform various penal duties, a directive was issued in 1849 that a separate Sunday service be held at the prison. When the District Military Prison was moved in 1856 from Fort George to Melville Island, chaplains visited every two or three days to hold service and communion, to read prayers, and to minister to individual prisoners. While turn-outs were small, numbering no more than twelve, one prisoner who took advantage of clergy visits was Gunner George Avis of the Royal Artillery. On March 18, 1883, Avis was punished for excessive talking, which was contrary to prison regulations; two months later he was again disciplined for the same infraction. Aware that "there is sanctuary in conversing with a clergyman," Avis requested regular audiences with the chaplain for the remainder of his Melville Island stay, thus satisfying his penchant for free speech while circumventing prison regulations.

An army prison, Melville Island was governed and policed by the military. Soldiers garrisoned at Fort George traditionally provided the Island's guard detail, which consisted of one sergeant, one corporal, and nineteen privates. The chief warden, two assistant wardens, and cook were civilians, generally retired soldiers appointed from the "Out Pension." Wardens were still under orders to salute officers and wore a uniform of sorts—a blue frock coat, trousers, and forage cap purchased from personal monies, with a greatcoat provided free of charge every two years. The cook did not wear a uniform but was allotted twenty shillings annually with which to buy a frock and apron; should one of the wardens resign or be dismissed, the cook was promoted to his position. Despite being required to function on a "semi-military footing," wardens were not armed. In one instance, the chief warden was provided with a sword but no belt, while the assistant wardens were given a belt with no sword and a bullet pouch without a firearm. For protection, wardens petitioned the War Office in London for wooden staves. Their concerns were apparently justified; in 1866, an irate Private Thomas Mahoney attacked the warden with a stone-breaking hammer for which he was sentenced to an extra 168 days.

7. INTERIOR OF OLD DETENTION BARRACKS, 1929. IN ITS DAY, MELVILLE ISLAND COULD ACCOMMODATE UPWARDS OF 1,500 PRISONERS, WITH MEN SLEEPING IN TIERS OF HAMMOCKS. A 1935 FIRE DESTROYED MANY BUILDINGS.

toes (or Indian meal substitute) with a pint of milk. By 1863, prisoners were allowed a meat dinner twice a week after completing twenty-eight days of their sentence. Conversely, anyone breaching prison rules could lose his meat diet for twenty-eight days.

Table fare in the nineteenth century military prison was generally bland. In 1859, the Commissariat posted this call for tenders to provide prison supplies:

"The following quantities and descriptions will probably be required, more or less....6 tons of oatmeal; 6 1/2 tons of Indian meal; 60 lbs. of Onions; 2 lbs. round pepper; 2,000 imperial gallons milk; 10 bushels of stove salt. The foregoing supplies to be all of the best quality, to be subject to the approval of the Chief Warden or Provost Serjeant [sic] in charge...and to be deliverable, on their Requestion, and at the Contractors expense, at the Military Prison, or Garrison Cells, in such quantities and at such times, as may be required...."

Prisoners were fed twice daily. Breakfast was twelve ounces of oatmeal or bread and half a pint of milk; supper was five pounds of pota-

8. SOLITARY CELLS, MELVILLE ISLAND PRISON, 1929.

A sentence of solitary confinement by court martial resulted in a reduction of daily rations by two ounces of oatmeal at breakfast and a pound of potatoes for supper. Solitary confinement for breach of prison rules carried a harsher penalty—one pound of bread a day with water ad libitum; this bread and water diet could not last for more than seventy-two hours. Solitary confinement gradually replaced flogging as a punishment but was condemned by reformists because it "sours a man's disposition." The inmate with the most violent of sour dispositions was reported to be Private Jeremiah Sullivan of the 62nd Regiment who, because of repeated infractions, received the first lashes for a prison offence on August 6, 1856. Sullivan immediately returned to his deviant ways, first punching in the warden's face, then threatening to brain the assistant warden. For this he was sentenced to another fifty lashes and 168 days hard labour. While awaiting punishment, Sullivan ransacked his cell, which cost him eight shillings (96 cents) from future pay to cover damages. Still unrepentant, Sullivan tried unsuccessfully to burn down the prison and was subsequently thrown into isolation for twenty-eight days. Only four days into this latest foray, he was shackled for undisclosed offences. How long his incorrigible behaviour was tolerated and what ultimately became of him remains a mystery, but he would have more than qualified for branding, transportation, or drumming out. When Canadian military authorities assumed control of the prison in 1905, there were reportedly still three prisoners remaining from the Imperial era. Although discipline had long since become more humane in 1909, the term "prison" was changed to "detention barracks," and "prisoners" became "soldiers in detention" to lessen the social stigma. On December 18, 1908, a Private Morton from the Royal Canadian Regiment was incarcerated at Melville. When released on May 28, 1909, he had the distinction of being "the last of the long list of prisoners to serve within the Military Prison at Halifax."

9. Photo of Melville Island Prison c.1890, showing forested knoll on mainland (right in distance) known as Deadman's Island, which served as a prison burial ground.

Within a stone's throw of Melville Island is a two-acre peninsula known as Deadman's Island, which served as a burial ground for prisoners of war and refugees in the early 1800s. Prison conditions during the War of 1812 were deplorable, with constant death from infected wounds, tuberculosis, pneumonia, typhus, and smallpox. The dead were wrapped in canvas, rowed to the point at night, and buried in shallow graves, only to have their bones exposed years later by erosion. Approximately 66 French and 9 Spanish prisoners from the Napoleonic Wars, 195 Americans from the 1812 War, 104 Black refugee victims of smallpox, and 37 Irish immigrants who succumbed to typhus are interred on Deadman's Island. Lost in the pages of time, their ghosts returned in recent years to haunt a proposed condominium development for the site, the mere mention of which raised the ire of many government and historical agencies at home and in the United States. As a result, Deadman's Island was purchased by the Halifax Regional Municipality to preserve its sanctity and the U.S. Department of Veterans' Affairs plans to erect a granite and bronze memorial.

CHAPTER 9

CHANGING OF THE GUARD

Britain completed its military withdrawal from Canada in 1905-06, a slow process that began in 1855 during the Crimean War, then accelerated in 1871 with the recall of remaining Imperial forces (except those needed for the naval dockyards at Halifax and Esquimalt). By the early 1900s, Britain's dominance of the high seas was being challenged by emerging world navies such as those of the United States and Germany. Despite keeping a wary eye south of the border, any realistic threat of war with the Americans had long since past, with Germany more worrisome to the British, who made a strategic decision to concentrate naval forces closer to home. A "virtual abandonment of the Western Hemisphere" began in 1904 with removal of the Pacific Fleet and North America and West Indies Squadron as well as closure of the two dockyards. Still requiring a safe Northwestern Atlantic port for coal and supplies, Britain negotiated the right of its warships to access Halifax. Intendant upon keeping the 1,700-man garrison in place to mount harbour defences, they requested that Canada shoulder some of the expense. A new 1904 Canadian Militia Act took control of the country's one thousand regular troops and thirty thousand part-time militia away from British army officers and placed it in the hands of civil authorities. Armed with this latest legislation, Prime Minister Sir Wilfred Laurier demanded a complete Canadian takeover of the Halifax garrison in lieu of a cost-sharing arrangement. Britain readily agreed, being only too happy to be rid of the added financial burden. The October 16, 1905 *Daily Echo* reflected on this change: "It is with a great deal of sentimental regret that we see the last of the last Imperial regiment. Although we feel that is better and more healthful for this young country that they should go, yet it means the severing of old ties and the passing of a picturesque element from our midst, which is always reason for regret."

The British force in Halifax at this time of change-over consisted of the 5th Royal Garrison Regiment, Royal Garrison Artillery, Royal Engineers, Army Service Corps, Royal Army Medical Corps, and Army Ordnance Department. Local newspapers announced that soldiers wishing to take their discharge and remain behind with Canadian forces could do so.

"A Militia order has been issued providing that officers, warrant officers, non-commissioned officers and men volunteering for transfer to the Canadian Permanent Force will, if their services are accepted, be released from their regular army engagements and will be required to relinquish all claim upon the Imperial Government for pay or pension earned by previous service. On the other hand, the Government of Canada are prepared to guarantee to all whose services are accepted, that their personal interests will be carefully safe-guarded, that their previous service in the regular army will be allowed to reckon towards increase of pay and pension under the Canadian regulations. That those who, under British Army regulations, were permitted to re-engage or extend their service, will be allowed to do the same in the Canadian Permanent Force, and that they will not be required to accept any lower rank, rate of pay, allowances or other emolument than they are in receipt of from the British Army funds at the time of transfer. Accepted applicants will be entitled to all the advantages allowed by the Militia regulations of Canada. The Minister of Militia reserves himself the right to accept the services of only such applicants as he may consider advisable."

One hundred and fifty-five men took the offer—seventy-seven from the Royal Garrison Artillery, sixty-three Royal Engineers, and fifteen from miscellaneous corps. Plans were to send one thousand Canadian soldiers from Toronto, Kingston, and Quebec in early December 1905 to form the new Halifax garrison, with seven hundred being infantry, two hundred artillery, and the remainder split between engineers, ordnance corps, medical corps, and clerical staff.

In November 1905, the Royal Garrison Regiment and Royal Garrison Artillery—along with 123 women and 318 children—left Halifax for Liverpool, England aboard the liner *Canada*. Fort George changed hands in 1905-06, and a formal transfer of the entire "Imperial Fortress of Halifax" to the Canadian Department of Militia and Defence was completed on January 16, 1906. Historian Harry Piers describes how, for several years prior to this shift, Imperial authorities spent large sums erecting new buildings and revamping defensive works, so when the time for departure arrived "the fortress had been put into a first-class condition and the entire establishment thoroughly renovated for a new tenant." There is an age-old saying that engineers are the first in and last out. True to form, the Royal Engineers left in March 1906, closing 157 years of Imperial military presence and influence. Behind them came the Royal Canadian Regiment, the Royal Canadian Garrison Artillery, and the Royal Canadian Engineers.

Manning the ramparts was not a concern for Canadian authorities as the country, and Halifax especially, had a long and storied history of militia service. They hoped in 1904 to create a permanent, five-thousand-man regular force army that could provide instruction to enthusiastic but largely untrained militia units. In the end, the force numbered only about 2,800, with half assigned to garrison Halifax. As a safe haven for the Royal Navy and a major shipping port, Halifax became "the Canadian Army's premier peacetime defence commitment." During World War One, 3,300 soldiers were stationed in the city, with most being older, married men with families or those ineligible for overseas duty because of a disability. In addition, some 1,700 others of the Canadian Expeditionary Force were either assigned to depot units or were recruits awaiting shipment overseas, who could be called upon if needed; this force of five thousand men comprised ten percent of Halifax's population at the time.

Being a maritime nation with hundreds of miles of coastline to defend, Canada had long depended upon the Royal Navy for protection. With its departure, Canada had two options—either pay large sums to the Admiralty to help build more British ships, or organize a Canadian Navy. The first option, being unpopular with the electorate, was deemed to be politically inexpedient. In 1907, the Halifax dockyard—including all associated buildings, wharves, and twenty-four acres of land—was officially transferred to the Canadian government (followed by Esquimalt in 1910). After much political wrangling and time delays, the Royal Canadian Navy (RCN) was founded on May 4, 1910 with the passing of the Naval Service Act, which provided, in theory at least, for a regular navy, naval reserve, volunteer force, and Royal Naval College.

One historian claims the birth of Canada's navy was surrounded by "almost farcical circumstances." The fleet consisted of two worn-out British cruisers—*Niobe*, assigned to Halifax, and the *Rainbow*, to Esquimalt. The Royal Naval College of Canada took over the old Dockyard Hospital and in November 1910 accepted its first class of twenty-one recruits into a three-year program (two years instruction and one year practicum). The controversial and fledgling Royal Canadian Navy ran aground almost immediately with the defeat of Laurier's ruling Liberals in the 1911 election and the subsequent funding cuts for proposed ship building programs, implemented by Robert Borden's victorious Conservatives. In 1912-13, the RCN recruited only 126 new bodies and lost 146 through desertion. At the outbreak of war in 1914, the extent of Canada's naval might (which reverted to British Admiralty control) included 350 men and the two cast-off cruisers. By 1915, *Niobe* was tied up to the dock as a depot ship, never to go to sea again. Canada doubled the size of her navy in 1917 by acquiring two submarines built originally for the Chilean government, then purchased by British Columbia's premier Sir Richard McBride to protect the west coast from possible German raiders. After a voyage of eight thousand miles to reach Halifax, the burned-out, obsolete vessels joined *Niobe* at dockside, where they remained out of action undergoing refit. None of this was of any grave concern as Britain was content to have Canada's wartime contribution focus on its army and shipyards while leaving maritime matters to the Royal Navy. Canada persevered, however, and by 1918 had "cobbled" together 9,600 naval personnel and 116 small craft comprised of armed fisheries patrol vessels, yachts, tugs, and a few borrowed American submarine-chasers to sweep the Halifax Harbour approaches for enemy mines and to provide coastal convoy duty against German long-range submarines operating off Nova Scotia.

The Royal Navy held Germany's High Seas Fleet in check but was overmatched when confronted with the submarine. There had not been a major world sea battle since the War of 1812 but this newest weapon made up for lost time. By 1917, German technology had produced a submarine capable of operating off the North American coast for up to three months. With the airplane proving efficient over the battlefields of Flanders, the British Admiralty pushed Canada to provide anti-submarine air patrols in support of convoys along the south coasts of Nova Scotia and Newfoundland. There was only one problem—Canada had no air force and would not until 1920. Canadians, however, took eagerly to flight in the pioneer days of aviation. In 1909, at Camp Petawawa, Ontario, two former members of the 2nd Field Company Canadian Engineers—J. A. D. McCurdy and F. W. Baldwin—"piloted the first military demonstration of aircraft flight in Canada." In World War One, nineteen thousand Canadians served in the Royal Naval Air Service and Royal Flying Corps (forerunner of the Royal Air Force), with Canada also providing training facilities for pilots, navigators, and air gunners on home soil in much the same way she would twenty-five years later for another World War.

In March 1918, a co-operative plan determined that the United States would increase the range of its coastal air patrols northward, providing airfields were established at Halifax and North Sydney. The Americans were to supply pilots, seaplanes, and kite-balloons until the hastily organized Royal Canadian Naval Air Service could assume responsibility. On August 15, 1918, Lieutenant-Commander Richard Evelyn Byrd, of later polar exploration fame, arrived in Nova Scotia to assume command of the United States Naval Air Station Halifax at Baker's Point in Eastern Passage. By August 25, four HS-2L flying boats were operational, and the first maritime patrol in Canadian aviation history was flown. Halifax and North Sydney were provided with four seaplanes, none of which were involved in any submarine interceptions before the war ended in November. Following the armistice, the Americans went home, leaving behind their planes and equipment for the Royal Canadian Naval Air Service personnel who had been training

in England and the United States. In typical post-war fashion, the RCNAS was disbanded within a month. Baker's Point lay idle until 1920, when the Canadian Air Force was officially organized and Canadian Air Board Station Dartmouth (Baker's Point) became one of six national stations. On October 7, 1920, the first Trans-Canada flight originated from Dartmouth; relays of planes and crews covered the 3,341 miles to Vancouver in 49 hours, 7 minutes flying time (spread over 10 days), with an average speed of 68 miles per hour. In 1924, the Canadian Air Force became the Royal Canadian Air Force, and Bakers Point, Canada's most easterly command centre, was renamed RCAF Station Dartmouth.

2. END OF AN ERA: MEMBERS OF THE ROYAL ARMY SERVICE CORPS POSE AT GATE TO QUEEN'S WHARF, A SHORT TIME BEFORE LEAVING, IN 1905.

The Royal Army Service Corps was one of the last army units to leave Halifax, departing in December 1905. Four of the men pictured here took their discharge and joined the Canadian Permanent Forces, the only one identified being E. H. Spearing (left, back row), who went on to become a Lieutenant-Colonel. The Royal Army Service Corps was responsible for all water transport and provision of services and supplies to the Halifax fortifications. In 1904-05, water transport duty was taken over by the Royal Canadian Army Service Corps, which was organized on November 1, 1901 as a branch of the Active Militia. Some men served upwards of forty-two years in water transport; crews wore civilian clothing until 1918, when navy blue uniforms were introduced (later replaced by army battle-dress). From only two small steamers—

SS *Alfreda* and SS *Armstrong*—water transport expanded to 14 vessels and 125 officers and men during World War Two. Ferry and freight service, target towing, and salvage were just some of the myriad jobs carried out. Due to post-war cuts, the water transport branch of the Canadian Army Service Corps was disbanded in March 1948.

2. END OF AN ERA: MEMBERS OF THE ROYAL ARMY SERVICE CORPS POSE AT GATE TO QUEEN'S WHARF, A SHORT TIME BEFORE LEAVING, IN 1905.

3. COAST ARTILLERY DEFENCE, POSSIBLY SANDWICH BATTERY, c.1942.

for British naval operations in the North Atlantic and a safe entrepot for the merchant shipping whose passage to Britain the Royal Navy protected." World War One harbour defences depended upon Imperial-era works, such as Fort Ogilvie and Cambridge Battery at Point Pleasant; Forts McNab, Ives and Hugonin on McNab's Island; Fort Charlotte at George's Island; and Sandwich Battery in Herring Cove. Armament varied from 6-inch and 9-inch breech-loading guns to 12-pounders and 4.7-inch quick-fire batteries. York Redoubt served as a barracks for troops awaiting shipment overseas and for infantry assigned to guard batteries on the west side of the harbour. The only new Canadian-built fortification was Connaught Battery, located between York Redoubt and Purcell's Cove, which was started circa 1912 but not completed until 1917.

4. COAST ARTILLERY DEFENCE, HALIFAX, 1941.

Canadian War Museum historian Roger Sarty writes that "Canada's most important contribution to the naval defence of the British Empire during the First World War was the fortified port of Halifax. Once again, as in the great wars of the last half of the eighteenth century and the early nineteenth century, the fortress became a secure principal base

5. ONE OF SEVERAL MOBILE BATTERIES THAT GUARDED HALIFAX IN WORLD WAR TWO, 1941.

Harbour defences moved farther out during World War Two, with four new batteries erected beyond the submarine net that stretched from York Redoubt to Sherbrooke Tower. Fort Ogilvie, Sandwich Battery, and Fort McNab were used again, with York Redoubt re-activated as the main fire-control post for the entire fortress system. York Shore Battery was built on the beach below York Redoubt and equipped with two 6-pounder duplex guns; a 4.7-inch battery guarded the submarine net. The most seaward battery was Fort Chebucto in Duncan Cove, operational from 1943 to 1945; nearby was the Outer RDF Radar Station and Lower Harbour Naval Signal Station. Strawberry Hill Battery, another new work between Fort McNab and Sherbrooke Tower, guarded the submarine net from McNab's Island. The last new gun emplacement was Devil's Point Battery (b.1941) at Hartlen Point in Eastern Passage, also home to an Observation Post and RDF radar station. Devil's Point was heavily armed with three 9.2-inch guns and a 40-mm anti-aircraft battery; there were at least three other anti-aircraft batteries using 3.7-inch guns strategically placed about Halifax.

5. ONE OF SEVERAL MOBILE BATTERIES THAT GUARDED HALIFAX IN WORLD WAR TWO, 1941.

The appearance and role of Fort George had changed dramatically by the time of this photo. Following the Canadian takeover, three new structures were erected on the east ramparts—a large drill shed in 1908 (left), a signal station circa 1916-20 (centre), and the small Time Ball House in 1908 (right); the building with peaked roof visible above ramparts is the Brick Block. The "time ball," a copper sphere two feet in diameter, was raised daily (except-ing Sunday), then dropped electronically at exactly 1 p.m. to provide accurate standard time for setting ships' chronometers. During World War One, Fort George served as barracks, general stores, and ammunition depot; it also housed German POWs from 1914 to 1916, when they were transferred to an Amherst internment camp. Little changed for World War Two. Again used for barracks and storage, the signal station was converted into an NCO's mess and the drill shed into a gymnasium. The closest Fort George came to active service was as a training centre for coastal and anti-aircraft artillery.

6. East slope of Citadel Hill, c.1929. The British War Office intended to demolish the Garrison Clock prior to withdrawing, but were persuaded against this "on account of its historical interest as well as its utility."

7. LINER *SS OLYMPIC* LEAVES HALIFAX FROM PIER 2 ON OCTOBER 12, 1916, WITH NOVA SCOTIA HIGHLAND BRIGADE BOUND FOR ENGLAND. HALIFAX WAS BRITAIN'S LIFELINE IN BOTH WORLD WARS, SERVING AS NORTH AMERICA'S PREMIER PORT FOR CONVOYS.

Canadian merchant shipping in World War One increased from an average of 45,000 tonnes of cargo a month in 1915 to 351,000 tonnes by 1918; nearly 2,000 vessels passed through Halifax in 1917 alone. A heavy price was paid, however, with 5,000 Allied ships, 11 million tonnes of cargo, and 15,000 Allied lives lost to German submarines.

Sixty-five million men from thirty nations fought in World War One; at least 10 million were killed with another 29 million wounded, captured, or reported missing. An average day for Britain and her allies claimed 2,500 dead, 9,000 wounded, and 1,000 missing in action. From a population of only 8 million people, 619,636 Canadian men and women served overseas, most shipping out from Halifax. Nearly one in ten Canadians did not live to see the port at war's end, with 66,655 killed and another 172,950 wounded. It has been said that World War One elevated the country from colonial status to nationhood, an idea borne out in Canada's signing of the 1919 Treaty of Versailles.

8. 85TH BATTALION NOVA SCOTIA HIGHLANDERS DEPOSIT THEIR COLOURS AT THE PUBLIC ARCHIVES OF NOVA SCOTIA (NOW THE CHASE BUILDING, DALHOUSIE UNIVERSITY), 1935. WITH A REPUTATION FOR COURAGE AND DETERMINATION, "THE NEVERFAILS" WON FOURTEEN BATTLE HONOURS IN WORLD WAR ONE.

Organizing the Nova Scotia Highland Brigade was "undoubtedly the most unique feature in the story of recruiting Canada's Overseas Forces" in World War One. The senior unit of the famed brigade was the 85th Battalion, authorized on September 15, 1915. The rush to enlist was so great that within a month the battalion was over-strength. Buoyed by the response, a province-wide recruiting campaign to organize a second highland regiment was initiated. The end result was "a record unsurpassed in any part of the Dominion." Within only three weeks, the 185th, 193rd, and 219th Battalions were raised, all over-strength; together with the 85th Battalion, they formed the Nova Scotia Highland Brigade on January 26, 1916. The 85th Battalion's motto—Siol Na Fear Fearail ("The Breed Of Manly Men")—was adopted by the brigade, which is claimed to have drawn a father, brother, husband, or friend from virtually every home in Nova Scotia. While training at Camp Aldershot near Kentville, NS, each of the approximately five thousand men had their photo taken for a lasting pictorial record of the brigade before departing overseas.

The 25th (Nova Scotia) Battalion was raised at Halifax in October 1914 by Lieutenant-Colonel G. A. Lecain (69th Regiment) from Roundhill, Annapolis County. Headquartered at the Armouries, recruiting offices were opened in Sydney, Amherst, New Glasgow, Truro, and Yarmouth. The battalion reached full strength by Christmas Day 1914, and embarked overseas on May 20, 1915 as a unit of the 5th (Eastern Canada) Brigade, 2nd Canadian Division. After more than three months of intensive training in England, "The Fighting 25th" left for Flanders in September 1915, where it fought "with great distinction" at the Somme, Vimy, Passchendaele, Arras, Amiens, the Scarpe, and Cambrai. Pictured here is battalion mascot Robert The Bruce, namesake of the warrior king who freed Scotland from British tyranny at the Battle of Bannockburn in 1314. Note the small silver breastplate hanging from a chain around the goat's neck; engraved upon it were names of battles in which the animal had been present—Ypres, Somme, St. Elol, Vermecilles, Courcelette, Hill 60, Zilleberke, Kemmel. The 25th Battalion returned to Canada in May 1919; Robert The Bruce retired to Cape Breton Island, where he died circa 1930.

10. POSTCARD PANORAMA OF 69TH REGIMENT AT CAMP ALDERSHOT, KENTVILLE NS, 1913.

A euphoria for things military swept Canada following the Boer War. Seizing the moment, Sir Frederick Borden, federal Minister of Militia and a native Nova Scotian who had lost a son in the South African campaign, convinced Parliament that better militia training facilities were needed in his home province. Twenty-five thousand dollars was subsequently allotted to purchase 2,500 acres of land in the Annapolis Valley near the town of Kentville. Camp Aldershot, named for the famous military base in the south of England through which so many Canadians would pass in future wars, opened in 1904. Infantry, cavalry, and field artillery militia units from across Nova Scotia trained annually at Aldershot during summer months; the camp, while closed in winter, remained operational until late autumn to accommodate cavalrymen who couldn't free up their farm horse until then.

Nearly thirty thousand Nova Scotians enlisted to fight in World War One with some twenty-five thousand "cleared" to serve overseas. Seven thousand troops were in Camp Aldershot at any given time during the war. More than thirty-five thousand Americans came north to sign up with the Canadian Expeditionary Force before the United States entered the war in 1917. One of these units was the 97th American Legion, which trained at Aldershot. For services rendered, a World War One private was paid one dollar a day, a major or general paid twenty dollars. A private totally disabled from combat received a monthly pension of $12.50; widows were entitled to thirty cents a day, and each of the first two children, ten cents a day. After enlisting, if a mother, father, or wife could show just cause, a soldier could be "bought back" for fifteen dollars or less.

Camp Aldershot was designed and constructed by Lieutenant John L. Cavanagh, an engineer. Facilities could best be described as spartan. A sea of tents housed the men, as seen here. Many married servicemen brought their families to the camp (then open year round), where they lived in tents away from the troops; with the onset of cold weather the

Panorama of Aldersh

69th Regiment Band

Hospital h

majority of families sought shelter in the surrounding community as boarders. A few temporary structures were erected at Aldershot (such as a hospital and mess buildings), but these disappeared soon after the war. Borden Hall, a sizable officers' mess overlooking the camp (visible in the distance) was erected in 1916 and was the only building that remained when Aldershot re-activated in September, 1939. One of the first units through the camp in World War Two was the West Nova Scotia Regiment. With militia roots dating back to 1717 and the 40th Regiment of Foot at Fort Anne, the West Novas organized in 1936 at Bridgewater by amalgamating the 69th Annapolis and 75th Lunenburg Regiments. Mobilized as an active service force battalion on September 1, 1939, the regiment shipped overseas from Halifax shortly after Christmas, following a month's training. The West Novas underwent further training at Aldershot, England, waiting years—as did most Canadians—to see combat. When combat came in the form of Operation Husky and the 1943 invasion of Sicily, the regiment was the first Allied unit to land and remain on the European continent for the duration of the war. The highly decorated West Novas were awarded twenty-six theatre and battle honours, the Distinguished Service Order, the Military Cross, and the Distinguished Conduct Medal. Other Nova Scotia regiments of note to come through Aldershot were the Halifax Rifles, Princess Louise Fusiliers, Cape Breton Highlanders, North Nova Scotia Highlanders, and Pictou Highlanders.

Camp Aldershot was designated 14 Advanced Infantry (Rifle) Training Centre in World War Two. Facilities had improved immensely since the Great War, with new assault courses, H-huts for barracks, canteens, a barber shop, laundry, even a theatre. Other camps sprang up around Nova Scotia. Basic training centres were established at Yarmouth and New Glasgow, and Camp Debert opened in 1941 outside Truro. This thirty-square-mile base acted as a staging area for troops awaiting shipment overseas from Halifax as well as a naval gunnery school and a training centre for coast defence and anti-aircraft artillery batteries. The adjacent RCAF Station Debert served as a reconnaissance and navigational school and a coastal command station.

11. Submarine net looking from York Redoubt toward Sherbrooke Tower on McNab's Island, 1940. Swedish Freighter Hjelmaren has just passed through the opened net between gate vessels *Arleaux* and *Festubert*. The tug *Foundation Jupiter* works on repairs in foreground.

German submarines were the scourge of Allied merchant shipping and naval escorts during both World Wars. To keep them at bay, two steel-mesh submarine nets were strung across the harbour in World War One, the first circa 1915 on both sides of George's Island, a second circa 1917 between Ives Point on McNab's Island and the breakwater at Point Pleasant. Entry was through a narrow passage controlled by gate vessels that opened and closed the net; minesweepers (converted herring trawlers and ocean-going tugs armed with six-pounder guns) ensured that outer unprotected channels were free of enemy mines possibly laid by lurking submarines.

During World War Two, only one submarine net was used between York Redoubt and Sherbrooke Tower. Twelve banks of remote-controlled, diesel-powered searchlights (Canadian General Electric 60-inch, 800-million-candle-power) flooded the harbour at night from close- and medium-range quick-fire batteries, while other powerful lights with concentrated beams were installed at the outer defences. Two electronically controlled minefields tightened security.

cent of the crews. Seventy-three Canadian merchant ships were sunk. Of the twelve thousand Canadian merchant seamen who served aboard Allied flagged vessels, two thousand were killed, making their death toll the highest proportionally of Canada's four fighting services.

Canadian General Andrew McNaughton prophesied in 1918, "We have them [Germany] on the run. That means we will have to do it over again in another twenty-five years." Twenty-one years later, Halifax again stepped to the fore as a convoy staging area. In World War One, Canadian shipyards built 161 merchant vessels. During World War Two, 80 shipyards across the country, employing 85,000 workers turned out 456 merchant ships, 176 of them sailing under the Canadian flag. By war's end, Canada possessed the world's fourth largest merchant marine. In six years, Allied merchant ships made 25,000 crossings of the Atlantic, carrying 180 million tonnes of supplies, much of it passing through Halifax. The cost was horrific, with nearly 4,800 merchant vessels and 21 million gross tonnes of shipping lost, along with fifty per-

13. SS *MARQUESA* NAVAL FLOATING DRYDOCK, HALIFAX C.1942.

In World War Two, Halifax earned the nickname "Cripple Creek" for the more than seven thousand damaged vessels that limped or were towed into port having survived the ravages inflicted by marauding "wolf packs" and the storm-tossed North Atlantic. The herculean task of repairs was shouldered by Halifax Shipyards Limited. Founded in 1918 to build vessels for the Canadian Government Merchant Marine, its war-time workforce of two thousand had shrunk to only a hundred by 1922 due to economic recession and labour strife, followed by depression in the 1930s. With another global war in 1939, the old Royal Navy Graving Dock was dusted off, and this six-hundred-foot long floating dock, with a capacity to lift twenty-five thousand tons, was built and launched at the shipyards. Smaller vessels under three thousand tons were hauled out for repairs on Dartmouth's five marine railways. Despite unfathomable political decisions in the early war years—awarding ship repair and construction work to ice-bound ports in the St. Lawrence and Great Lakes—"a significant part of the Battle of the Atlantic was fought and won in the workshops of Halifax harbour."

14. CANADIAN 1ST DIVISION EMBARKS FOR ENGLAND AT PIER 21 IN DECEMBER 1939. PIER 21 TODAY IS A DESIGNATED NATIONAL HISTORIC SITE INTERPRETIVE CENTRE IN RECOGNITION OF ITS IMPORTANCE AS THE IMMIGRATION GATEWAY TO CANADA FROM 1928 TO 1971.

personnel left Pier 21 on thirty-seven ships, some being ocean liners like the *Queen Mary*, which could carry fourteen thousand in one sailing. Forty-five thousand Canadians lost their lives in World War Two. Of the 55,000 wounded, most returned to Canada via Pier 21, which also processed 48,000 war brides and 22,000 children.

Canada's Army was woefully prepared for the task ahead when war came on September 10, 1939. Regular forces totalled only 4,500 troops armed with twenty-nine bren guns, twenty-three anti-tank guns, five mortars, sixteen tanks and zero modern artillery. Within one month, 70,000 men volunteered. From a male population of only 2.5 million between eighteen and forty-five years of age, 1 million answered the call to arms, the highest per capita of any Allied country. Within six years, five army divisions and two armoured brigades had shipped overseas. With the declaration of war, Halifax's Pier 21 was taken over by the Department of National Defence as the primary overseas embarkation point through which 494,000 men and women would ultimately pass. From August 8 to December 27, 1942, approximately 58,820 armed forces

15. ROYAL NAVY AND ROYAL CANADIAN NAVY "TOWN" CLASS
DESTROYERS AND "FLOWER" CLASS CORVETTES ALONGSIDE
JETTY NO. 4 AT HMC DOCKYARD, OCTOBER 16, 1942.

Historian Thomas Raddall writes that World War Two "brought cata-
clysmic change" to the dockyard and by 1945 "all the ancient buildings
were swept away…[and] the familiar, picturesque dockyard had van-
ished." The Royal Canadian Navy also experienced a metamorphosis.
Because of the Canadian government's indifference to its military forces
between wars, the RCN in 1939 consisted of only eleven ships. In six

years its fleet would grow to be the world's third largest, with nearly
four hundred vessels ranging from motor launches to aircraft carriers
and cruisers. More than a hundred and thirty were corvettes, the
"workhorses of the North Atlantic" convoy escorts. Only one corvette
survives today, *HMCS Sackville*, berthed near the old Queen's Wharf at
the Maritime Museum of the Atlantic in Halifax, a restored naval
memorial to the thousands of men who fought submarines, weather,
claustrophobic living conditions, and seasickness to keep open the life-
lines of the world. The RCN sank thirty-three U-boats but lost twenty-eight ships of its own, two from submarines at the very harbour
approaches—the minesweepers *Clayoquot* and *Esquimalt*.

16. INSPECTION OF DIVISIONS BY CHIEF OF NAVAL STAFF AT DOCKYARD STADACONA, AUGUST 11, 1942. IN 1941-42, HMCS STADACONA WAS ESTABLISHED AS BASE DEPOT HALIFAX WHEN THE DOCKYARD AND PORTIONS OF NAVY-OWNED LAND WERE EXPANDED TO TAKE IN WELLINGTON BARRACKS FOR DESPERATELY NEEDED HOUSING.

One hundred thousand men and women served with the Royal Canadian Navy in World War Two; two thousand were killed. Training facilities to handle such numbers were sorely lacking at the outset. In May 1942, HMCS Cornwallis, a recruit training school, was established at Halifax. Within a year, however, the dockyard space used by the school was needed for other wartime purposes. In June 1942, construction began on a new $9 million training base in Deep Brook on the shores of the Annapolis Basin. On April 14, 1943, HMCS Cornwallis officially transferred to the new facility, the largest of its kind in the British Commonwealth. The base opened with a complement of 2,539 and—with time in short supply—staggered courses lasted only six to eight weeks. From 1943 to 1945, HMCS Cornwallis turned out sailors and Wrens at an amazing rate, with one thousand instructors drilling ten thousand recruits at a time in the finer points of boat pulling, seamanship, knots and splices, marks of respect, self-defence, assault courses, and rifle drill. At war's end, the base served as a Discharge Transit Centre for thousands of naval personnel.

17. AIR CREW AT ELEMENTARY FLIGHT TRAINING SCHOOL, STANLEY, NS. WITH ITS WIDE OPEN SPACES, RELATIVELY CLOSE PROXIMITY TO BRITAIN, STRONG INDUSTRIAL CAPACITY AND EASY ACCESS TO U.S. AIRCRAFT PARTS, CANADA WAS A NATURAL CHOICE FOR THE BRITISH COMMONWEALTH AIR TRAINING PROGRAM.

Britain was in desperate need of trained air crews at the outset of World War Two. With neither the resources nor facilities to meet demand, a call for help went out to the Dominions. On December 17, 1939, Canada, Australia, New Zealand, and Britain agreed to undertake an ambitious plan known as the British Commonwealth Air Training Program (BCATP). Between 1940 and 1945, one hundred and fifty-one elementary and advanced flight instructional schools were established at airfields across Canada. Stanley was one of twenty-nine civilian-run Elementary Flight Training Schools in Canada that enabled the RCAF to draw upon expertise and facilities already in place at local flying clubs to get the BCATP up and running. The massive project required more than 8,000 buildings (700 being aircraft hangers), 300 miles of water mains, storage facilities for 26 million gallons of aviation fuel, and ground crews totalling 104,113 men and women. By war's end, 131,553 pilots, wireless operators, navigators, and air gunners from the Australian, New Zealand, British, and Canadian Air Forces had completed the intensive training regime. Canada carried the lion's share of costs, picking up $1.6 billion of the $2.2 billion price tag. The British Commonwealth Air Training Program was, according to historian J. L. Granatstein, "the major Canadian military contribution to the Allied War effort."

18. ELEMENTARY FLIGHT TRAINING SCHOOL AT STANLEY, NS OPERATED FROM MARCH 1941 TO JANUARY 1944. A BREAKDOWN OF NUMBERS SHOWS THAT 72,835 ROYAL CANADIAN AIR FORCE PERSONNEL GRADUATED FROM THE BRITISH COMMONWEALTH AIR TRAINING PROGRAM, FOLLOWED BY 42,110 RAF, 9,606 RAAF, 7,002 RNZAF AND 5,296 NAVAL FLEET AIR ARM.

Several RCAF stations across Nova Scotia not only trained air crews but played a critical role in providing air cover for convoys and hunting down German U-Boats. RCAF Station Sydney was responsible for patrolling the Cabot Strait and the waters south of Newfoundland. RCAF Station Debert had the distinction of operating the first British Commonwealth Air Training School in Canada. In 1942, a new air-training base for pilots, navigators, and gunners opened at Greenwood Village in the Annapolis Valley, which flew submarine surveillance patrols over the Bay of Fundy. Planes from Debert and Greenwood routinely flew practice missions to a bombing and gunnery range at Economy on the Minas Basin. RCAF Station Yarmouth trained one thousand men between 1942 and 1944, the majority being air gunners for the Royal Navy Fleet Air Arm; Yarmouth also provided anti-submarine bomber reconnaissance. The most important base in Eastern Canada was unquestionably RCAF Station Dartmouth. The first mission of the war originated there on September 10, 1939, when a Stranraer Flying Boat searched for enemy vessels off Halifax harbour. In May 1941, North America's first radar station was built at nearby Preston. During the course of the war, nine RCAF long-range Bomber-Reconnaissance squadrons flew hundreds of missions into the northwest Atlantic and the Gulf of St. Lawrence. And six RCAF Fighter Squadrons were stationed in Dartmouth to protect the ocean and harbour approaches from possible air attack.

19. SAILORS CHECK OUT ONE OF THE TOO FEW SPOTS AVAILABLE TO ENTERTAIN THE THOUSANDS OF FORCES PERSONNEL INHABITING HALIFAX DURING WORLD WAR TWO.

Not since Wolfe captured Louisbourg and Howe sought refuge from Boston had Halifax been swamped with so many uniforms as it was during World War Two. A peacetime population of sixty-nine thousand swelled to a hundred thousand as military forces vied with civilians for overtaxed space and services. Accommodation was in short supply; complete strangers shared double beds in boarding houses, while many waited three days for a hotel room. Inflation was rampant, with monthly rental of rooms that went for twenty dollars in Toronto hitting sixty dollars in Halifax. There were line-ups for everything and not enough of anything. Strict liquor laws were enforced, as was a six-year nightly black out. "All this is very hard on the nerves," wrote censor H. B. Jefferson. Frayed nerves severed in May 1945 when peace triggered the infamous VE Day Riot, described by author Stephen Kimber as "a two-day orgy of boozing, looting, window-smashing, dancing in the streets, public fornication and mindless mayhem…." A black mark on an otherwise impeccable war record, the VE Day Riot left Halifax with three dead and 211 arrests plus damages of $5 million, with 564 businesses looted.

20. UNIQUE POSTCARD IMAGE OF MUSHROOM CLOUD FROM THE 1917 HALIFAX EXPLOSION, TAKEN FIVE MILES AWAY AT YORK REDOUBT.

TAKEN FROM YORK REDOUBT
IMMEDIATELY AFTER THE
EXPLOSION.

ON ACCOUNT OF THE ABOVE WE
WERE DELAYED IN SENDING
GREETINGS.

Throughout its history, Halifax was an accident waiting to happen, with vast stores of munitions scattered about in magazines, forts, merchant vessels, and warships. Several times there were near misses, such as the World War Two incident when the munition ships *Trongate* (British) and *Volunteer* (American) caught fire in the harbour; the fires were, fortunately, contained. Two explosions—the Central Magazine in 1857 and Bedford Magazine in 1945—caused considerable property damage but claimed just two lives. Such was not the case, however, on December 6, 1917, when the French munitions ship *Mont Blanc* blew up after colliding with the Belgian relief ship *Imo*. The story of the 1917 Halifax Explosion has been told and retold, its causes and central characters analyzed, criticized, and immortalized. More Nova Scotians died that day (1,600) than were killed on the battlefields of World War One, with another 9,000 injured and 6,000 left homeless, out of a city population of 65,000. Three hundred and twenty-five acres were leveled resulting in $35 million damage. Soldiers of the British Expeditionary Force stationed at the Armouries awaiting shipment overseas were the first to mobilize into action. They scoured ruins for survivors, piecing together make-shift stretchers to carry the injured to first-aid stations. Every available military medical unit and hospital was pressed into service. Camp Hill hospital for convalescent veterans treated 1,400 people within twenty-four hours of the explosion; doctors from the Cogswell Street military hospital established emergency first-aid stations on the Halifax Commons. American doctors, nurses, and orderlies provided much-needed expertise; two vessels having already left port turned around five miles out and returned after seeing the post-explosion mushroom cloud and feeling the aftershock. More than thirty merchant ships were anchored in Bedford Basin at the time, awaiting convoys due to leave on Friday December 7 and Monday December 10. Damage to these ships was minimal and—despite the fact dockyard facilities and provisioning stores were either destroyed or in a state of confusion—the first convoy sailed on December 11, only four days after the largest man-made explosion in history before the advent of the atomic bomb, dropped in World War Two, twenty-eight years later.

21. DEDICATION OF WORLD WAR ONE CENOTAPH ON GRAND PARADE, NOVEMBER 11, 1929. PRIOR TO THIS, HALIFAX HELD ITS REMEMBRANCE DAY SERVICES AT THE BOER WAR MEMORIAL ADJACENT PROVINCE HOUSE.

Founded in war, forged by war, Halifax was a cornerstone of the British Empire for nearly two hundred years. From colonial garrison town to an east coast port of the Dominion, sacrifices and contributions made by Imperial and Canadian forces are remembered in numerous cenotaphs, monuments, plaques, and cairns throughout the city. Long silent but preserved now as national historic sites, "the Halifax harbour defence system has been recognized as unique on the North American continent because it contains a complete conspectus of shore defences from the mid-18th century to the Second World War." Museums dedicated to army, navy, air-force, and merchant navy history graphically portray Halifax's storied past. For twenty-five years, the Nova Scotia International Tattoo has showcased its rich military legacy. "The greatest misfortune that can happen to any people is to have no noble deeds and no heroic personalities to look back to," wrote Scottish Professor Dr. Blackie in 1900. "For as a wise Present is the seed of a fruitful Future, so a great Past is a seed of a hopeful Present."

SOURCES AND PHOTO CREDITS

Sources

Akins, T. B. *History of Halifax City*. Halifax: Nova Scotia Historical Society, 1895.

Allen, Ralph. *Ordeal By Fire: Canada 1910-1945*. Toronto: Popular Library, 1961.

Arbuckle, Lt. (N) Graeme. *Customs & Traditions Of The Canadian Navy*. Halifax: Nimbus, 1984.

Armit, Capt. W. B. *Halifax 1749-1906: Soldiers Who Founded And Garrisoned A Famous City*. Army Museum, Halifax Citadel, n.d.

Armstrong, John Griffith. *The Halifax Explosion and the Royal Canadian Navy*. Vancouver: UBC Press, 2002.

Baker, Raymond. *The Early Citadels at Halifax 1749-1815*. Parks Canada Manuscript Report #107 (Miscellaneous Historical Reports On Sites in the Atlantic Provinces), n.d.

Bell, Ken, and C. P. Stacey. *100 Years: The Royal Canadian Regiment 1883-1983*. Don Mills: Collier Macmillan Canada, 1983.

Boileau, John. *Internees, Evacuees, and Immigrants. The Beaver: Canada's History Magazine*. Vol. 84:1 Feb/Mar 2004.

Brett, Capt. W. *Hints On Bivouac and Camp Life*. London, England: T. & W. Boone, 1856.

Brown, W. M. *Recollections of Old Halifax*. Collections of the Nova Scotia Historical Society, Vol. 13. Halifax: McAlpine Publishing, 1908.

Colaiacovo, Tony, Ed. *The Navy Times: Ninety Years of History—A Salute to the Canadian Navy*. Halifax: Effective Publishing, 2000.

———. *The Navy Times: A Celebration of Our History, Culture and Traditions*. Volume 4, No. 1, Second Edition. Halifax: Effective Publishing, n.d.

———. *The Times of Halifax: A Celebration of Our History, Culture and Traditions*. Halifax: Effective Publishing. Volume 3, No. 3, 1999.

———. *The Times of Pier 21: A Celebration of Our History, Culture and Traditions*. Halifax: Effective Publishing. Volume 3, No.1, n.d.

———. *The Times of Tall Ships: A Celebration of Our Maritime History, Culture and Traditions*. Halifax: Effective Publishing, 2000.

Conlin, Dan. *A Private War In The Caribbean: Nova Scotia Privateering 1793-1805*. Halifax: M.A. Thesis. St. Mary's University, 1996.

Cuthbertson, Brian. *The Halifax Citadel: Portrait of a Military Fortress*. Halifax: Formac, 2001.

Douglas, W. A. B. *The Sea Militia of Nova Scotia 1749-1755: A Comment On Naval Policy*. Canadian Historical Review, Vol. 47, 1966.

Duncan, Francis. *Our Garrisons in the West*. London: Chapman & Hall, 1864.

Dunlop, Allan C. *The Levee and Other New Year's Festivities*. The Nova Scotia Historical Quarterly, Vol. 10, Nos. 3 & 4, September & December. Halifax: Public Archives of Nova Scotia, 1980.

Dunn, Brenda. *The Halifax Citadel, 1906-51: The Canadian Period*. Manuscript Report No. 284. Ottawa: Parks Canada, 1977.

Edwards, Major Joseph Plimsoll. *The Militia of Nova Scotia, 1749-1867*. Collections of the Nova Scotia Historical Society, Vol. 17. Halifax: Wm MacNab & Son, 1913.

Elliott, Shirley B. *A Library For The Garrison And Town: A History Of The Cambridge Military Library, Royal Military Park, Halifax, Nova Scotia*.

———. *Domestic Life in Early Halifax*. Halifax: The Nova Scotia Museum, 1976.

Fingard, J., J. Guildford, and D. Sutherland. *Halifax: The First 250 Years*. Halifax: Formac, 1999.

Fingard, Judith. *The Dark Side Of Life In Victorian Halifax*. Halifax: Pottersfield Press, 1989.

———. *Jack in Port*. Toronto: University of Toronto Press, 1982.

Foster, J. A. *Heart of Oak: A Pictorial History of the Royal Canadian Navy*. Toronto: Methuen, 1985.

Fraser, D. G. L. *The Origin and Function of the Court of Vice Admiralty In Halifax 1749-1759*. Collections of the Nova Scotia Historical Society Vol. 33. Kentville Publishing, 1961.

German, Tony. *The Sea Is At Our Gates: History of the Canadian Navy*. Toronto: McClelland & Stewart, 1990.

Graham, Brigadier-General C. A. L. *The Story of the Royal Regiment of Artillery*. Royal Artillery Institution, 1962.

Greenough, John Joseph. *The Halifax Citadel 1825-60: A Narrative and Structural History*. Canadian Historical Sites No. 17. Ottawa: Parks Canada, 1977.

Hadley, Michael L., and Roger Sarty. *Tin-Pots & Pirate Ships*. Montreal: McGill–Queen's University Press, 1991.

Hammond, M. M. *Memoir of Captain M. M. Hammond, Rifle Brigade*. London: James Nisbet & Co., 1858.

Hardy, Campbell. *Sporting Adventures in the New World*. 2 Vols. London: Hurst & Blackett, 1855.

———. *Forest Life in Acadie*. London: Chapman & Hall, 1869.

Hawkins, John. *The Founding of Halifax*. Halifax: Goldcloth Publishing, 1999.

Heal, S. C. *Conceived In War, Born In Peace, Canada's Deep Sea Merchant Marine*. Vancouver: Cordillera Publishing, 1992.

Johnston, Andrew. *Defending Halifax: Ordinance, 1825-1906*. History and Archaeology No. 46. Ottawa: Parks Canada, 1981.

Jones, Martin. *Hockey's Home Halifax–Dartmouth: The Origin of Canada's Game*. Halifax: Nimbus, 2002.

Kimber, Stephen. *Sailors, Slackers and Blind Pigs: Halifax At War*. Doubleday Canada, 2002.

Kitz, Janet, and Gary Castle. *Point Pleasant Park: An Illustrated History*. Halifax: Pleasant Point Publishing, 1999.

Kroll, Robert E. ed. *Intimate Fragments: An Irreverent Chronicle of Early Halifax*. Halifax: Nimbus, 1985.

Lamb, James B. *On The Triangle Run*. Toronto: MacMillan Canada, 1986.

———. *The Corvette Navy*. Toronto: MacMillan Canada, 1977.

Lawrence, Hal. *A Bloody War: One Man's Memories of the Canadian Navy, 1939-45*. Toronto: Macmillan Canada, 1979.

———. *Tales of the North Atlantic*. Toronto: McClelland & Stewart, 1985.

Lawrence, Ian. *Historic Annapolis Royal*. Halifax: Nimbus, 2002.

LeBlanc, J. P. *A Brief History of Melville Island*. Research Division, Halifax Defence Complex, 1994.

Logan, Major H. Meredith. *Melville Island, The Military Prison of Halifax*. Address given before the United Services Institute of Nova Scotia at the Armoury, Halifax, March 24, 1933.

Lotz, Jim. *Canadians At War*. London: Bison Books, 1990.

Lynch, Thomas G. *Canada's Flowers: History of the Corvettes of Canada, 1939-1945*. Halifax: Nimbus, 1981.

MacLean, Grant. *Walk Historic Halifax*. Halifax: Nimbus, 1996.

Marquis, Greg. *In Armageddon's Shadow: The Civil War And Canada's Maritime Provinces*. Montreal: McGill-Queen's University Press, 1998.

———. *Mercenaries or Killer Angels? Nova Scotia in the American Civil War*. Collections of the Royal Nova Scotia Historical Society, Vol. 44. Halifax: McCurdy Printing, 1996.

Martell, James Stuart. *The Romance of Government House*. Halifax: Information Services, Dept. of Government Services, Revised Edition 1973.

Major, Marjorie. *Melville Island*. The Nova Scotia Historical Quarterly, Vol. 4, No. 3, September. Halifax: Petheric Press, 1974.

McDonald, R. H. *The Royal Artillery in Halifax, 1860-1875*. Halifax Defence Complex manuscript, 1981.

McDonald, R. H. *Hastings Doyle and the Anti-Confederates.* The Nova Scotia Historical Quarterly, Vol. 6, No. 4, December. Halifax: Petheric Press, 1976.

Metson, Graham. *An East Coast Port...Halifax at War 1939-1945.* Toronto: McGraw-Hill Ryerson, 1981.

Millington, Elsie. *Purcell's Cove: The Little Place That Helped Build Halifax City.* Victoria, B.C.: Desktop Publishing, 2000.

Milner, Marc. *North Atlantic Run: The Royal Canadian Navy & The Battle for the Convoys.* Toronto: University of Toronto Press, 1985.

Morrison, James H. *Wave To Whisper: British Military Communications in Halifax and the Empire, 1780-1880.* History and Archaeology No. 64. Ottawa: Parks Canada, 1982.

———. *Soldiers, Storms and Seasons: Weather Watching in Nineteenth Century Halifax.* The Nova Scotia Historical Quarterly, Vol. 10, Nos. 3 & 4, December. Halifax: Public Archives of Nova Scotia, 1980.

Morton, Desmond. *A Military History of Canada.* Toronto: McClelland & Stewart, 1999.

Nicholson, G. W. L. *The Gunners of Canada: The History of the Royal Regiment of Canadian Artillery Vol.I 1534-1919.* Toronto: McClelland & Stewart, 1967.

Nova Scotia Archives and Records Management. *Halifax And Its People 1749-1999.* Halifax: Nimbus, 1999.

O'Neil, Patrick. *Halifax and the Garrison Theatrical Tradition.* Collections of the Nova Scotia Historical Society, Vol. 44. Halifax: McCurdy Printing, 1996.

Pacy, Elizabeth. *Halifax Citadel.* Halifax: Nimbus, 1985.

———. *Historic Halifax.* Willowdale, Ont.: Hounslow Press, 1988.

Parker, Mike. *Running the Gauntlet: An Oral History of Canadian Merchant Seamen In World War II.* Halifax: Nimbus, 1994.

———. *Guides of the North Woods: Hunting & Fishing Tales From Nova Scotia 1860-1960.* Halifax: Nimbus, 1990.

———. *Where Moose & Trout Abound: A Sporting Journal.* Halifax: Nimbus, 1995.

Paul, Daniel N. *We Were Not The Savages.* Halifax: Fernwood, 2000.

Payzant, Joan M. *Halifax: Cornerstone of Canada.* Windsor Publications, 1985.

Picart, Lennox O'Riley. *The Trelawney Maroons and Sir John Wentworth: The Struggle to Maintain Their Culture 1796-1800.* Collections of the Royal Nova Scotia Historical Society, Vol. 44. Halifax: McCurdy Printing, 1996.

Piers, Harry. *The Evolution of the Halifax Fortress 1749-1928.* 1947. Revised by G. M. Self and Phyllis Blakeley. Halifax: Public Archives of Nova Scotia, Publication No. 7, n.d.

Pulsifer, Cameron. *The 78th Highlanders in Halifax, 1869-71: The Experiences of a Highland Regiment in a Garrison Town, Vol. 1.* Halifax Defence Complex manuscript, 1982.

Queen's Own Highlanders, Seaforth and Camerons. John G. Eccles Printers Inverness, 1978.

Quigley, John G. *A Century of Rifles The Halifax Rifles 1860-1960.* Halifax: William MacNab, 1960.

Raddall, Thomas H. *Halifax, Warden of the North.* Toronto: McClelland & Stewart, 1971.

———. *Hangman's Beach.* Toronto: McClelland & Stewart, 1966

———. *West Novas.* Self-published, 1947.

Razzolini, Esperanza Maria. *The British Army and Black Gunpowder in the Mid-Nineteenth Century.* 1979 Parks Canada Manuscript Report # 395 FC215 M36 No.395 c.1 NSHlAP.

Reed, R. H. ed. *East Camp RCAF Station Yarmouth, Nova Scotia, Memories of World War II No. 1 Naval Air Gunnery School. A British Commonwealth Air Training Plan Base.* Yarmouth: Sentinel Printing Ltd. 1984.

Ripley, Donald F. *The Home Front, Wartime Life in Camp Aldershot and Kentville, Nova Scotia.* Hantsport: Lancelot Press, 1991.

Ross, David, and Rene Chartrand. *Cataloguing Military Uniforms.* Saint John: The New Brunswick Museum, 1977.

Ruck, Calvin. *Canada's Black Battalion No. 2 Construction 1916-1920.* Halifax: The Society for the Protection and Preservation of Black Culture in Nova Scotia, 1986.

Sarty, Roger. *The Maritime Defence of Canada.* Toronto: The Canadian Institute of Strategic Studies, 1996.

———. *The Halifax Military Lands Board: Civil-Military Relations and the Development of Halifax as a Strategic Defended Port, 1905-1928.* The Northern Mariner, XlI, No. 2 (April 2002).

———. *The Battle of the Atlantic.* Ottawa: CEF Books, 2001.

Saunders, Ivan J. *A History of Martello Towers in the Defence of British North America 1796-1871.* Parks Canada. History & Archaeology #15, 1976.

Schmeisser, B. *Town Clock 1803-1860, A Structural and Narrative Study.* Halifax Defence Complex manuscript. 1984.

Schull, Joseph. *Far Distant Ships: An Official Account of Canadian Naval Operations in World War II.* Toronto: Stoddart, 1987.

Smith, Marilyn Gurney. *The King's Yard: An Illustrated History of the Halifax Dockyard.* Halifax: Nimbus, 1985.

Stanley, G. F. G. *Canada's Soldiers 1604-1954: A Military History of an Unmilitary People.* Toronto: MacMillan, 1954.

States, David W. *William Hall, V. C. of Horton Bluff, Nova Scotia, Nineteenth-Century Naval Hero.* Collections of the Royal Nova Scotia Historical Society, Vol. 44. Halifax: McCurdyPrinting, 1996.

Steppler, Glen A. *Powder Barrel Markings for Halifax Citadel.* 1980 Parks Canada Manuscript Report #395 FC215 M36 No. 395 c.1 NSHlAP.

Stubbing, Charles H. *Dockyard Memoranda 1894.* Collections of The Nova Scotia Historical Society Vol. XIII. Halifax: McAlpine Publishing Co., 1908.

Trider, Douglas W. *History of Dartmouth And Halifax Harbour 1415 to 1800 Volume I.* Dartmouth: Self-Published. 1999.

Tucker, G. N. *The Naval Service of Canada: Its Official History Vol. I Origins & Early Years.* Ottawa: King's Printer, 1952.

Unknown. *Halifax: Its Sins and Sorrows.* Halifax: Conference Job Printing Office, April 8, 1862.

Vieth, Frederick Harris D. *Recollections of the Crimean Campaign and the Expedition to Kinburn in 1855 including also Sporting and Dramatic Incidents in Connection with Garrison Life in the Canadian Lower Provinces.* Montreal: John Lovell & Son, 1907.

Visitor Services. *Guide Handbook Halifax Defence Complex Historical Background.* Parks Canada, 1985.

Watts, Heather, and Michele Raymond. *Halifax's Northwest Arm: An Illustrated History.* Halifax: Formac, 2003.

Whitfield, Carol M. *Tommy Atkins: The British Soldier in Canada, 1759-1870.* History and Archaeology No. 56. Ottawa: Parks Canada, 1981.

Williams, Jeffrey. *Princess Patricia's Canadian Light Infantry.* London: Leo Copper in association with Secker & Warburg, 1985.

Wright, A. Jeffrey. *The Halifax Riot of April 1863.* The Nova Scotia Historical Quarterly, Vol. 4, No. 3, September. Halifax: Petheric Press, 1974.

Young, Richard J. *Blockhouses in Canada 1749-1841: A Comparative Report & Catalogue.* Parks Canada. History & Archaeology #23, 1980

Photo Credits

NSARM – Nova Scotia Archives and Records Management
PAC – Public Archives of Canada
PCC – Parks Canada Citadel

INTRODUCTION

1. NSARM   Army-Forts: Citadel   Acc.5938

CHAPTER 1: SENTINELS OF THE PAST

1. NSARM   Royal Engeneers #93   Acc.6990
2. Piers, Harry. *Evolution of the Halifax Fortress 1749-1928*
3. NSARM   Army 5357
4. NSARM   Royal Engineers #202   Acc. 6962
5. NSARM   J.A. Irvine Collection   Album 37, #24
6. PAC   C-8080
7. NSARM   Royal Engineers #303   Acc. 6818
8. NSARM   Army : Barracks
9. NSARM   Royal Engineers #178   Acc. 6805
10. NSARM   Royal Engineers #297   Acc. 6814
11. NSARM   Notman #9605   Loc. 33.2.1
12. NSARM   Royal Engineers #185   Acc. 6967
13. NSARM   Royal Engineers #384   Acc. 6889
14. NSARM   Royal Engineers #262   Acc. 6892
15. NSARM   Royal Engineers #4.1   Acc. 6823
16. NSARM   Royal Engineers #25   Acc. 6932
17. PCC   108-07-2-880-0333
18. PCC   108-04-2-878-0209
19. PAC   625530
20. NSARM   Royal Engineers #255   Acc. 6995
21. NSARM   Notman #1692
22. NSARM   Royal Engineers #209   Acc. 6830
23. NSARM   Army : Forts   N-2026
24. NSARM   Army : Forts
25. NSARM   Royal Engineers #222   Acc. 6907
26. PCC   108-87-2-895-0261
27. PCC   108-87-2-895-0260
28. NSARM   Army : York Redoubt
29. NSARM   Army : Forts   (Notman)
30. NSARM   Royal Engineers #241

CHAPTER 2: THE KING'S YARD

1. NSARM   Notman #13295   Acc. 6990
2. NSARM   Navy : Dockyard   Acc. 5887   N-1177
3. PAC   C 4480
4. NSARM   Notman #67467   N-197
5. NSARM   Navy : General   Acc. 6383
6. NSARM   Halifax City Atlas 1878

7. NSARM   Navy : Dockyard   Loc. 55.4
8. NSARM   Royal Engineers #327
9. NSARM   Royal Engineers #336   Acc. 6843
10. NSARM   Royal Engineers   Ad.#23   Acc.6835
11. NSARM   N-1174
12. NSARM   Navy
13. PAC   Grant Collection 127288/1974-470
14. NSARM   N-1281
15. NSARM   Navy : Ships
16. NSARM   Navy : Ships   N-2595
17. NSARM   Notman #61690
18. PCC   000-71-2-894-0202
19. PAC   28471
20. NSARM   Navy : Ships   Acc. 9272   N-2602
21. NSARM   Notman   #[11] 130

CHAPTER 3: MANNING THE RAMPARTS

1. NSARM   Notman O/S#100,005
2. PCC   108-99-2-800-0214
3. NSARM   Notman #68091
4. PAC   11716
5. PCC   108-97-2-871-0221
6. NSARM   Notman #41212
7. NSARM   Notman #44969
8. NSARM   Notman #40673
9. PCC   108-97-2-895-0267
10. PCC   000-58-2-870-0396
11. NSARM   Army : General (Tom Conners) #695
12. NSARM   Notman #40451
13. PCC   108-61-2-890-0230
14. NSARM   Cogswell #104
15. NSARM   "Fixed in Time" #226
16. PAC   C-85764
17. NSARM   Cogswell #149
18. NSARM   Cogswell #159
19. NSARM   Army : General
20. PCC   108-97-2-860-0273
21. PCC   108-97-2-860-0273
22. NSARM   Misc. N.S. Photographers #1
23. NSARM   Army   Acc. 9241
24. NSARM   Army : Regiment
25. NSARM   Andrew King 1979 74.6
26. NSARM   Notman   O/S #14090
27. NSARM   Notman O/S #9492
28. NSARM   Notman O/S #100,033   Loc.33.3.2
29. NSARM   Notman O/S #8073
30. NSARM   Notman #3591

CHAPTER 4: ROYAL COUPLE

1. NSARM   Royal Engineers #104   Acc.6978
1. NSARM   Royal Engineers #112
2. NSARM   Army : Forts
3. PCC   108-03-2-873-0215
4. PAC   PA 28481
5. NSARM   Royal Engineers #273   Acc.6831
6. NSARM   J.P. Porter   N-140
7. PCC   108-60-2-914-0205
8. PAC   PA 28407 (Notman)
9. NSARM   Notman #3457   Loc. 55.3
10. NSARM   Army : Forts
11. NSARM   J.A. Irvine Album 35, #30
12. NSARM   Royal Engineers #85 Acc.6984 N-2028
13. NSARM   Notman (reverse of #68091)
14. NSARM   Army : Artillery

CHAPTER 5: A GARRISON TOWN

1. NSARM   Royal Engineers #400 Loc. 31-2-3 Acc. 7035
2. NSARM   Notman #9169
3. NSARM   Notman #1940   Loc.33.2.1
4. NSARM   Gauvin & Gentzell #10
5. PAC   C-19387
6. NSARM   Series 5 #97   Loc.33.5.7
7. NSARM   Album 5 #55   Loc.31-1-2
8. NSARM   Halifax City Atlas 1878
9. NSARM   Army   Acc. 6277
10. NSARM   Royal Engineers #78   Acc. 6877
11. NSARM   Album 29
12. NSARM   Album 29
13. NSARM   Album 29
14. NSARM   Royal Engineers #40   Acc.6969
15. NSARM   Army : Barracks
16. NSARM   Royal Engineers #187 Acc.6788 Loc.44.3.2
17. NSARM   Royal Engineers #49 Acc.6895
18. NSARM   Army : Barracks
19. NSARM   Royal Engineers #200   Acc.6972
20. NSARM   Royal Engineers #153   Acc. 6903
21. NSARM   Gauvin & Gentzell #26   N-4414
22. NSARM   Notman O/S # 35208   N-2972; N-338
23. NSARM   Notman #10196   N-6112
24. NSARM   Cogswell #293
25. NSARM   Notman   1983-310 N-3835
26. NSARM   Rogers #32   Loc. 31.2.3
27. NSARM   Royal Engineers #93A Acc. 6834
28. NSARM   Royal Engineers #248 Acc. 6886
29. NSARM   Royal Engineers #249

30. NSARM   Halifax City Atlas 1878
31. NSARM   Royal Engineers #246
32. NSARM   Royal Engineers #247
33. NSARM   Royal Engineers #245
34. NSARM   Army : General #7560
35. NSARM   Royal Engineers #216 Acc. 6938
36. NSARM   Royal Engineers #189 Acc.6918
37. NSARM   Royal Engineers #38
38. NSARM   Notman #61589
39. NSARM   1987-265 Loc. 37.3.1 N-8962
40. NSARM   Notman #53 [2]
41. NSARM   Notman #1966 Loc. 33.2.1
42. NSARM   Waltar Kauzman #10 1989-268 Loc. 33.5.5
43. NSARM   Notman #8323
44. NSARM   Notman O/S #100,029
45. NSARM   Notman #68837
46. NSARM   Norwood #380 Acc. 1987-480
47. NSARM   Royal Engineers #381
48. NSARM   Army : General #5985
49. NSARM   J. A. Irvine Album 35 #91
50. NSARM   Notman 1983-310/12123
51. NSARM   Notman #6334

CHAPTER 6: NO LIFE LIKE IT

1. PCC   108-04-2-875-0206
2. NSARM   Notman #62189
3. NSARM   Notman $40258
4. NSARM   J.A. Irvine Album 35 #76
5. NSARM   Royal Engineers #111 Acc. 6944
6. NSARM   Notman #65711
7. NSARM   Notman #16758
8. PCC   108-85-2-900-0267
9. PCC   108-85-2-890-0203
10. NSARM   Notman O/S #8510
11. NSARM   Army : General Loc. 55.3
12. PCC   000-97-2-865-0201
13. NSARM   Notman #36403
14. NSARM   Notman #71432
15. PCC   108-89-2-885-0240
16. NSARM   Cogswell #283
17. PCC   108-97-2-875-0250
18. NSARM   Notman #44369
19. NSARM   Notman #48319
20. NSARM   Halifax : Churches

CHAPTER 7: REST AND RELAXATION

1. PAC   C-11719
2. NSARM   Notman #8884
3. NSARM   Notman "Fixed in Time"
4. NSARM   Notman #98397 "Fixed in Time" #33
5. PCC   108-89-2-880-0275

6. PCC   108-85-2-890-0259
7. NSARM   Ferdinand James Odevnine #21 Loc. 31.1.7
8. NSARM   Royal Engineers #10.c.2 Acc. 7003
9. NSARM   Notman #8853
10. PCC   108-61-2-890-0274
11. NSARM   "Fixed in Time" #27
12. NSARM   Army : General   Loc. 55.3
13. NSARM   Notman O/S # 7838
14. NSARM   Army : General
15. NSARM   Royal Engineers #155 Acc. 6791 Loc. 44.3.2
16. NSARM   Notman #59736
17. NSARM   F.W. Johnson Loc. 47-2
18. NSARM   Army : General Acc. 4737 Loc. 55.2

CHAPTER 8: CRIME AND PUNISHMENT

1. NSARM   Navy: Dockyard
2. NSARM   Royal Engineers #188 Acc.6896
3. NSARM   Army : General Acc. 6480
4. NSARM   Army : General Acc. 6481
5. NSARM   Army : General Acc. 6484
6. NSARM   Army : General
7. NSARM   Army : General Acc. 6482
8. NSARM   Army : General Loc. 35.3
9. NSARM   Notman #53167 Loc. 33.3.7

CHAPTER 9: CHANGING OF THE GUARD

1. NSARM   Notman 1983-310 #11121 Loc. 33.2.1
2. PCC   108-97-2-905-0208
3. PAC   DND Army WRC-564
4. NSARM   Bollinger 1941 # 328 G Acc. 1975-305
5. NSARM   Bollinger 1941 #328 B Acc. 1975-305
6. PCC   108-01-2-929-0201
7. PCC   108-93-2-916-0271
8. NSARM   Army : Battalions & Regiments
9. NSARM   Carson Acc. 1987-214.1 Loc. 37-16
10. NSARM   Army N - 6899, 6901, 6905, 6906, 6907
11. PCC   108-68-1-940-0328
12. NSARM   Navy : General #0-93-1
13. PAC   HS-1662-3
14. PAC   Army WRA-12
15. PAC   PA106063
16. PAC   NP-1277
17. NSARM   Stanley Flying School Loc. 37.2.2
18. NSARM   Stanley Flying School Loc. 37.2.2
19. PAC   PA105173
20. PCC   108-98-2-917-0240
21. NSARM   Army : General   N-4385